Pictorial History of Swords and Bayonets

Pictorial History of Swords and Bayonets

including Dirks and Daggers

R. J. Wilkinson-Latham

LONDON
IAN ALLAN

To Christine and Edward

First published 1973

ISBN: 0 7110 0394 7

Published by Ian Allan Ltd., Shepperton, Surrey and printed in the United Kingdom by Morrison and Gibb Ltd., London and Edinburgh

CONTENTS

INTRODUCTION

In this volume, I have endeavoured to trace the history of the sword, bayonet, dagger, dirk and knife from earliest times up until 1918 when the sword was no longer considered as an effective weapon of war. Every effort has been made to illustrate and mention as great a variety of the above weapons as possible in the space available. Besides the enthusiastic assistance received from numerous museums and private collectors, who are all mentioned in the illustration credits, I would like especially to thank the following for their help: Peter White; Herman A. Maeurer; Jack Cassin Scott; Jack Blake; R. D. Haines, Dennis Lipscombe and Jack Wells of Wilkinson Sword Ltd, and above all my father, Major John Wilkinson-Latham, who from his deep knowledge of edged weapons of the world, aided and guided me throughout the preparation of this book.

Note to the Nomenclature of Weapons

Military weapons are usually known by their date of introduction but the method of denoting this varies from country to country and from one author or collector to another. In Britain especially, weapons are known as the 'Pattern of' a certain date whereas other countries prefer and use 'Model of' a certain date.

In order not to confuse by continual references to patterns and models, a uniform nomenclature of the 'Pattern of' a certain date has been chosen when describing military weapons of all countries. I apologise, in advance, to those who feel that this is not correct.

September, 1972 R. J. WILKINSON-LATHAM

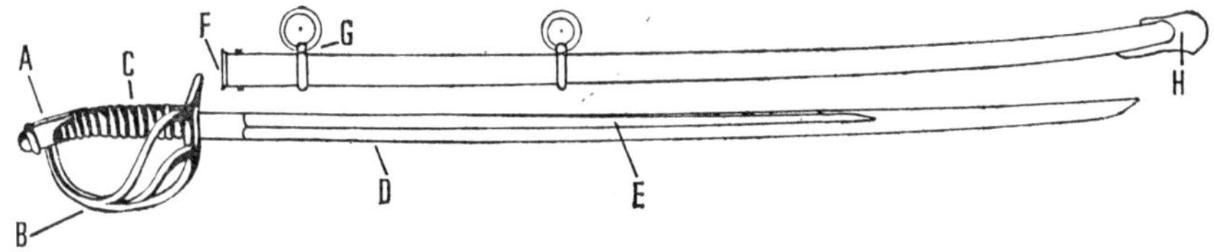

Fig. 1 Parts of a sword: A. Cap pommel; B. Guard; C. Grip; D. Cutting edge; E. Fuller; F. Mouthpiece; G. Band and ring for suspension; H. Shoe.

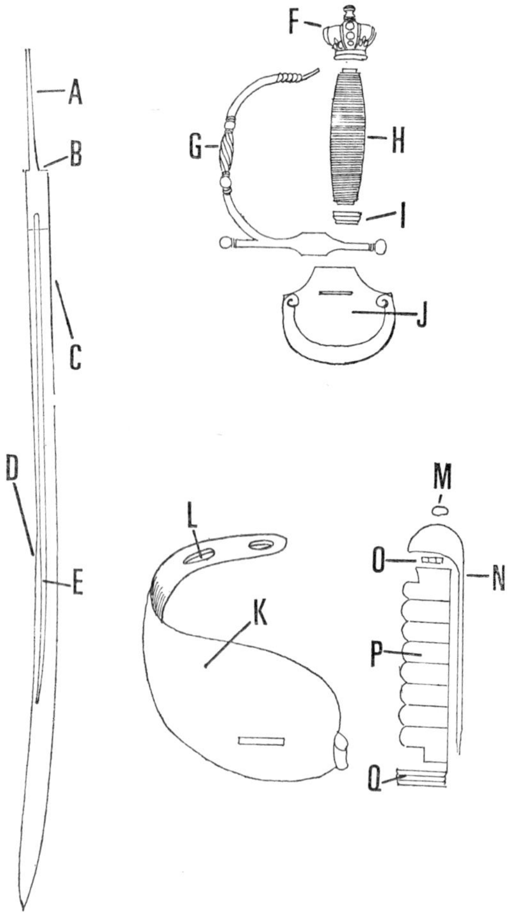

Fig. 2 Parts of a sword: A. Tang; B. Shoulder; C. Cutting edge; D. Back of blade; E. Fuller; F. Pommel; G. Knuckle guard with quillons; H. Grip; I. Ferrule; J. Shell guard; K. Guard; L. Slot for sword knot; M. Top nut; N. Pommel and backpiece; O. Under nut; P. Grip; Q. Ferrule.

1: SWORDS

Evolution and History up to 1750

In the armoury of ancient man, the sword was perhaps one of the last edged weapons to be invented, except of course for the bayonet which only made its appearance in the 17th century AD. The reason why the sword formed no part of primitive man's weapons, both offensive and defensive, was the lack of any suitable material from which to fashion a blade. Flint was too brittle in any suitable length and not strong enough for the work of a sword, while wood, which was suitable for spears and could be hardened to a certain extent with fire was completely inadequate. It was not, therefore, until the discovery of copper and the man-made metal bronze that sword blades of a rudimentary nature were able to be made, but it was still to be many years before the discovery of iron and later the secrets of steel making enabled this form of weapon to be perfected.

Copper was used to a certain extent to make knives and daggers but it was not until the discovery of bronze, the amalgam of copper and tin, that swords were made in any quantity. The bronze sword was typified by its heaviness which was due to the thickness of the blade required to make the weapon firm, rigid and able to withstand the usage to which it might be put. Because bronze is a soft metal, a way had to be found to make a blade which was strong and durable and this was done by making the blade thick and consequently heavy. Ways were sought to lighten the blade and this was done either by making it leaf shaped or by making the sides parallel with a central rib for strength. The leaf-shaped blades appear to date from the latter years of the bronze age (Plate 3). The blade was formed with the tang already shaped and it only required two pieces of wood or bone riveted to it for the weapon to be ready for use.

The shape the blade took very much depended on the fighting tactics of the country or area concerned and so we find that the Greeks preferred a narrow bladed weapon for cutting, whereas the Romans and Scandinavians used the leaf shaped blade for thrusting, which without the central ridge gave better penetration. Some weapons were naturally intended for both cutting and thrusting and it is very difficult to define the preferences of a particular nation or area even with the aid of surviving specimens, vases, statues and wall paintings. Suffice it to say that the bronze sword was not a particularly effective weapon because the nature of the material and the time and expense in manufacture meant that the majority of the armies relied on the spear or lance as their primary weapon, with the sword secondary, to be used when two opposing armies came to grips.

The discovery of iron and its infinite capabilities heralded the dawning of a new age in the history of man. Iron, which at this period could only be smelted and not cast, produced harder and more durable objects which, although subject to rust or oxidisation, provided better utensils and weapons. A knife or sword was now thinner in the blade yet stronger and capable of holding an edge far longer than it would if made of bronze; the armour and helmets worn by the soldiers was lighter and more resilient. Bronze weapons still continued to be made and used during the early years of the Iron age, as the discovery took a great number of years to infiltrate into all the various civilisations. Once blades started to be made in iron, bronze was reserved for the hilts and on occasion, the scabbards of swords.

Scabbards of swords have changed very little in principle since these early days, except for the introduction of the all leather scabbard with metal mounts which came at a slightly later date. Early scabbards were either made from cast bronze which enabled the craftsman to embellish his work with raised decorative designs or from two pieces of suitable wood, grooved on the inside to take the blade and bound around the outer surface with either cloth or leather. This latter method of covering a wood body in leather can still be seen in use today in the 'Sam Browne' scabbard.

The early iron age swords did not change in shape for many years but about the first century BC, the Roman sword or *gladius* changed into a weapon with a narrow double edged blade with parallel sides and an obtruse angled point. This sword was essentially used for thrusting while that used by the Greeks, with a slightly curved blade and cutting edge on the inner curve, was used for cutting.

During the conquest of Gaul by Julius Caesar, the Roman legions were armed with the spear or *pilum* and the *gladius* or short sword whereas their adversaries were equipped with a double edged weapon with a far longer blade. This weapon was used for hacking and by all accounts seems to have been of very inferior quality, many being soft and bendable. Even though the longer bladed sword was favoured by the Gauls, the Romans,

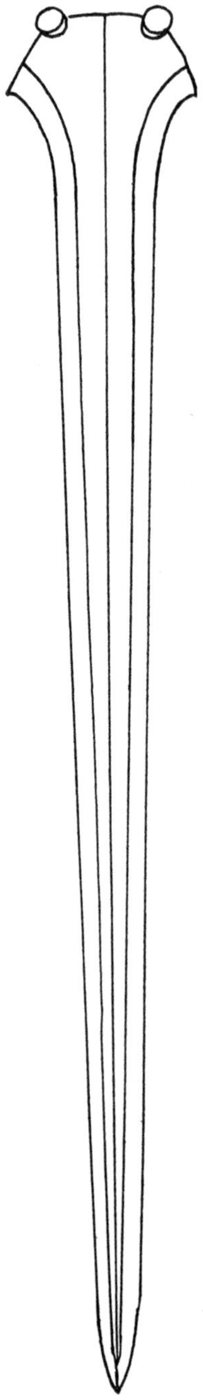

Fig. 3 Early Bronze Age thrusting sword (drawn from an example in the London Museum).

who based their fighting tactics on their highly disciplined legions preferred the short bladed weapon and it was only during the third century AD that it was realised that the mounted man with a long bladed sword was more than a match at close quarters for the legionary.

It was only after the defeat of the Romans and the break-up of their once vast empire by the barbarious hordes that the short bladed sword used by the foot soldier lost popularity. The victorious hordes brought with them the style of the long sword and everywhere in Europe where these tribes settled, the double edged bladed long sword prevailed. Throughout Europe and the British Isles, the invaders established themselves in their new lands and set about defending themselves against other intruders. The Saxon style sword, as it is generally termed, had a double edged blade with a heavy cross guard and pommel and a wood grip bound with leather or cloth. The cross guard and pommel were invariably made of horn or bone and served to stop the hand from sliding on to the blade during combat and to prevent the grip slipping through the hand.

In the sword of the period up to the 10th Century, the cross guard and pommel assumed another more important role. Being made of iron, they were used to ward off blows of an opponent and to give balance to the heavy blade; although the pommel and cross guard varies in style and decoration, the blade remained the same. The pommel of the Viking sword changed considerably in shape and had, unlike the Saxon weapon, a taper to the double edged blade. A great number of hilt types and variations have been identified and classified by R. E. Oakeshott in *Archaeology of Weapons.*

When the Normans invaded Britain in 1066, their swords differed very little from those of the Vikings, from whom they had descended. The weapon had a double edged blade with rounded point, a wood or bone grip, a straight longish cross guard and a brazil nut shaped pommel. The scabbards were made of two pieces of wood which were covered in leather and then decorated. This basic style of cross hilted sword remained in use for many years with only slight variations such as the curving forward of the cross guard during the 12th century and the adoption of a round or wheel shaped pommel at the same period. The ornamentation of swords became more complexed during this period and the shaping and decorating of the pommel and cross guard varied. During the 14th century triangular and conical pommels were used but in the hundred years that followed the pear shaped pommel came into vogue.

The saying 'necessity is the mother of invention' is certainly very apt in describing the evolution of the sword as, had defensive armour remained as chain mail, no further evolvement would probably have taken place. But this saying is just as apt for the evolution of armour and from the various defences of *cuir boulli* (boiled leather), chain mail and studs sewn to leather jerkins, plate armour appeared during the 14th century to try and provide absolute protection. To penetrate this, the sword had to be stronger and heavier, and so evolved the two handed and hand-and-a-half sword (Plates 9, 11, 13, 14). These weapons had long blades and proportionately longer hilts which could be grasped in two hands and swung, delivering a formidable blow. While the two handed sword was favoured by men fighting on foot for obvious reasons, the hand-and-a-half could be used by a mounted man, but usually this weapon was only used when his lance or spear had been broken or dropped. From these large weapons, which were the favoured swords of the Swiss and the Germans, the Scottish Claymore or 'Claidheamh-mor' developed, which had a long double edged blade, a plain grip and pommel and either straight or slightly down pointed quillons ending in trefoils.

The alternative sword used at this period was the *estoc* (Plate 6), a conventional length weapon with a diamond sectioned blade with a reinforced and sharp point. Later, the blade length increased and the sword was used as a supplementary weapon to the cross hilted sword by placing the pommel against the shoulder and gripping one side of the cross guard and using it as a lance.

It was at this period that the simple straight bar cross guard began to develop into a more complexed shape. The sword used by the German mercenaries, the *Landsknechts* had the quillons curved each side of the guard horizontally to form an 'S' while other types had one quillon turned up and the other turned down in the same shape. This was the beginning of the hand guard on swords which deviated from the straight or slightly curved cross guard. Because the sword was used with two hands, the top portion of the blade was left unsharpened so that the hand gripping it could not be cut. This section of the blade was known as the *ricasso*.

The cross guard developed further with the addition of rings each side of the guard which were later supplemented with the addition of further rings or bars. Towards the end of the 15th century, bars were sometimes replaced by sheet metal hand guards. The two handed sword had its *ricasso* covered in leather and on certain examples had a downward projection of metal each side of the blade below it which in effect formed a secondary hand guard. The need for further development of the two handed sword was arrested by the spread in the use of firearms, which heralded the demise of armour. It was now no longer practical for the mounted man to be armoured against the musket ball, as this would entail a huge weight of iron and subsequent loss in mobility. Consequently the need for the powerful two handed swords died with the armour it was designed to combat.

The basic military sword, however, remained a cut and thrust weapon with a simple cross guard and a double edged blade tapering to a point. There were no set patterns for this style of weapon, regulation swords not becoming a feature until the 18th century.

The emphasis at this period had been on the use of both the cut and the thrust but with priority being given to the former. However, with the decline in the wearing of armour, swords became lighter in the blade even though they were still used for cutting and thrusting. The rapier or *espada ropera* (the Spanish for a dress sword) appears to have originated in Spain and was the term, used by the middle of the 16th century, applied to a long bladed cut and thrust weapon with a hand guard of rings and bars. Towards the end of the 16th century, the blade tended to become slimmer and lighter but even so, some were as long as five feet! The Italians concentrated on the use of the point in their method of sword play and their teaching of the art of 'the fence', or what we term today as fencing. With the widespread influence of the Renaissance throughout Europe, the Italian method of fighting was adopted in many countries which led to use of the cut being abandoned in all but military swords.

At first the blades were long and diamond sectioned but by the 1570s they were shortened to a more manageable length, and used in conjunction with either a left hand dagger or a gauntlet to parry the opponents' blade. The emphasis on the point also effected the guard which became more complexed to give added protection to the hand. During the middle of the 17th century, the bars of the swept hilt rapier were often replaced with a shell each side of the base of the grip, which eventually evolved into the so-called cup hilt rapier with a bowl guard that was largely favoured in Italy and Spain. The effect of the Renaissance can also be seen in the decoration of both swept and cup hilt rapiers, many being lavishly chiselled and inlaid with gold or silver. There is an infinite variety in the shapes and designs of cup and swept hilt rapiers depending either on the country of origin or on the wishes of the purchaser. A cross section will be found illustrated in Plates 16, 17, 18, 22, 24, 25.

Although the rapier remained popular in Italy and Spain as late as the 1720s, its use declined in England and France in about the 1660s and its place taken by the 'Town' or 'Walking sword' (Plate 26). It had been realised that all things being equal in a duel or fight, the man with the lighter sword would be in a far better position than his opponent and as the rapier was carried as part of the daily attire, a lighter weapon would also be more convenient. The lightening and shortening of the sword was also brought about by the creation of standing armies formed with professional soldiers and officers as the likelihood of a gentleman being called on at short notice to fight in a battle was negligible and even if so, he could replace his slender bladed weapon with a cut and thrust fighting sword.

The Court sword or small sword (also referred to as a Town or walking sword) was probably first used in France where it was worn at the Court of Louis XIV in place of the rapier. The influence of Louis XIV in fashion and other matters soon spread throughout Europe and with it the Court sword. In England, the French influence arrived with the Restoration of Charles II, who during his exile had spent many years travelling throughout Europe.

There was naturally not an immediate change from one style of sword to another, the gap in the evolution being filled by a style of sword often referred to as a *flamberge*. This transitional weapon had a long blade of square or diamond section with a simple hilt without knuckle bow and two short quillons fitted above a small shell guard. In some cases the shell guard was omitted and these swords are referred to as pillow swords as legend has it that they were meant to be kept either under the pillow or at the head of the bed in case of intruders at night. (Plate 28, right).

The small sword had a blade of about 32ins with a hilt consisting of a shell guard, quillons (which now touched the shell and were called *pas d'âne rings*), a knuckle bow, pommel and grip. As the small sword had now become an indispensable part of the gentleman's dress, the hilt fittings and scabbard mounts became very decorative, and the grips were bound with wire in patterns which terminated each end in a woven collar of wire known as a 'Turks head'.

There are many variations in design, decoration and metals used in the small sword but even though the weapon was carried throughout Europe from the mid-1600s until the late 1780s, there is little variation in the basic shape. Although the earlier forms of small sword had employed a blade based on that of the rapier, it was not long before a new blade evolved with which nearly all small swords and later court and diplomatic swords were fitted. This blade was a slim tapering blade with three edges with each face 'hollow ground'. The top portion of the blade or *forte* was wide for about 8ins and then abruptly narrowed to a blade of a width of $\frac{3}{4}$ins. The *forte* was usually about 1$\frac{3}{4}$ins wide and hollow ground in the same manner as the slimmer portion of the blade. The name given to this blade form was 'colichemarde' which is reputed to have derived from the name of the inventor, Count Von Konigsmark, a well-known Swedish adventurer and duellist. The 'colichemarde' blade appears to have fallen into disuse by about 1730, although examples of small swords of the 1780 period are known with this blade form.

From about 1725, the wide *forte* disappeared and the blade tapered gradually from shoulder to point. The manufacture of hollow ground blades appears to have been an exclusive German secret, and their fine blades were used not only in England but elsewhere on the Continent. Sword blade making in England had fallen to a sorry state by the late 17th century and in order to try and revive this craft, the Government had imposed a heavy tax on the importation of foreign blades. Although the sword makers of Hounslow, who had been operating since 1620 were able to turn out the cut and thrust blades required for the fighting soldier, the greatest demand was for hollow ground blades. Because the secret of hollow grinding was exclusively German, a syndicate of business men petitioned for the granting of a patent for their manufacture, promising to bring over from Germany, skilled smiths who would teach the art in England. Although the patent was granted in 1688, the political situation hindered the implementing of it. However, by 1690, the Hollow Sword Blade Company was formed with a factory at Shotely Bridge in County Durham. However, the Company seems to have only turned out military blades and swords and never to have made the type of blade it was set up to manufacture.

In 1703, the syndicate decided to cut its losses and disposed of the factory to one of the German workmen, Herman Mohll, but retained the Charter, which was the most valuable asset. The syndicate then went into land speculation in Ireland and after that sold the Charter to Sir George Caswall and Jacob Sawbridge who set up the Sword Blade Bank, which foundered in 1720 when its principal customer the South Sea Company failed. Mohll continued the business but got into trouble with the Customs through smuggling partly finished 'hollow ground' blades without payment of duty. He immediately liquidated the company only to start it again as Herman Mohll and Son who specialised in the manufacture of military blades. In 1742, the factory passed to Robert Oley, one of Mohll's employees whose family ran it until 1832 when Robert Moll, a descendant of the original Mohll purchased it and moved to Birmingham where he changed his name to Mole and continued as a Government sword and bayonet contractor until 1922, when the sword making business was acquired by Wilkinson Sword Co.

By the 1780s, the small sword had been abandoned by civilians, except for diplomats and was used by the military as a dress sword. The small sword, or the descendant of the small sword still survives today in the court and diplomatic swords. A curious revival of the small sword occurred in Britain in 1825, when Surgeons, Secretaries and Pursers of the Royal Navy were ordered a gilt hilted small sword. These patterns lasted only seven years. Some fine examples of presentation of small swords exist which were presented long after the wearing of this style had ceased.

Apart from the use by diplomats, swords were now used nearly exclusively by the military with one notable exception: the hunting sword. This style of weapon usually had a short, slightly curved, single edged blade and either a hilt with simple cross guard or with knuckle bow. The grip was either of stag horn or tortoise shell covered wood but, by the late 18th century, ivory was also used. Many of these weapons were silver mounted and those without knuckle bows often had a chain guard fitted to pommel and cross guard. It was not unusual during the late 18th century for officers, especially in the Navy to carry these hunting swords, a notable example being Captain Cook who carried a silver mounted ivory hilted hunting sword. (Plate 32).

As was mentioned above, the Military did not use the fine rapiers or small swords, except of course at court or other suitable occasions, and the fighting sword continued to be a rather heavy cut and thrust weapon. The hilts of these swords were far more protective and had intricate guards of bars and panels which became known as the basket hilt. (Plate 40). This form first appeared in Germany during the mid-1500s and was soon adopted by the cavalry throughout Europe. The construction of the basket varied greatly, some being akin to the later and more well-known Scottish Broadsword, now called a claymore, while others had pierced baskets or half baskets. Others had pierced shell guards with a knuckle bow that broadened out from the pommel to where it met the shell guard. A well-known type of this pattern was the so-called Mortuary sword, (Plate 40), whose basket hilt was decorated with embossed heads meant to represent the execution of Charles I, hence the name, but as examples of this style are known well before 1649 (the date of Charles I execution), the name of Mortuary sword can be considered as a description that has crept into use, probably during the 19th century.

By the end of the 17th century, the hilt had become more simplified, losing many of its bars and retaining only a shell guard, and a knuckle bow with perhaps a few auxiliary bars. During the following century, except for certain regiments, this form of sword hilt remained as the basic military pattern but, as supply was a matter for the Commander of the Regiment, a variety of styles and designs were in use. The full basket hilt also continued in use up until the late 18th century, when the regulating of uniforms and equipment ousted the personal choice of Commanders and substituted a regulation weapon of a fixed design, for both heavy and light cavalry, the former retaining a straight cut and thrust weapon with a fairly heavy hilt for protection, while the latter adopted a curved sabre with a simple stirrup hilt.

Another form of basket hilted sword, mainly used in Italy where it was first designed was the *schiavona*. (Plate 39). These swords had an elaborate hilt composed of interlaced bars with a distinctive pommel which more often than not was in brass. The blades of these swords were heavy and of the cut and thrust variety.

Even though the true basket hilt had been largely abandoned by the beginning of the 19th century, it still remained in use with Scottish regiments who still wear it today.

Swords of Europe 1750–1918

Although the three most dominant European powers, Britain, France and Germany (before 1871, Prussia), exercised a certain sway over military uniform styles of other countries, they tended to retain their own patterns of swords, although naturally, under the Hanoverian rule in Britain, German influence was bound to be fairly strong. Allied to this was the sorry state of the British sword making industry which necessitated the ordering of sword and bayonets from Solingen in Germany. France, who herself had a large arms making industry, procured little from other countries and Germany, at this period had the largest sword making industry in the world. The German influence on swords was also spread by craftsmen who were either persuaded to set up business in a foreign land or who were forced to emigrate due to lack of work at home. These German craftsmen went to England, Sweden, Russia, North America, France, Belgium and Austro-Hungary during the 17th and 18th centuries; their influence can be seen in many features of the swords of those countries.

In Britain, as in other countries, the sword was used mainly by mounted men of this period. Infantrymen who had been armed with a short hanger, (Plates 41 and 42) since the early part of the 18th century had this weapon withdrawn in 1767, only grenadiers retaining it. Scottish regiments also carried a basket hilted weapon, (Plate 43), and this was also withdrawn in the same year except for Sergeants. The Infantry officer does not appear to have been ordered a special sword until 1786. Prior to that date, it was the commanding officers who decided on the style that should be worn, which was usually based on the 'Town' or walking sword of the period.

In 1786, an order issued by George III stipulated the pattern to be carried by Infantry Officers, *viz* 'A strong cut and thrust weapon with blade 32in long and 1in wide at the shoulder, the hilt to be steel, gilt or silver according to the buttons of the uniform'. Although there is no further evidence concerning the design of the sword, it is thought by most authorities to be a spadroon with a five bead guard. (Plate 44). The grip was in either ivory or dark horn and bisected by a metal band which matched the hilt and which bore a cartouche on which was engraved the title of the regiment, a crown and GR or left blank. In some cases the knuckle guard was plain without the five balls or beads. (Plates 44 and 45).

In 1796 a new pattern of sword was ordered. (Plate 47). This time a description of the weapon was given which enabled its immediate identification. 'The sword, to have a Brass Guard, Pommel & Shell, gilt with Gold; with the grip or Handle of Silver Twisted Wire. The Blade to be straight, & 32 inches in length, conformably to former orders, given out in April.' This pattern of sword was widely copied throughout Europe and Russia and was probably first adopted by the Prussians in the 1750s. There are three basic styles which help in identifying the country of origin and these are the French style, the Russian style and the Prussian style each differing in small details of pommel and shell design. The French style was what was copied by the British and the Danes. The Russian style was distinguished by the ball pommel with flattened top piece, while the French, British and Danish weapons have what it termed an 'Adam' pommel.

In 1803, another pattern of sword was ordered for wear by Infantry Officers. This weapon had a curved single edged blade similar to that adopted on the 1796 Light Cavalry sword with a single bow to the hilt and a lion head pommel and backpiece. (Plate 159). The guard incorporated the Crown and Royal cypher GR and in the case of Flank company officers the bugle horn stringed for light companies and the grenade for grenadier companies. The grip was in wood, bound with fish skin and blackened, but examples with ivory grips are known, being on the pattern of this sword prescribed for General Officers and on some of the versions of this sword that were carried by officers of the Volunteers. There were also a number of differing types of sword that incorporated the lion head pommel and backpiece of this pattern with the knuckle bow of the light cavalry sword, all in gilt brass, these being worn by Rifle Officers and officers of rifle volunteers. (Plates 51 and 52).

Although the sword was prescribed in 1803, there is adequate proof that the 1796 sword continued in use for some years after that date.

The Royal Navy had up until 1805 followed the army style of sword, the most popular being the bead hilt spadroon with five balls incorporated in the guard and the anchor in the side ring. (Plate 168). Some officers also wore the 1796 and the 1803 sword, the latter with a foul anchor above the crown and GR on the knuckle bow. Prior to 1786, when the bead hilt sword was adopted various types of sword and hanger were worn by naval officers.

In 1805, the Admiralty ordered a pattern of sword to be worn by the various ranks of naval officers, although it is thought that the sword was in use prior to this date. It had a lion head pommel and backpiece and a stirrup hilt with a langet each side of the base. On this langet was engraved the crown and foul anchor badge. Flag Officers had ivory grips while those of the other officers had blackened fish skin. Warrant Officers sword had a plain backpiece and pommel. (Plate 166). This pattern was carried up until 1827 when it was replaced by a version of the 'Gothic' hilt pattern adopted by the Infantry Army in 1822. Unlike the army sword, the naval version had a filled in guard, the crown and anchor in the cartouche as well as retaining the lion head pommel and backpiece of the earlier pattern. (Plate 168, centre). This hilt, with minor changes in shape and in the crown in the cartouche remains the pattern carried by Naval Officers today. (Plate 170). Various blades were used with this hilt, the pipe or quill back blade, (Plate 169), was used until 1846 when replaced by the slightly curved single edged 'Wilkinson' pattern. In the late 1870s, many officers had Scottish broadsword blades fitted to this hilt although this was never sanctioned by regulation. In 1929, the slightly curved blade was ordered to be straight. (Plate 170).

The infantry had adopted a new sword in 1822, (Plate 55), which had a gilt half basket hilt with, in the oval cartouche, the Crown and Royal cypher. This sword was also carried by the Foot Guards and the Rifles.

The Guards carried this pattern until 1855 when a steel hilt of the same design, but with the Royal cypher in the cartouche being replaced by the badge of the regiment, was approved. The Rifles, however, had obtained permission to have a steel hilt with a stringed bugle horn in the cartouche in 1829. Both these last mentioned patterns are still worn today.

Up until 1845, all the blades on infantry, Guards and Rifle swords were piped back which, according to Henry Wilkinson, was 'the worst damned blade ever' because the pipe or quill back interfered with its cutting power. The new design of blade which was single edged and slightly curved was approved by the War Office in a letter to Wilkinson dated 10th March 1845, although it did not come into general use until 1846.

In 1892, after 70 years service with the Infantry of Britain, and until 1862 with the Honourable East India Company and afterwards with the Indian Army, a new sword was approved which had a sheet steel hand guard impressed with the Crown and Royal cypher (Imperial cypher for the Indian Army). The blade was straight with no cutting edge until the final few inches of the point. In 1895, an amendment was made to the hilt which involved lapping down the inside edge of the guard to avoid wear to the uniform. This pattern, with a change in the crown and cypher is still worn today by Infantry, Royal Engineers and various other Corps. (Plate 68). It is also, again with a change of the crown and cypher for the national badge worn by numerous Commonwealth countries.

In 1822, General Officers also adopted this sword with a 'Gothic' hilt, but with the badge of a Crown surmounting a laurel wreath with, inside it, a crossed sword and baton in place of the Royal cypher in the cartouche. (Plate 56). In 1831, they adopted the mamaluke hilted scimitar which is still worn today. (Plate 61). The old pattern was in 1834 relegated to Staff Officers. (Plate 56).

The cavalry, which was divided into heavy and light, had a particular sword for each. The light cavalry had adopted a steel stirrup hilted sabre in 1796, (Plate 49), which was modified in 1820 by lightening the blade, and was gradually replaced after 1829 with a new pattern sword. The 1796 sword was also carried by the officers until 1822 when they were ordered to adopt a new pattern with a three bar hilt and thinner blade. (Plate 60). This sword continued to be the light cavalry officers sword until 1896 when a sword was approved for all cavalry officers. This pattern was also carried by the Royal Artillery, Royal Horse Artillery and Royal Army Service Corps, who all retain it to this day.

The troopers sword adopted in 1829 had a three bar hilt with a plain steel backpiece with ears that were pinned through the grip. The blade was slightly curved and single edged. In 1853, it was decided that all cavalry troopers would wear the same sword regardless of whether heavy or light, and a new pattern was adopted. (Plate 64, left).

The heavy cavalry had adopted the 'disc' hilt sword in 1796. This weapon had a straight single edged blade with a hatchet point and a

Fig. 4 Drawing of a guard of the Shropshire Yeomanry Cavalry from the Pattern book of Wilkinson Sword Ltd. *Circa* 1895.

round steel guard with knuckle strap that was pierced with holes around the edge of the steel guard. (Plate 50, left). In 1822, the hilt was modified by cutting away the inside edge of the guard and reshaping the point of the blade.

In 1830, a sword with a plain steel bowl guard and slightly curved single edged blade was introduced and continued in use until 1853. (Plate 50, right.) Officers of heavy cavalry were ordered a new sword in 1822 which had a straight single edged blade and a gilt hilt with knuckle bow and boat shell guard. This was also carried by Household Cavalry Officers. (Plate 162, centre). In 1834 a sword with a pierced bowl guard similar in outside dimensions to the troopers sword of 1830 was adopted. (Plate 57, right). In 1856, this pattern was replaced by a sword with a scroll hilt guard, slightly smaller than the previous pattern and a slightly curved single edged blade. This sword, but with the hilt in gunmetal, was ordered for Royal Engineers. (Plate 63).

In 1896, both light and heavy cavalry officers adopted a sword with an adaptation of the design of the 1834 heavy cavalry officers sword and with the blade adopted in 1856. In 1912, officers were ordered the newly approved version of the sword that all troopers had been armed with in 1908 but with the large bowl guard decorated with the honeysuckle designs used on the 1834 and 1896 swords. (Plate 70).

In 1853, all troopers adopted the three bar hilt sword which had a slightly curved blade. (Plate 64, left). The novelty of this sword was that the tang did not narrow to allow the grip to pass over it, but was the same width as the grip and had two pieces of leather fitted each side. In 1864, the same blade was fitted to a new pattern which had a sheet metal guard pierced with the design of a Maltese Cross. (Plate 64, right). In 1882, a new version of this pattern was adopted with lapped down sides to the guard. From 1882 until 1908, various committees sat to try and decide on the ideal sword for the cavalry. The first committee was set up after the sword scandal of 1884 when it was discovered that a large number of the army's swords were unserviceable and liable to bending and breakage when used in action.

The result of the various committees was the further modification of the 1864 pattern, in 1885, (Plate 65, left), 1889, and in 1890. In 1899 a new sword was adopted which still used the same blade, but had a larger unpierced guard which soon proved too flimsy. (Plate 65, right). Finally, after the limited issue of an experimental sword in 1904, the 'Patt 1908' was approved which is considered to be the finest sword ever designed. (Plate 69, left).

One prominent feature of French swords is that, with only a few exceptions, they are all brass or gilt hilted. The most well-known and widely copied types were those used by the light and heavy cavalry, these styles being either copied faithfully or slightly adapted by The United States, Belgium, Spain and some South American countries, amongst others.

The cavalry sword of the 1750s was very similar to that employed in most armies at this time. The hilt consisted of a shell guard with a knuckle bow and auxiliary bars while the blade was straight and either single or double edged. An iron hilted sword with a half basket guard was introduced in 1781, but superceded by a brass hilted version in 1784. The hilts of these last two swords were constructed from sheet metal bars fitted to a single cast knuckle bow and small shell guard. The blades were straight with a single cutting edge and a rounded point. Officers carried a somewhat more elaborate version of that issued to the men with the bars cast in brass and then gilded.

On November 24th 1793, it was decided to adopt the Republican Calendar in place of the Gregorian Calendar and this was to start from the day on which the first Republic was proclaimed. It is useful to know the various years of this calendar because swords and other military weapons were and are often described as being of the pattern of An XI etc.:

> An I Sept 22nd 1792/93; An II Sept 22nd 1793/94; An III 22nd Sept 1794/95; An IV Sept 23rd 1795/96; etc. up until An XIV 23rd Sept 1805/December 22nd 1805 when it was decided to restore the Gregorian calendar.

A sword with a cast brass hilt with four bars was adopted in An XIII and used up until 1815 by the Dragoons while the Cuirassiers sword, which was similar, was adopted in An XI. In the same year a light cavalry sabre was adopted with three cast brass bars to the guard and a backpiece to the grip. This pattern can also be recognised by the small brass lozenge in the middle of each side of the leather bound grip, and the langets fitted each side of the base of the guard. This style was copied and used by the Russians.

In 1816, the light cavalry adopted a further pattern of sword which had a hilt similar to the heavy cavalry sword of An XIII but with only three bars to the cast brass hilt. The new sword did not have a backpiece to the grip but a cap pommel, which was a feature of French cavalry swords during the 19th century. In 1822, the light cavalry sword was fitted with a new type of blade which was more curved than the previous pattern. In 1882, the light cavalry sword underwent yet another change in blade design and this time a straight blade was adopted. The mounted artillery also used a similar style of sword, but with a single cast knuckle bow and a blade with a more pronounced curve to it. This pattern was adopted in 1829.

The heavy cavalry were issued with a new sword in 1816 which had a four bar hilt similar to the pattern of An XIII, but with a cap pommel of differing shape. Whereas the sword of An XIII had a straight single edged blade with two fullers and a hatchet point, the new pattern had a double edged straight blade terminating in a rounded point. In 1822, the heavy cavalry were given a new weapon which had an altered hilt and a curved blade. The grip shape now leaned forward and the hilt bars were joined to the base of the guard without any round ornamentation that the previous pattern possessed. In 1854, however, a return was made to the straight double edged blade with two fullers that had been used on the sword of 1816.

There were also a variety of other swords used by mounted men, some for the *Gendarmerie* and others for the Royal or Imperial body guards.

Many French swords are marked on the back of the blade with the date and place of manufacture and also, in a number of cases, with the pattern or model date. A typical inscription might read: *M^{re} d'Armes de Chat^{t} Février 1879-Cav^{rie} L^{re} M^{le} 1822* which meant that the sword was made at the arsenal at Chatellerault in February 1879, and was of the light cavalry pattern of 1822. These marks are also to be found on officers swords of the Army and Navy.

The French infantry of the 1790s were armed with a hanger as well as musket and bayonet. This weapon had a cast brass hilt consisting of grip and knuckle bow and a short curved single edged blade. In An IX, a new pattern was adopted which had a hilt cast in one piece. (Plate 75). This pattern was extensively copied throughout Europe and also by Russia. Britain adopted a version of this weapon to arm the Foot Artillery in the 1830s. During the Revolution, there were a great variety of side arms differing in small detail from each other. The basic hilt had three bars to the guard and a leather bound grip, but the backpieces and the badges superimposed on the guard varied. Illustrated are two slightly differing variations. (Plate 74.)

The Foot Artillery also adopted a short hanger with a double edged leaf shaped blade. (Plates 72 and 75). Once again this weapon was copied in Europe and the United States. Britain adopted this pattern for the Land Transport Corps during the Crimean War (1854–6). In dating French weapons it must be remembered that the various changes which occurred in the political situation effected the badges and emblems on the weapons. Weapons bearing the 'Fleur de Lys' fall into the periods when France was ruled by the House of Bourbon, ie. 1717–1792 and 1814–1830. Those weapons with the cockerel fall into the period of the rule of the House of Orleans, ie. 1830–1848. The dates of the Republics were: First Republic 1792–1804, Second Republic 1848–1852 and the Third Republic 1870 to date. The First Empire was 1804–1814 and the Second Empire, 1852–1870.

After the Napoleonic wars a new pattern of sword was adopted for Infantry officers in 1821. (Plate 74). During the wars, a variety of patterns had been used in the Army by both officers and NCOs. This new sword had a hilt with a single knuckle bow which widened into an ornamented shell guard. The pommel of the weapon was the typical French cap variety. In 1854, a new pattern was adopted which was similar in shape but was less decorative. (Plate 74). This style continued to be carried up until 1882, when a steel hilted sword with a four bar guard was adopted, which was the sword carried during the First and Second World Wars. (Plate 77).

In the Navy, as in the British Navy, swords during the eighteenth century were a matter of choice and no fixed patterns were worn. During the last quarter of the century regulations ordered officers to carry the same sword as the military but in 1800 a special pattern was adopted. This took the form of a simplified version of the light cavalry officers' sword in having a single knuckle bow guard and a curved single edged blade. The langets of the guard bore each side a foul anchor. In 1805 a variation of this weapon was adopted which had a shorter blade and the langets replaced by plates. (Plate 174).

In 1837 a new sword was ordered to be worn which had a half basket guard with decorative shell guard incorporating the anchor badge and crown. The various changes in regime necessitated the removal of the crown in 1848 and the restoration of a slightly different version between 1852 and 1870. (Plate 175).

Besides the fighting swords described in the previous pages, officers of all branches of the Army and Navy wore dress swords. These took the form of the typical diplomatic adaptation of the small sword and usually bore distinctive designs or badges on the shell guard. This type of sword was also adopted by the United States and Belgium. Illustrated are a selection of these weapons from various periods and branches of the service. (Plate 76).

The Belgian armed forces largely tended to copy the French patterns of swords and often adopted new patterns within a year of their being adopted by the French. The cavalry used the identical patterns of swords employed by the French, although British weapons were imported from time to time. British swords which may be found with Belgian markings are the heavy cavalry sword of 1796 and the Cavalry pattern of 1908 which were supplied in large numbers during the First World War, although not much liked by the Belgian cavalry because it could only be used for thrusting.

The infantry copied all their swords from the French patterns and there is often little to distinguish one from the other except for the Royal cypher on the Belgian models. Illustrated in Plates 78, 79 and 80 are a cross-section of swords used by the Belgian forces.

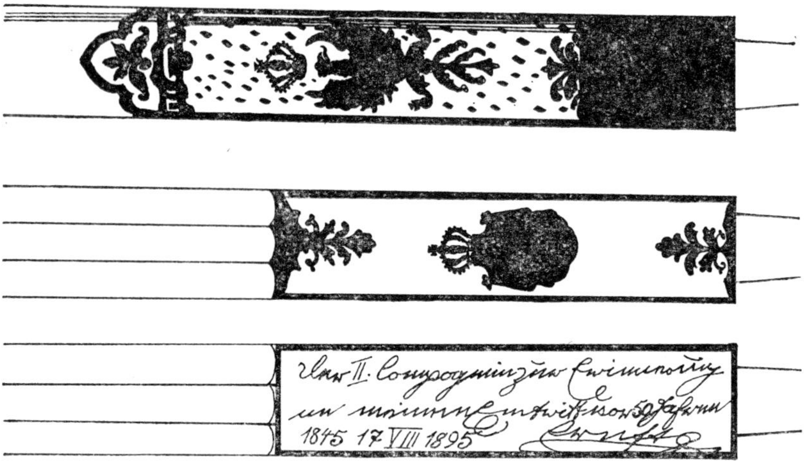

Fig. 5 Examples of presentation and decorative embossing on German military swords. *Circa* 1900.

German swords are perhaps the most numerous in variety than any others owing to the large number of states that were allied together during the 19th century which eventually, in 1871, were unified into one nation. Each state maintained its own army and had its own patterns and variations of swords, which many still retained after the unification. Another reason for the great number of small variations encountered between two swords of supposedly the same pattern was that regulations allowed differences in decoration on sword and scabbard, not according to rank, but according to the amount of money an officer was willing to spend on the weapon.

The leading state in the confederation and later the unification, was Prussia and its uniforms and weapons were copied or adapted by the other states, but usually with the addition of their own badge.

The Prussian dragoon sword adopted in 1735 was similar to that used by Russia and Denmark, but the Prussian sword had an eagle head pommel whereas the Russian sword had a lion head and the Danish weapon had a plain ball pommel. The hilt was in brass and composed of a number of intersecting bars reinforced at the intersection with a small disc. The blade was double edged with a spear pointed on the original pattern, which gave way in 1797 to a single edged blade. The scabbard was in brown leather with internal mouthpiece and partially hidden chape. Other states also had heavy straight bladed weapons for their cavalry, but with a variety of hilts composed mainly of bars which sometimes incorporated a shield with the ruler's monogram or the badge or emblem of the state.

Following the campaign of 1815, a large number of French cavalry swords were obtained as part of reparation and were used by a number of the Guard Cuirassier regiments and the *Garde du Corps* until the middle of the 19th century. The Russian style of heavy cavalry sword was also adopted and used by certain regiments up until 1880.

In 1854, the Prussian cuirassiers were issued with a new pattern of sword which was based on the French pattern of the beginning of the century. The hilt of four bars was cast in brass and the typical French pattern cap pommel was retained. The blade was straight with a single fuller running down the centre and a single cutting edge. The Prussian light cavalry had adopted a sword similar to that used in Britain since 1796. The hilt with its single knuckle bow guard was in steel. This pattern served as a model for the Uhlan sword of 1873 and various other weapons for both infantry and cavalry which were adopted in the last quarter of the 19th century. All these models are similar in that they use a single stirrup knuckle bow.

The rest of the Prussian heavy cavalry had been issued with a new sword in 1852 which had a steel bowl guard pierced to give the impression of being composed of a number of flat bars. The blade was slightly curved with a single fuller each side and a single cutting edge. The cavalry of the State of Saxony had adopted a sword with a three bar hilt spaced rather wider apart than the British light cavalry sword of 1822, in 1831, and Mecklenburg had also followed suit but with a sword based closer on the British pattern.

The infantry, like other nations had armed the private soldier with a sidearm as well as a musket and bayonet. There is very little to distinguish the 18th century patterns from those used by the British, except for the markings on blade and hilt. The hilt consisted of a cast brass grip and pommel and a small double shell guard. The blade was short, curved and single edged. By 1818, a pattern almost exactly the same as the French hanger had been adopted. Although these were manufactured during the 1820s, the first supplies were weapons captured from the French after Waterloo.

The infantry officer carried a sword that was similar to the 1796 sword of the British infantry, although the Prussian weapon seems to have served as the model, being adopted in the 1750s. Although this type was used during the 19th century as a dress sword, it was discarded during the last quarter except for a few regiments, mainly Guard regiments, who retained it. In 1889, a new pattern of sword was adopted for the Prussian infantry officer, which was also used by infantry officers of Wurtenberg, and Mecklanberg. The sword had a straight single edged blade with a gilt brass guard consisting of three narrowly spaced bars on which was fitted the badge of the state. The grip was bound in black fish skin and topped with a French style cap pommel. The Prussian version had the crown and cypher of the Emperor fitted to the middle of the grip. Jaeger and Fusilier officers had adopted a sword with a single stirrup hilt with a backpiece that incorporated a lion or eagle as a pommel depending on the state.

The cavalry and artillery had also adopted a sword with a single stirrup hilt with a lionhead pommel and backpiece. On each side of the lower part of the guard there was a langet on which was placed a motif to show the arm of the service; crossed swords for cavalry and crossed cannon barrels for artillery.

The illustrations show a wide variety of differing types of swords worn

Fig. 6 Examples of blade embossing. Left to right: Turkish Navy; 2nd Bengal Lancers; Imperial German Guard Cavalry; Geraldton Rifle Volunteers.

by officers of various states and united Germany during the 19th century. (Plates 81–89). Also illustrated is an army officer's sword of the Nazi period which shows that the same patterns were adhered to with a change only in the design on the langet. (Plate 89).

On the formation of the *Deutsche Marine* in 1848, a sword was adopted for officers that was based on the British pattern of 1827. The German sword had in the cartouche a foul anchor and a bone grip in place of the fish skin on the British sword. The blade was slightly curved, single edged and piped backed. In 1871, with the proclamation of the German Empire, the Imperial crown was placed in the cartouche above the foul anchor. There was a great variety of German naval swords from rather plain versions to highly elaborate swords which in some cases incorporated coloured stones in the eyes of the lionhead pommel, green for starboard and red for port! (Plate 176).

To show the extent of the variations that might be encountered, the Carl Eickhorn catalogue, *Musterbuch der Waffenfabrik* of 1908 illustrates 10 different styles of sword and seven different versions of the scabbard! In 1919, the Imperial crown was removed from the cartouche which now only contained the foul anchor. This style remained in use throughout the Nazi regime without change.

Space does not permit a detailed description of swords of other European countries but a cross-section of weapons have been illustrated. (Denmark: Plates 92–100; Sweden: 101–107; Austria: 108–114; Spain: 115–122.)

Swords of America 1770–1918

America, both North and South, came under various European influences during the 19th century, the foremost being French in North America and German in South America during the latter years of the century. While Britain did not influence the armies of the Americas, she had a profound effect on various navies, their dress and swords.

UNITED STATES OF AMERICA

During the War of Independence, Washington's forces were armed with a variety of swords. Officers used either small, hunting or military swords while the infantry mainly utilised the British pattern of hanger. The cavalry used what they could either buy or capture on the field of battle from the British or German troops. As with other armies, the cavalry was divided into heavy and light, the former having a straight bladed rather heavy sword with a basket or full guard while the latter used a curved bladed weapon with simple knuckle bow. (Plate 123).

In the United States Navy, regulations for swords were issued in 1813,

Fig. 7 Examples of badges found on United States and Confederate States of America swords made in England. *Top:* United States Cavalry 1864. On reverse of the blade, the Flag and the word 'Union'. *Left:* From a sword presented to Captain John Henry Mickler, 11th South Carolina Infantry, Confederate States of America. *Centre:* From a sword presented to Captain Raphael Semmes, Confederate States Navy by officers of the Royal Navy and friends in England to commemmorate the engagement with an ironclad ship of the Union, June 19th 1864. *Right:* United States Navy *circa* 1864.

but these were so vague as to allow plenty of latitude in design. In 1827, a sword based on the British infantry pattern of 1822 was adopted having an eagle with outspread wings in place of the cartouche, and an eagle head backpiece. In 1841, a further pattern was ordered which had an eagle head backpiece, a decorative knuckle bow and a small down pointing shell decorated with oak leaves and acorns. In 1852, a sword based on the French pattern was introduced having the letters USN incorporated in the design of the half basket guard. (Plate 134). This pattern was also carried by officers of the Revenue Service with the letters USRM in place of USN. This weapon was carried from 1862 until the early 1870s and then from 1890 to 1915 when the Revenue was amalgamated with the Coast Guard. The new sword was exactly the same as that of the Navy in appearance except that the letters USN were replaced with USCG. (Plate 134).

Officers of the United States Marine Corps were ordered swords in 1804 referred to in the order as 'yellow mounted sabres'. In 1825, a new pattern sword was sanctioned. This had a mamaluke hilt with the ivory scales held to the tang with brass stars. In 1859, this sword was withdrawn and officers ordered to carry the sword 'of the pattern adopted by the War Department, April 9th 1850'. In 1875, permission was given for officers to once more adopt the mamaluke hilted sword which is still retained to this day. (Plate 133). Enlisted men of the Corps carried the same sword as the US infantry which had a half basket guard, cap pommel and letters US incorporated in the foliage of the guard.

As in most other armies, there was a variety of sword used according to the arm of the service to which the officer was attached. The earlier styles of sword were based on the contemporary British patterns but it was not long before the French influence prevailed. Not only were the swords copied from the French patterns but also the bayonets, muskets and uniforms.

The heavy cavalry had a three bar hilted sword similar in style and shape to the British light cavalry sword of 1829, the Americans adopting theirs in 1833. By 1840, this had been replaced by a typical French style sabre which was to continue in use throughout the 19th century. The light or horse artillery were armed with a sabre modelled on the French equivalent. (Plate 128). This also continued in use throughout the 19th century. The grip was leather covered wood and the hilt components cast in brass. The heavy cavalry sword had a three bar guard and cap pommel while that of the artillery had a single knuckle guard. The foot artillery had a single knuckle guard. The foot artillery were armed with a short double edged bladed hanger, again modelled on the French pattern but with the eagle on the pommel in place of the *fleur de lys* or cockerel. (Plate 127).

By 1864, various departments had their own style and pattern of sword and the following extract from equipment regulations of that date shows the patterns in use.

Sword and Scabbard

73. *For General Officers* — straight sword, gilt hilt, silver grip, brass or steel scabbard.
74. *For Officers of the Adjutant-General's, Inspector-General's Quartermaster's, and Subsistence Departments, Corps of Engineers, Topigraphical Engineers, Ordnance, the Judge Advocate of the Army, Aides-de-Camp, Field Officers of Artillery, Infantry and Foot Riflemen and for the Light Artillery* — the sword of the pattern adopted by the War Department, April 9th 1850; or the one described in General Orders No 21, of August 28th 1860, for officers therein designated.
75. *For Medical and Pay Departments* — small sword and scabbard according to pattern in the Surgeon-General's office.
76. *For Medical Cadets* — the sword and belt plate will be the same as for non-commissioned officers.
77. *For Officers of Cavalry* — sabre and scabbard now in use according to pattern in the Ordnance Department.
78. *For Artillery, Infantry and Foot Riflemen* — except for field officers — the sword of the pattern adopted by the War Department, April 9th 1850.

In 1902, a nickle plated four bar hilted sword with black shaped plastic grip was approved for officers of the US Army. (Plates 131 and 133). In 1913 the troopers sword of the cavalry was replaced with a new pattern which appears to have been influenced by the British cavalry troopers sword of 1908. The American sword had a double edged blade with a central fuller and a large bowl guard with beaded edge. (Plate 132).

SOUTH AMERICA

The study of the swords of South American countries is very difficult because of the sparseness of information and surviving examples. Except for a few instances, the swords used by both army and navy were modelled on those of either Britain or Germany; Brazil alone basing its navy sword on that of the United States. While the British pattern dominated in South American navies, Germany's influence can be seen in many of the military swords, although some countries seemed to have a mixture of styles with one arm of the service following Germany and another Britain.

Plates 135 to 142 show a selection of swords of the following South American countries: Argentine, Brazil, Chile, Costa Rica, Cuba, Equador, Guatemala, Mexico, San Salvador and Venezuela. Although taken from catalogue sheets and drawings of the 1927–1935 era the swords were those worn during the late 19th century and 20th century. Many of the patterns illustrated are still worn today and except for a few, made by Wilkinson's, are of German manufacture.

A number of South American countries which have military and naval academies award annual sword prizes to the top cadets and although these are the standard Navy, Army and Air Force pattern swords, they bear the appropriate inscription on the blades. All these 'specials' are made by Wilkinson Sword Ltd.

Swords of Asia Including Russia 1800–1918

Only military and naval swords will be discussed in this section; native or national weapons being described under non military and native swords (see page 34).

The dominant power in Asia from 1800 was undoubtedly Russia and it was not until the 1860s and 1870s that China, Japan and Siam attempted to organise their forces or part of their forces along European lines and to adopt uniforms and weapons of European design. In the organising of their forces, China, Japan and Siam relied on advisers of the leading European powers and so it is not surprising to find that their swords were in the main modelled on those of advisers. In this respect, Britain dominated the design of naval swords of all three powers.

RUSSIA

Until the liberation of the serfs in 1863 by Czar Alexander II, all Russian swords were made in Government factories for officers and men, unless the former secured a sword from abroad. It was not until after this date that private manufacturers were set up by some of the liberated armourers to supply highly decorative and more elaborate weapons for officers.

About 1800 the Prussian influence was prevalent in the design of military weapons but this gave way by 1825 to the French influence which, later in the century, was replaced by the Caucasian influence; this, combined with some points from the French patterns, evolved into the *Shashka.*

The Russian swords in use in 1800 are typical of the styles to be found in a number of European armies, the cuirassiers having a straight bladed weapon with basket hilt of bars with a circle at the intersection bearing the badge of the double headed eagle, (Plate 145), while the Guard Cuirassiers replaced this hilt with a more elaborate one. (Plate 144). Placed over the bars was a large cast double headed eagle surmounted by a crown, which gives the sword a similar appearance to the 1814 pattern adopted by the British Life Guards and the cuirassier sword adopted in Denmark. The light cavalry, as would be expected, had a stirrup hilted sword in steel or brass with a wire bound leather grip. The scabbard, as that for the cuirassier pattern, was in the French style of covering the body of the scabbard with large mounts, which gave the appearance of a solid metal scabbard with pierced out panels showing the leather covering beneath.

The infantry sword was the same in style as that adopted by countless other countries including Britain, France, and Prussia to name a few. It was a straight bladed weapon with a gilt brass urn shaped pommel with a knuckle bow and boat shell guard. In Britain this was the 1796 pattern while in Spain it was adopted in 1822. In Russia, the sword was adopted by the horse artillery and as a dress sword by the cavalry.

In 1806 and again in 1809, swords based on the French influence were introduced. The Dragoons received theirs in 1806 and the cuirassiers and the rest of the cavalry their new weapons in 1809. (Plate 146). The sword of the cuirrasier and the dragoon was the same except for the scabbard. The former had leather and the latter, metal. The sword had a brass cap pommel and a three bar brass guard. The blade was straight with two fullers extending from the shoulder to the point. The cavalry had a similar sword but with a forward leaning pommel and guard and a curved blade.

Under Nicholas I, the French influence continued with the introduction in 1826 of a number of new patterns for the army. The infantry discarded their small sword for a curved bladed weapon modelled on the French pattern of 1821. (Plate 148). The cuirassiers sword now had a guard with four bars and a heavy straight blade similar to its French counterpart while the officers' version was similar, but much lighter. The cavalry sword was a copy of the French model of the *System AnXI* and in fact a large number of captured French weapons were repaired where needed and issued. (Plate 148). This pattern had a three bar hilt with pommel and backpiece in brass. The grip was wood bound in leather with a brass stud in the middle of the grip on each side. The guard was fitted with two brass langets each side at the top of the blade. The blade was single edged and curved with a deep central fuller and carried in a heavy steel scabbard with two bands and rings.

The first sword of the 'Asiatic pattern' as it was called, or what we term today as the *shashka*, was introduced in 1834. From that date onwards, the French influence slowly decreased as this new form of weapon came to the fore and continued in use up to 1917 and later. The true Caucasian *shashkas* had a plain grip with no knuckle bow or cross guard fitted to a single edged curved blade. The pommel was invariably beak shaped and incorporated a hole to fit the sword knot. The scabbard was in wood with a leather covering and brass mounts. Some patterns have additional rings in which the bayonet was fitted, but all have the rings on the outer curve of the scabbard so that when worn the sword hangs with the hilt upwards and not downwards as was normal. This method was copied from the traditional method of carrying this style of sword, which allowed the weapon to be in the correct place for drawing it.

A variation for Cossacks was introduced in 1838 and another variety, but with knuckle bow, for dragoons in 1841, this latter pattern having a hilt not dissimilar in appearance to the French pattern infantry sword of 1821. Under Alexander II, these styles continued in use with a new pattern with knuckle bows being introduced in 1865 and 1868. In 1881, a commission was appointed to design a sword to replace the numerous variations and varieties in use in the different branches of the army which resulted in the pattern of 1881 being adopted. This pattern was destined to replace all the other weapons in use for all branches of the service and for both officers and men. (Plate 149).

As soon as the universal pattern sword had been approved, it was decided to allow the Cossacks to retain their traditional style of sword which, under the new system, took on many points of the universal pattern. The pommel and back of the hilt were in brass and the grip of diagonally lined wood. The blade and scabbard were the same as the universal pattern. There were versions in both types for officers and men, differing only in the quality of finish and having engraved blades and pommels. (Plate 150).

In 1909, a slightly different version of the pattern 1881 was issued and a new sword based on the cavalry pattern of 1826 was adopted by the cavalry. Cossacks, while having a new pattern approved in 1910, were allowed, by Imperial command to wear and use swords that had been family heirlooms and were not forced to adopt the regulation weapon. These swords, together with a version of the pattern of 1910 which was approved for infantry officers in 1913, were carried until the revolution in 1917. Under the new regime, these swords continued to be carried but without the Czarist emblems and cyphers.

The Russian Navy had no specific sword until the 1820s, before that date the officers had used military weapons. During the 1820s a sword was approved for Naval Officers. This appears to have been a straight bladed weapon with a brass three bar hilt with a brass backpiece with a pronounced top nut and a wire bound leather grip. In the 1860s, the straight blade was replaced by a curved one. This pattern continued to be worn for many years, before and after the 1917 Revolution.

SIAM

In both the military and naval swords, Siam copied the British style of weapon. The newly organised forces, under British instructors had their swords designed for them by Wilkinson and Son and because of this and the British influence, the infantry sword was based on the British infantry pattern of 1822, the cavalry sword was modelled on the British heavy cavalry pattern of 1856, the artillery were armed with a version of the 1822 light cavalry sword and the Navy copied the contemporary British model. (Plate 151).

The infantry sword had in place of the slightly ornate backpiece on the British pattern one that had an elephant head pommel with the trunk following the line of the strap of the guard. The guard was what was called the 'Gothic' pattern having three bars, which incorporated the arms of Siam in place of the cypher of Queen Victoria which would appear in the British pattern. The blade was slightly curved with a single cutting edge and a fuller in each side. The decoration of the blade was an exact copy of the British style except that the crown and Royal cypher were replaced with the arms of Siam. The main difference besides the elephant head and the Siamese arms was that the hilt was silver plated and the blackened fish skin grip was bound with three strands of silver wire. There was also another version of this sword with the British style pommel and backpiece and with the arms engraved on the guard. This model was issued to senior NCOs.

The cavalry version, also carried by the Royal Guard utilises the heavy cavalry hilt of 1856 but with the Siamese arms incorporated in the scroll work. The backpiece was the same as on the infantry sword and again the hilt was silver plated. (Plate 152).

The Navy adopted a copy of the British pattern, but with a plain foul anchor in the cartouche on the guard and the elephant head pommel and backpiece in place of the lion head pommel and backpiece. In all cases with Siamese swords they are much smaller than their corresponding British counterparts. The hilts and blades used were those utilised for dress swords in the British service being lighter and smaller than the full size fighting weapon.

CHINA

It was only a few years before the end of the 19th century that China had a small number of troops dressed and equipped in Western fashion, and it was not until 1911 with the establishment of a Chinese Republic, that the entire army was modelled on western lines. In about 1897, those units dressed and fitted out in western style copied the uniform and equipment of the United States and therefore probably their style of swords, but in 1903 the Russian style was adopted, and continued in vogue after the formation of the Republic.

As early as 1867, efforts had been made to form a fleet but it was not until 1881 that this was accomplished. The sword carried at this time was an adaptation of the country's traditional sword, but with the formation of the Republic and the issue of Dress Regulations, the British pattern of sword was copied as would be expected due to the influence that Britain had exercised in Chinese naval affairs. The gilt half basket hilt had in place of the crown and foul anchor in the cartouche, a foul anchor within a corn wreath. The pommel and backpiece were also different from the British pattern having a *li-ting*, an ancient Chinese symbol resembling a tripod cauldron with handles and lid, in place of the lion head. There was also a version for Warrant Officers which had a black grip and plain pommel.

While discussing the Chinese naval sword, it is well worth looking at the sword adopted and worn by the Chinese Maritime Customs as, in the past, this sword has often been confused with the Chinese navy sword. The Maritime Customs was essentially a British formed and administered force to combat the vast amount of piracy along the miles and miles of Chinese coastline. Formed in 1867 with Chinese other ranks and British officers, the new force adopted the current British pattern of uniform, but naturally with certain distinctive alterations. Although swords were carried by the officers at this time, it was not until 1872 that the various badges, buttons and sword were approved. In November 1871, Wilkinson's made a claymore bladed naval sword with dragon head pommel and a plain anchor in the cartouche on the guard. This weapon, (Plate 178), was supplied to Captain J. Cocker of His Imperial Chinese Majesty's Gun Boat '*Ling Ting*' (*Author's note:* Although the name of the boat is recorded by Wilkinson's as *Ling Ting*, it should perhaps be *Likin*, one of the three gun boats ordered in 1868). The sword had an ivory grip but, other than the pommel and cartouche, was akin to the British naval sword of the period.

In 1872, the design of the sword was slightly revised. The cart uche now bore the badge of an anchor with a dragon superimposed on it and the grip was white fish skin bound in gilt wire. There is a drawing in Wilkinson's pattern book showing this sword with an anchor and dragon badge on the top two mounts of the scabbard. The swords appear to have been purchased in bulk from Wilkinson's as also were the badges and buttons. A quotation dated 1875 prices the sword at £6-10-0(£6.50) but £5-15-0(£5.75) if ordered in a quantity. From a subsequent order by Wilkinson's to Thomas Donler, a Birmingham button and badge maker, it appears that 13 swords were purchased and the necessary embroidery, buttons and badges for 13 uniforms. The National Maritime Museum possesses a sword of this type but with a lion head backpiece. This is thought to be a mistake on the part of the supplier and not a change in pattern. Ratings were armed with British pattern cutlasses.

JAPAN

Japanese military and naval forces were only organised along European lines in the late 1860s with the re-creation of the Imperial authority under the new Emperor Mutsuhito and the abolition of the Samurai, the Japanese nobility who had been undoubtedly the sword maker's best customers. With the Western influence and the organisation of an army and navy, modern weapons including swords were adopted in place of the traditional style Japanese weapon. The army adopted a sword based loosely on the French infantry pattern on whose uniforms the Japanese based their own. The hilt was somewhat elongated with a thin knuckle bow and pommel. In later years, the use of the traditional blade shape crept into use and these were mounted with the hilt described. The French influence was ousted by the Germans in the last quarter of the 19th century and German military advisers naturally tended to impose their country's designs on the army. NCOs carried a sword not unlike the contemporary German pattern.

The Japanese Navy styled its uniforms and swords on the Royal Navy but it was not until January 1872 that sword, belt and buckle were approved. Wilkinson's pattern book gives the complete details for the sword and belt. (Plate 179). The weapon approved was an exact copy of the British pattern except that the cartouche bore a foul anchor and crossed cherry blossom device. Ordinary officers had a plain edge to the oval whereas Admirals had a roped edge which joined to the ring on the top of the anchor. The fouling on the anchor differed from the British pattern in that the rope entwined around the top bar of the anchor (stock). The admiral's sword belt and scabbard had, in place of the oak leaf pattern on the British examples, the cherry blossom design.

As in the case of the army, the traditional style blade came back into use and was similar in design to the sword carried by the United States Navy having a pommel and knuckle guard in gilt and a white fish skin grip. Both this style and the more traditional style weapon were in use until 1945.

Siamese, Chinese and Japanese diplomats, like their western counterparts carried a court sword based on the European style which itself was based on the Town or Walking sword carried in the late 18th century.

Swords of India 1850–1918

Although the swords used by the officers of the East India Company's armies were the same patterns as those carried in the British army, there were many interesting regimental variations besides the main difference of the Company's arms in place of the Royal cypher. The main regimental differences were for the cavalry in the hilt design and for the infantry in the scabbard. Infantry regiment variation continued up until the close of British rule in 1947 but, with the issue of the universal pattern cavalry officers' sword and the universal pattern troopers' sword during the second decade of the twentieth century, the number of variations were reduced.

Under the rule of the Honourable East India Company, the army was divided between the three Presidencies; Bengal, Bombay and Madras and each one maintained an army, clothed and equipped by the Company. Officers' swords of the period 1850–1862 differ from their British counterpart in having the crest of the East India Company in place of the Royal cypher on the guard of the 1822 Infantry sword and on the blades of other patterns. In 1862, when the Company's forces were taken over by the Crown and reorganised (some regiments being taken on the British Army establishment and others disbanded) the crest of the Company was replaced by the Royal cypher. In 1876, Queen Victoria was proclaimed Empress of India and the cypher on the sword hilt and blades was changed to an intertwined VRI, the Royal and Imperial cypher.

It would be impossible in the limited space available to describe all the regimental patterns and variations and a number of the more common differences have been discussed.

CAVALRY

The swords of the cavalry of the East India Company had always been supplied from England, but in many cases without the scabbard which, except if it was steel, were made up locally. Thomas Gill, in a booklet he published in 1790 in an attempt to prove that his swords were superior to all other makes, stated that the East India Company issued an order for 10000 horsemen's swords 'indiscriminately amongst English and German manufacturers' but not, it appears, to Mr Gill. Subsequently, it would seem, he did secure a part of the order only after some of the other manufacturers' goods had proved to be defective. The pattern of weapon supplied seems to have been the same style as adopted by the British light cavalry, namely a simple stirrup hilt knuckle bow, plain backpiece and curved single edged blade.

For many years after, this pattern of sword seems to have been used in the Company's cavalry, but with a slight change to the hilt in 1796. After the Indian Mutiny and the formation of various irregular cavalry units who in some cases favoured the native tulwar, this pattern of stirrup hilt was still in use and continued with a number of regiments up until the 1914–1918 war. In the 1860s, a sword with the same curved blade, presumably to utilise the existing scabbards, but with a three bar hilt was adopted. (Plate 155). This hilt was smaller in size than the British pattern that had been adopted many years previously for the light cavalry, to accommodate the small Indian hand. This pattern became fairly universal throughout the Indian Cavalry until the introduction of the troopers sword based on the British 1908 pattern. (Plate 69, right). Some of these weapons had ears to the backpiece while others did not and also the design and style of the scabbard differed from one regiment to another. Some regiments adopted the British pattern of sword with the Maltese cross hilt (see Swords of Europe 1750–1918, page 8) but as various amalgamations took place, the number of differences decreased and the three bar hilt sword became almost universal.

State troops, raised and maintained at the expense of their rulers did not always follow the style used in the regular army and many variations exist in this category, some weapons engraved with the state badge while others had distinctive hilt designs made for them by British manufacturers. (Plate 154).

Officers' swords also varied but were in the main confined to two patterns, the light cavalry of 1822 and the heavy cavalry pattern of 1856 and 1896. Dress swords were either like the British style levée swords or copies of the native tulwar pattern.

Listed below are the differences encountered in cavalry swords from about 1870–1914. The regimental titles given are those adopted after the re-organisation of 1903.

1st Duke of York's Own Lancers (Skinner's Horse) — Tprs. (Troopers= Sowars) three bar hilt, black scabbard with three mounts. Native officers, same sword with scroll hilt.

2nd Lancers (Gardener's Horse) — Tprs. 1882 British pattern in leather scabbard with top mt. and chape.

3rd Skinner's Horse — As 1st Duke of York's Own Lancers.

4th Lancers — Tprs. three bar hilt, black leather scabbard with three mounts.

5th Cavalry — Tprs. three bar hilt, black leather scabbard with three mounts.

6th Prince of Wales Cavalry — Tprs. three bar hilt, black leather scabbard with three mounts (long chape). Native officers — stirrup hilt with ears to backpiece leather scabbard, three mounts.

7th Lancers — Tprs. three bar hilt.

8th Lancers — Tprs. three bar hilt.

9th Hodson's Horse — Tprs. three bar hilt with extra curved blade.

10th Duke of Cambridge's Own Lancers (Hodson's Horse) — Tprs. three bar hilt, wood scabbard covered black leather with 10ins chape, no shoe.

11th Prince of Wales's Own Lancers — Tprs. stirrup hilt with ears to backpiece, black leather scabbard, three brass mounts. Native officer — three bar hilt.

12th Cavalry — three bar hilt.

13th Duke of Connaught's Lancers — Tprs. stirrup hilt, black leather scabbard with 8ins chape.

14th Murray's Jat Lancers — Tprs. three bar hilt, scabbard with two mounts with stud on the top mount, no rings.

15th Lancer's (Cureton's Multanis) — Tprs. three bar hilt. Native officers, scroll hilt with black leather scabbard, three mounts.

16th Cavalry — Tprs. three bar hilt.

17th Cavalry — not known.

18th Tiwnana Lancers — three bar hilt, wood scabbard covered in black leather with stud on 4ins top mount and 9¾ins chape.

19th Lancer's (Fane's Horse) Tprs. — three bar hilt. Native officers 1853 British pattern in leather scabbard.

20th Deccan Horse — Tprs. three bar hilt. Native officers scroll hilt with brown leather scabbard with two mounts and a ring each side of top mount.

21st Prince Albert Victor's Own Cavalry — Tprs. three bar hilt, scabbard wood covered in brown leather, three mounts.

22nd Cavalry (Frontier Force) — as 21st.

23rd Cavalry (Frontier Force) — Tprs. three bar hilt, scabbard wood covered in black leather with 6ins chape.

25th Cavalry (Frontier Force) — Tprs. three bar hilt, wood scabbard covered in black donkey skin with top mount with two rings and 6ins chape.

26th Light Cavalry — Tprs. three bar hilt.

27th Light Cavalry — Tprs. three bar hilt.

28th Light Cavalry — not known.

29th Lancers, Deccan Horse — Tprs. 1882 British pattern in leather scabbard with three mounts. Long chape.

30th Lancers, Deccan Horse — not known.

31st Duke of Connaught's Own Lancers — Tprs. 1853 British pattern in leather scabbard with brass mounts.

32nd Lancers — As 31st.

33rd Queen's Own Light Cavalry — Tprs. three bar hilt with 33ins blade.

34th Prince Albert Victor's Own Poona Horse — not known.

35th Scinde Horse — Tprs. three bar hilt with black scabbard with three mounts but short chape.

36th Jacob's Horse — Tprs. three bar hilt with 37ins curved blade and black scabbard with two rings on top mount and 6ins chape.

37th Lancers (Baluch Horse) — Tprs. three bar hilt with black leather scabbard, three mounts but with short chape. Native officers scroll hilt with wood scabbard covered brown leather with 9ins chape, and stud on top mount, no rings.

38th Central India Horse — Tprs. three bar hilt with black leather scabbard with two mounts and no shoe to chape.

39th Central India Horse — three bar hilt.

The Infantry were less varied in the pattern of sword, but had more variations in the style and type of scabbard. The standard sword was the 1822 brass hilted 'Gothic' pattern but in 1895, a new steel hilted sword with 'dumbell' pattern blade was adopted, the Crown and Imperial cypher being impressed on the face of the guard. Once again the differences quoted below are not those of the British Officers but of the pattern worn by Warrant Officers. These styles were also sometimes used by British and Viceroy Commissioned Officers for wear when the steel scabbard was not used. The list is not complete but a cross section. The Regiments shown below have not been placed in any order of precedence but have been listed alphabetically.

Baluch — Rifle pattern sword with plain oval to cartouche.

Bengal Police — Steel hilt rifle pattern with scrolled 'BP' in cartouche. Solid brown leather scabbard with 4ins steel top mount and chape.

Bombay Rifles — Rifle pattern with plain oval to cartouche. Steel scabbard for dress but wood scabbard covered with black leather with top mount and 3ins chape otherwise.

Burma Rifles — Rifle pattern sword with black leather scabbard with 6ins nickle plated chape.

Ceylon Tea Planters Rifles — Rifle pattern with plain oval to cartouche and special badge in place of bugle.

Fig. 8 The Royal and Imperial cypher of George V. From an official India Stores Depot drawing.

38th Dogras — Steel hilted 1895 pattern with brown leather scabbard and 6ins brass chape.

1st Gurkha — Plain oval to cartouche, black scabbard with 7½ins chape.

2nd Gurkha — As 1st but scabbard with German silver mounts, top 5½ins, chape 6 ins, no shoe.

4th Gurkha — As 1st.

5th Gurkha — Wreath oval to cartouche, brown scabbard with 8¼ins chape.

6th Gurkha — As 1st but scabbard with 3½ins top mount and 7⅜ins chape.

Jahore Police — Nickel plated rifle pattern hilt with crescent and star badge with Jahore crown in cartouche. Royal Artillery curved blade

32ins × 1ins in brown scabbard with three mounts and Jahore badge on middle mount.

Maharatta Infantry — 1895 steel hilted infantry with Imperial cypher.

40th Pathans — Plain oval to cartouche on rifle pattern sword.

4th Punjab Infantry — Plain oval to rifle sword, black asses skin scabbard, no top mount.

5th Punjab Infantry — Steel hilt 1895 pattern with Wilkinson patent tang hilt, pipe backed blade 36ins × 1¼ins. Black imitation donkey skin scabbard with 4½ins top mount, 3½ins middle mount and 8ins chape with large shoe. Top and middle mount with band and ring.

33rd Punjab Infantry — Plain oval to cartouche on rifle pattern sword. Brown scabbard with nickle plated chape and 2ins top mount.

56th Punjab Infantry — Plain oval to cartouche on rifle pattern sword. Black leather scabbard with 6ins chape. Top and middle mounts with band and ring.

Punjab Police — Trade quality 1822 light cavalry sword.

2nd Queen's Own Sappers and Miners — Brass hilted 1822 pattern up to 1914.

5th and 6th Rajputana Rifles — Plain oval to cartouche on rifle pattern sword. Black leather scabbard.

2nd Sikh Rifles — As 5th Rajputana but scabbard with 6ins top mount, 3ins middle mount and 6½ins chape.

3rd Sikh Rifles — As 2nd but with 5½ins top mount, 3½ins chape, no shoe.

15th Ludiana Sikhs — Brass hilted 1822 pattern with Imperial cypher, black leather scabbard when all steel not worn. Top mount 5½ins, middle mount 3¾ins, 9ins chape with large shoe.

(The above lists for cavalry and infantry were compiled from patterns, drawings and notes in the pattern books and details taken from the contract books of Wilkinson Sword Ltd.)

In the infantry, an all steel scabbard with fixed rings and an iron or gilt hilted sword, similar in pattern to that approved in 1889 for Staff Sergeants of the British Army was introduced in 1893. The above variations still continued for the swords of native officers and warrant officers, in spite of pressure being put on regiments to conform to the pattern of 1893.

In the cavalry, the hilts and scabbards varied but the blades were mainly of a standard pattern. Native Bengal cavalry had a 33ins blade to their swords while Madras and Bombay had a 31½ins blade described in an India Store Department order of September 1883 for 2304 blades to Robert Mole of Birmingham as 'India Stores Pattern 6480, Native India Cavalry/ Madras and Bombay/Blades tulwar. Paget pattern'.

Two other swords which could be mistaken for cavalry weapons were the Havildar and the Mountain Battery or Artillery swords. (Plates 156 and 164). The former was before 1894 used in the Indian Army for arming the men of Mountain Batteries as well as Havildars (Native sergeants) and drummers. Although a new pattern with same grip and blade but a steel hilt was approved in 1894 for the Indian Mountain Batteries and in 1896 for the Royal Artillery Mountain Artillery, it did not appear to come into full scale use in the Indian service. Both swords have a cast iron grip, curved cavalry style blade, but the Havildar sword had a brass stirrup guard and the Mountain Artillery sword had a steel one. Both were carried in a brass mounted brown leather scabbard and worn in a cross belt and frog with the cutting edge uppermost.

Both patterns continued to be ordered throughout the First World War.

Non-Military and Native Swords

Besides the large number of types of military and naval swords used in the period 1750–1918, there were also others carried by *quasi* military bodies such as the police. Many of these patterns were based on military swords such as those of the German Police and the swords carried by high ranking officers in the British Police. In Germany and some South American countries not only were the police armed with swords but this weapon was also issued to members of such organisations as the fire brigade. In Britain, the Thames Division of the Metropolitan Police was issued with short hangers with brass two bar guard and solid cast grip; a further style with single knuckle bow with a wood grip and cap pommel in either brass or steel was issued to Prison warders, with occasionally the name of the prison engraved on the blade. (Plate 186). Swords were also carried by such bodies as the Yeomen of the Guard, the Scottish Archers (The Sovereign's Bodyguard for Scotland) and by numerous others connected with the Royal Household. (Plate 183).

Large numbers of swords were worn by Consuls and Diplomats of various countries, the style of these weapons being mainly based on the small sword. (Plates 181, 182 and 184). At Court a cut steel court sword was worn. This sword was a close copy of a small sword in polished steel with faceted steel studs inlaid in the grip, pommel and shell guard. Diplomatic swords were usually in gilt brass with a small downward pointing shell guard with a beaded edge. (Plate 184). Many countries adopted this style of sword but with either distinctive shaped pommels or badges and emblems fitted to the shell guard. The Consular sword had a pommel in the shape of a closed helmet and was also constructed along the lines of a small sword but with, on occasion, mother of pearl sides to the grip. There were many styles of this weapon but all conformed to the basic small sword pattern, some even having the triangular sectioned hollow ground blade while others had the biconvex blade. This style of weapon has not changed in the last 100 years or so. Swords of this type were, and still are, carried by Royal Academicians, elected members of the *Academie Française* Officers of the Scottish Archers, Equerries to the Queen and other dignitaries in Court dress.

Presentation swords were usually modelled on the style of sword of the period and in the late 18th and 19th centuries, these were mainly military or naval but a number of small sword types, elaborately decorated in enamels were presented by the City of London and other corporate bodies to high ranking and distinguished officers.

In Russia, the custom was for the Czar to give honour swords, decorated with a small enamelled badge of a particular order for gallantry or distinguished conduct whilst in other countries such conduct was rewarded by an order alone. Besides individual presentation swords, made and bestowed to commemorate a certain battle or war, perhaps the best known type is the sword presented by the Patriotic Fund at Lloyds.

For a number of years, merchants and ship insurers had presented swords to officers who, through their actions, had either protected the merchants' or insurers' property or had rendered services to such merchant companies as The Honourable East India Company. On 20th July 1803, at a meeting of underwriters, subscribers and merchants at Lloyds, the Patriotic Fund was established for the purpose of awarding those who conducted themselves with valour in the defence of the nation. Dependant relatives of those awarded were to be provided for and it was further decided that the awards would take the form of silver plate and presentation swords. The money for these awards was raised by public subscription and by the end of the first month, some £100,000 had been raised. The swords given were in three classes, £30, £50, and £100 to which a fourth class was added in 1805 when a meeting of the fund decided that: 'Swords of the value of £100 each, with appropriate inscription, be presented to the surviving Captains and Commanders of His Majesty's Ships, who served in the dangers and glory of the memorable action with the combined fleets of France and Spain off Cape Trafalgar on 21st of October 1805, viz . . .'. This was then followed by a list of the 29 recipients. The 'Trafalgar' swords differed slightly in design from the normal £100 swords, of which 30 were given between 20th July 1803 and 24th May 1809 when the awarding of swords was discontinued. In the same period, 16 £30 swords, and 88 £50 swords were also presented which, together with the 'Trafalgar' awards makes a total of 172 Lloyd's swords. With the discontinuance of the awarding of swords, money was given instead but a number of officers so awarded, privately commissioned Richard Teed, the maker or supplier of these swords, to provide them with a sword according to the scale of their award. Although the Lloyd's swords, except for those bespoken weapons, were discontinued in 1809, the Fund continued until July 1st 1825.

All categories of sword were similar in design, differing only in some small detail of the blueing and gilding on the blade but the main difference between the various grades was in the decorative nature of the scabbard, the £30 sword having three large gilt mounts, the £50 sword having a scabbard where the three mounts were joined together leaving only two panels of the actual scabbard visible and the £100 sword had a similar scabbard but with more decorative mounts and the panels filled with elaborate ornamentation.

Presentation swords were also awarded by the Corporation of the City of London but these were of no special set pattern, each being designed and made for the occasion.

Other forms of presentation swords were either slightly more elaborate versions of the regulation weapon or, more commonly, the standard pattern with the presentation inscription on the blade. During the Victorian period in Britain, swords were not only awarded for valiant deeds or actions but, it seems, from the large numbers of surviving examples, for practically any pretext whatsoever. Edward VII, when Prince of Wales, was a prolific giver of swords, judging from the records of Wilkinson and Son, such as the large numbers given during his tour of India in 1875–6 and he appears to have handed them out to relatives such as the King of Greece, King of Spain, the Kaiser and many other kings and princes on birthdays, visits, or just as 'a token of affection'. Swords were also presented by regiments and corps to long serving officers on promotion or retirement and by sergeants and NCOs when a warrant officer received his commission. The variety of presentation swords is large and besides the types mentioned above there were swords presented for skill at arms, regimental prizes, and swords presented by the Commanders in Chief India to officers of the army and political services, not to mention the police in connection with minor tribal fights and incidents.

Presentation swords were also given in other countries and these were either the regulation weapon with an engraved blade or scabbard or a more elaborately made sword, which usually incorporated motifs and badges relating to the action or the reason for the award.

Native made weapons, especially Indian, are to be found with presentation engravings. These weapons are usually fine examples of the native swordmakers art and the engraving which is on the scabbard or hilt will probably relate that the sword was presented by a Prince to a British officer or regiment or perhaps a return gift when a British style weapon was presented.

JAPANESE SWORDS

The types of Japanese swords changed hardly at all during their long life. The basic style was adhered to in practically every example but with differences in the decorative nature of the fittings and scabbard. Japanese sword blades, for these are in many cases the most valuable and ancient part of the weapon, were grouped in periods of time and from the writing which sometimes appears on the tang of the blade, it is possible to attribute the weapon to a particular period, area and bladesmith. Blades forged before 1537 fall into the *Koto* period while those made from 1537–1876, which are largely found today, are the *Shinto* period. Blades made from 1876 onwards fall into the *Showato* period and it is in this latter era that most of the military swords that had hilt fittings modelled on the western style fall, except where perhaps an old ancestral blade was used with modern made fittings.

The earliest types of Japanese sword blades before the 9th century AD were mainly straight in the Chinese style but from about that period onward, the blades adopted a slightly curved shape due to the thrust being abandoned in favour of the cut by the *Samurai* or warrior.

Japanese swords fall into four main categories, each with a different blade length and decoration and carried in a different manner. The longest sword was the *nodachi* which could be anything up to five or six feet long and was carried across the back in the same way as a rifle or musket would be slung. Next in size came the *tachi* which was shorter and slung from a belt, while the *katana*, (Plate 194), with its plainer fittings was pushed through and held by the waist sash. The smallest of the swords, between one and two feet long was the *wakishashi* which was a short version of the *katana* with a sheath fitted to take two small tools, one a general purpose knife and the other for putting up the hair.

The *Samurai*, or the warrior class of feudal Japan, carried their weapons in pairs called a *daisho* which could consist of a long and short sword or a short sword and dagger depending on the choice of the warrior. The privilege of carrying more than one weapon was peculiar to the *Samurai*, but on rare occasions might be conferred on someone lower in the feudal scale.

Besides the blade of the Japanese sword, which was itself unique in both shape and method of manufacture, there were various component parts of the hilt and scabbard. The grip of the sword was made of two pieces of wood, grooved on the inside to fit the tang of the blade and glued together. This grip was held to the tang by means of a small wooden peg which passed through the grip and a corresponding hole in the tang. Over the wood grip was stuck a layer of ray fish skin called the *same* and then a criss-cross of braid which held to each side of the grip a small metal ornament known as the *menuki*. A small cap or pommel (*kashira*) was fitted to the top of the grip and held by the braid binding while a ferrule (*fuchi*) was fitted to the other end. Before this grip was slipped on to the tang, a small washer made in copper (*seppa*) was placed between the *fuchi* and the hand guard (*tsuba*) and the other side of the guard resting on the shoulder of the blade. Each of these fittings was decorated ensuite, the most elaborate being the *tsuba*, which was mostly made from iron and decorated with relief work and piercing and sometimes inlaid with gold or silver. *Tsubas* that had three holes in them were usually for the smaller swords such as the *wakisashi*, as the two holes each side of the central slot were intended for the *kodzuka* or small knife and the *kogai*, the implements for dressing the hair which were accommodated in the scabbard. So elaborate are the designs of the *tsuba* that these alone are collected. (Plate 197).

On occasion, the sword blade was mounted in a plain all wood scabbard with plain wood grip. This was not worn but was purely a storage case for the blade, which was, if an old blade, handed down in a family for many generations with perhaps only the scabbard and hilt fittings being changed. Some of these old blades often turn up in military swords of the *Showato* period. One of the most difficult parts of collecting Japanese swords is the reading and interpreting the writing on the tang. Sometimes the writing when deciphered will reveal that the blade was the work of a famous smith and that it dates from the 17th or 18th century, but sometimes it may only say such phrases as 'Made in 1939 using the steel from a smoothing iron'. The inclusion of a signature on the tang of a blade or the lack of it does not automatically mean that the blade is either very old or vice versa as the above example shows.

The making of a sword blade was a highly skilled and complex operation taking many weeks to complete before it was ready for testing or proving, which was accomplished either on the bodies of convicts or on other materials such as bales of hay, iron etc.

The unique property of a Japanese sword blade was its hardness and ability to hold and edge for a long period without having the brittleness normally associated with very hard steel. This extraordinary virtue was accomplished by the method of manufacture employed which combined hard steel and iron together, and tempered the result in a special way. The steel and iron could either be heated and hammered together with a variety of powders and clay and then folded and allowed to cool before the process was repeated as many as 20 times before the blade was forged, or the blade could be made with a soft inner core. In this latter method, the steel ingot was heated, hammered and folded about 10 times and then a soft iron plate was placed on the steel and the two metals folded in the centre with the iron innermost. This was then forged to the blade shape. The next step in the manufacture was perhaps the most crucial as this was the hardening process. The blade was covered in a layer of wet clay mixture and a line drawn about ½in from the edge and the clay covering this portion removed. When the clay had hardened, the blade was placed in a furnace with the bladesmith watching the change in colour of the metal as it heated. When the required colour of metal had been reached, the blade was withdrawn, the clay covering removed and the blade plunged into tepid water. The blade was withdrawn and the metal allowed to cool. The line where the clay had stopped appeared slightly wavy and crystallised and the area between this and the cutting edge was known as the *yakiba*. The rest of the outer layer of steel was hard but to a much lesser degree than the edge. The blade was now sharpened and polished to a mirror finish, a process that could take many weeks to accomplish. It was then marked on the tang with the maker's name, province and date before being mounted with the fittings and scabbard.

In 1876, the Imperial edict forbade the carrying of swords by anyone except the military and the art of the sword maker nearly died out under the pressure of the mass produced military item. The mass produced weapons with their knuckle guards and western style scabbards were of the *Shin-Shinto* period but in 1937, a return was made to the more traditional style sword and this was known as the *Shin-Gunto* era. Many of these last war military swords have the traditional style of hilt and blade but with brown leather covered scabbards while NCOs had a sword with an all steel scabbard and a cast alloy hilt in the form of the traditional shape but with the braid painted in brown paint. (Plate 153).

NATIVE INDIAN SWORDS AND OTHER NATIVE WEAPONS

The basic style of sword predominant on the Indian subcontinent was the tulwar. (Plate 189). This style of weapon had been carried for many hundreds of years by the warrior who relied mainly on it for both attack and defence, other items such as daggers, axes etc., being secondary to this main armament. Although today, Indian swords of this type are loosely grouped under the name of 'tulwar', there are many variations in blade shapes and size and in the style of hilt. All tulwars have a curved blade of some variety being intended for cutting rather than thrusting. The thrusting sword of India was the *pata*, which had a straight blade. (Plate 238). This 'gauntlet' sword had the grip enclosed in an armoured gauntlet, usually highly decorated in the Indian style and was used in the way one would deliver a straight left in boxing.

The predominant feature of the tulwar besides the curved blade, was the all metal hilt with its distinctive disc pommel, usually, even on the most common types, engraved with typical Indian designs. (Plate 196). The metal hilt consisted of a cast grip with cross guard and langet each side and a disc pommel with a nut on the top. This nut, however, did not hold the hilt to the tang as in western-made swords, but was purely to hold the disc to the top of the grip and to finish off the tang. The grip, incorporating the cross guard was usually held to the tang with shellac or another form of hard glue or fixative. On occasion this top nut took the form of a spike sometimes curving forward.

Another form of Indian sword, akin to the *tulwar* was the *Firangi* which was basically used like the European two handed sword. The blade of the *Firangi* was like the *pata* and straight, but the hilt was similar to the *tulwar* except that the cross guard and langets were replaced by a slight bowl hilt with a knuckle bow and a flat disc top with a spike projection. (Plate 190). The grip was held with one hand and the spike with the other and the sword wielded in this way. The inside of the bowl guard was usually padded and langets protruded from the bowl guard to stiffen the top of the blade. Some examples have the two separate grips and knuckle guard like the one illustrated but, in this case, the top spike is not included. (Plate 195).

On all Indian weapons a variety of blades can be found, some, if not most, made locally in India by native craftsmen, while other swords used European blades either imported to India for sale by one of the trading companies, or discarded military blades either captured or picked up on the battlefield. Many curved blades found in *tulwars* will be found with either French or British military blades in them; these can be identified from the original marks and engravings which are usually left intact with native engraving, embossing and inlaying being added. Some blades were especially made in Europe for the Indian market and these were usually marked, as were nearly all blades made in either Germany and England for this type of trade, with the marks of famous swordmakers such as Andrea Farrara, (fig 16c), and with such marks as the running wolf of Passau, (fig. 15a), as this enhanced the value of the blade to the native purchaser.

Another form of curved bladed sword found not only in India but in neighbouring countries was the *shamshir*. (Plate 188). The curves of the blades of these weapons varied enormously, some being slight while others were curved so irregularly that the scabbard had to have a slot in the back to enable the sword to be drawn, or sheathed. The basic style of hilt of the *shamshir* was the design called *mamaluke*, akin to the modern British and Indian Army general's sword. It is interesting to note that in the 19th century some officers entitled to wear the mamaluke style scimitar on occasion adopted a native made weapon instead of the regulation one, or had a particularly attractive or old native blade mounted with the regulation hilt. The grips of the *shamshir* could be horn, bone, ivory, brass or precious metals and the cross guard of silver, gold, or inlaid iron. The cross guard usually terminated in two acorn or ball shaped finials and had a langet each side, which not only came down over the top part of the blade but also indented upwards into the grips.

Another most distinctive blade shape was found on the *kora*, the native sword of Nepal. The hilt had a simple disc pommel and cross guard with a plain grip but the blade widened from the hilt and had a distinctive cutaway point which, in some examples, was decorated with an eye.

From further east than India come such swords as the *Mandau* of the Borneo Dyak's and the *dha* from Burma. (Plate 194). The former weapon was carried by the head hunting tribes of Borneo and had a blade which widened towards the rounded point rather like a *machete*, and was usually concave in section and decorated with chiseling and other designs. The hilt was fairly simple being a carved bone or horn grip, sometimes fashioned in the form of an animal's head to which was attached tufts of hair which, although popularly believed to be human, were more often than not from animals. The sheath, as with most sheaths for native weapons was made from two pieces of wood bound together with thongs made from creeper or grass. Like many other styles of sword used for many other purposes than fighting, a smaller sheath attached to the main one housed a supplementary knife. Usually attached to the scabbard, which was decorated with hair and other forms of binding, were the user's talisman or good luck beads and charms.

The Burmese *dha* had a slightly curved blade which was single edged and fitted with a long hilt, rather like the Japanese but less ornate and likewise without a cross guard. The top of the hilt was crowned with a metal cap, as was the base. The grip itself was wood bound in fish skin or other suitable material. The scabbard was again not unlike that found on Japanese swords and was of similar construction but bound together with metal bands or thongs. A thick cord was wound around the top of the scabbard and ended in a long loop which was worn over the shoulder.

Beside the weapons mentioned above, there are others based on these designs or which differ little from them.

AFRICAN SWORDS

The two common styles of African sword were those carried by the Sudanese, the Arab and the Abyssinians, all more often than not found with European trade blades made in Germany or England. The Sudanese and Arab sword had a straight double edged blade which terminated in a rounded point, although some of the Arab swords had curved blades, with a simple cross hilt. The hilt had a round leather disc pommel with a plain leather bound grip and a metal cross guard with straight faceted bars and a double langet pointing upwards and downwards, the former usually covered by the grip binding. The scabbards which were made of leather and tooled with lines down and across, broadened to a spear shaped point at the end and had two rings held to the body with leather thongs which served to attach the carrying loop. Some hilts of these weapons can be found with the grip in bone and the mounts in gold or inlaid with precious metals. The blades may be marked with not only names of famous smiths but with the sun, moon and stars symbols and impressed makers' marks which has led to speculation that the blades were those captured during the crusades but, except for the very rare case, this is a myth and the blades were especially made for the African market.

The swords found with a very curved sickle-like blade with the cutting edge on the inner side were those used in Abyssinia, although straight blades of varying widths and even wavy blades were carried. The hilt of the Abyssinian sword was usually one piece of horn through which the tang passed. This grip swelled out towards the top on which was placed an ornamented piece of metal before the tang was held in place by either burring over or a small nut. The many variations of blade shape and size found mounted with these hilts is due to the large scale importation of blades from Germany and Britain during the 19th and 20th centuries. The Wilkinson Sword Company produced a whole series of blades for the Abyssinian market, embossed with the Lion of Juda and decorative scroll work, and on occasion, some were blued and gilt. Wilkinson's also made a 'flame' blade which was double edged and waved, embossed and inlaid to give the impression of a burning flame. The inlays were in blueing, brass and copper and the effect was most realistic. These blades were hilted up in Abyssinia and were used to arm Emperor Haile Selassie's personal bodyguard. (Plate 164).

Another style of sword encountered emanated from the West Coast of Africa and usually consisted of a leaf shaped blade, of rather poor quality, decorated with various designs and with a small grip and ball pommel. The blades on some could be highly decorative but this style of weapon was more used for ceremonial occasions and executions rather than fighting.

2: DAGGERS, KNIVES & DIRKS

Evolution and History up to 1750

In following the evolution of daggers and dirks, we must also include the knife which was, perhaps, one of the first edged weapons used by early man. The knife, from the old Norse *knifr* and later the old English *cnif*, was usually a short bladed weapon with a single cutting edge, whereas the dagger, from the 14th century English word *dag*, meaning to stab, was an equally short bladed weapon with two cutting edges and the blade tapering to a point. The dirk, a type of weapon normally associated with the Scottish knife of that name and known in the 17th and 18th centuries as a *durk*, could be either single or double edged and with a varying blade length.

The earliest forms of knife were made from flint with probably a small piece of animal skin wrapped around the part that was gripped in the hand. Wood slats or even sides made from bone were fitted to the foot long blades and later, flint daggers had a more shaped handle made from wood, which swelled out towards the top ensuring a better grip and giving the appearance of having a pommel. The blades, instead of being narrow and thin, were leaf shaped and flat but thick enough to be used in combat.

The early forms of knives and daggers mentioned above were not really effective because of the brittle nature of flint, but with the discovery of copper and later its amalgamation with tin to form bronze, a more robust and useful form of knife and dagger were made. The main drawback to copper was that it was a soft metal and to have a blade that would not bend or break when used, it had to be fairly thick. The early forms of copper knives and daggers were cast in one piece and then finished by hand with the grips of either wood or bone riveted to the tang. The edges of the blade were beaten to give the weapon a suitable cutting edge. With the improvement in casting methods and the advent of the two piece mould, daggers were made with lighter blades, but with a central rib or bar stretching from shoulder to point that gave the copper blade the strength it needed and replaced the more wasteful methods of using a fairly thick blade.

The discovery of tin, and how, when blended with copper the resultant amalgam was not only stronger but just as easy to work, led to the use of bronze for weapons of early civilisations. The majority of the discoveries and improvements in edged weapons up until this time had taken place in the near and Middle East where the great civilisations all existed. Because of this new metal, blades could be made longer, thinner but yet just as strong or even stronger than the copper blades with a central rib. The grip, which was cast as an integral part of the blade was more elaborate in shape and was fitted with scales of horn, bone or ivory. The blade shapes in the North remained wide at the shoulder and tapered to a point, but in the Southern European areas the dagger tended to follow the shape of the sword with more of a leaf shaped blade. Even though bronze was superior to copper for the making of edged weapons, it was still a soft metal liable to damage if wielded too strongly or used to hack rather than thrust.

The discovery of iron about 3000 years before the birth of Christ gave the metal worker a far stronger, more lasting metal with which to make his swords and daggers and supplied the warrior with a superior weapon with more potential than the bronze sword. The one drawback with iron was that, at this time anyway, it could not be cast but only smelted and the hilts were invariably cast in bronze in two piece moulds and so it was possible to make them into pleasing and comfortable shapes. Decorated with horn or bone, they were riveted to the tang of the iron blade. The hilts and scabbards were sometimes made in copper or bronze and became more ornate and were decorated with inlaid precious metals and stones. There is some doubt whether the scabbard was used with copper and bronze age swords, except in the case of chieftains or other high ranking members of the community, when it was unlikely to be in the same metal as the sword and was more probably in wood, bound with either cloth or leather. The iron bladed dagger was still double edged at this period and the designs of the hilts, grips and pommels were many and varied though usually conforming in design to the sword of the particular area where they were made and used.

The two edged bladed dagger in iron with a copper or bronze hilt riveted to the blade or slipped over and riveted to the tang, began to lose popularity around 400 BC although double edged swords continued in use for many hundreds of years after this period. The dagger was now replaced by the short bladed knife with a single cutting edge which could be used for hacking, cutting and even thrusting when necessary. The decline in popularity of the dagger could possibly be attributed to the success of the Greek hoplites, heavy infantrymen grouped in a unit of 16 ranks of 256 men called a phalanx, who, under Alexander the Great, swept across the Persian Empire as far as India, from 334–331 BC. The favourite weapon of the hoplites was the *sarissa*, a pike with a point at each end of the staff with an overall length of 16 feet; they also carried a short sword but dispensed with daggers or knives.

During the era of Roman domination covering the period of approximately 300 BC to AD 400, when the legions were defending Italy against the onslaught of the savage barbarian hoards, neither the dagger nor the knife were included as part of the soldiers' fighting equipment which consisted solely of the spear or *pilum* and the *gladius* or short sword.

Vikings, Norsemen and other Germanic tribes employed the knife in a form called a *scramasax*, a single edged weapon of no set blade length; other than for this use, it remained a household implement until the 12th and 13th centuries when the dagger was revived as a fighting weapon. Contemporary evidence shows that the daggers that were carried during the 12th and 13th centuries were mainly triangular sectioned and double edged, although examples are known with single edged blades. From about 1250, the cross guard and pommel were crescent shaped but by about 1300 another form had appeared having a lozenge shaped pommel, a small simple cross guard slightly down pointing and a double edged blade which was rather long and slim.

By the latter years of the 14th century, the dagger had become part of the equipment of the knight and man-at-arms and various forms can be seen on contemporary monumental effigies in churches. The predominant style had a broad tapering double edged blade about 12ins long with a wood or horn handle, with the tang of the weapon shaped to the basic grip so as not to need a cross guard and the grips covering both the pommel and cross guard shapes. The most popular style of knife worn by civilians was the 'Ballock' knife or dagger, (Plate 198), depending on whether the blade was single or double edged, which had a grip with two large protuberances where it joined the blade. Although termed a 'Ballock' knife or dagger during the Middle Ages, the Victorians referred to it as a kidney dagger, a term still occasionally used today. The 'Ballock' knife had a sheath with, in some cases, a small integral sheath for a knife. This weapon is thought to be the forerunner of the Scottish dirk.

Another basic style of dagger in use in the 14th century had a simple pommel and a slightly pointing down cross guard. The blade was of diamond section and the pommel and cross guard very similar to the style of sword in use at this time (see Swords, Evolution and History up to 1750, page 3). During the first half of the 15th century the 'Rondel' dagger was in use and although similar in size and shape to the above weapon, it differed in that the pommel and cross guard were round discs of metal. (Plate 198). Another variation had the guard with one side turned up and the other turned down and this latter style seems to be the most common; it can be presumed to be the type carried by the normal fighting soldier. (Plate 198).

The style of dagger in use during the 16th century was the simple cross hilted variety, a pattern that seems to have been widely used in Europe. Daggers are mentioned in the reign of Elizabeth I as part of the equipment of the ordinary soldier and are noted in contemporary documents of the period. The 'quotas of certain Hundreds', subdivisions of counties or shires having their own court, in 1559 mention the dress and arms of certain levies as 'a cassock of watchett a $\frac{3}{4}$ yard, a white doublet, white hose, shoes, garters and points, a scull cap, a sword, dagger and girdle'. A muster proclamation for Liverpool in 1567 similarly stated that the men were to be armed with a sword and dagger.

Two other forms of dagger appeared in the last half of the 16th century and were called the *stiletto*, (Plate 202), and the *main gauche*. The former was a thin bladed weapon with a narrow triangular or square sectioned blade, being rather entirely of metal or similar to the more conventional dagger. Some examples were very ornate and had carved and chiseled work on the cross guard and pommel. The *main gauche*, (Plates 201 and 202), or left hand dagger was used in conjunction with the sword in fighting and duelling. The blade was double edged, strong enough to be able to check the blow of the opponents sword and the cross guard usually curved downwards on each side. Later examples had small rings each side for added hand protection and for use by horsemen who plunged the dagger into the ground and tied the reigns of their horse to the ring as a tether. Another variety of *main gauche*, prevalent in Spain and Spanish territories had much longer straight quillons and a triangular shaped metal guard for the hand. (Plate 205). Some examples also had an additional shell guard, conforming to the companion rapier. (Plate 18). The *main gauche* went out of fashion in the 1660s as the rapier declined in fashion but still continued in use in Spain until the early 1700s. After this date nearly all forms of fighting knives were discontinued due to the different fighting tactics imposed by the general use of firearms.

The 'Ballock' knife or dagger enjoyed a longer life, although the shape of the grip altered slightly and became rather long and narrow. In the 1650s, the Northern English version began to develop into the dirk, the two side balls on the grip becoming larger and the pommel flattened at the top. (Plates 206 and 207). During the early part of the 18th century, the grips were carved with Celtic interlacing and decorated with small nails between the strap work; the two balls now tended to be flat at the front and back of the grip and the scabbard made to accommodate a small knife and fork. Following the 1715 rebellion in Scotland attempts were made to ban all Scottish weapons and, following the 1745 uprising, an act was passed against highland dress.

Daggers and knives having African and Eastern origins which are most readily available today in antique markets are dealt with in 'Other Daggers and Knives', pages 54–59.

Scottish Dirks

The Scottish dirk, evolved from the 14th century 'Ballock' knife, seems to have already taken on a special form in Scotland as early as 1512. A contemporary account of that year stated that Highlanders were noted for their 'large daggers sharpened on one side only, but very sharp'. Early examples did not usually carry a companion knife and fork in the scabbard but a few instances of this are known. The grips of dirks were made from bog oak, a particularly hard and dark wood, and usually topped by a brass or iron pommel.

The dirk was an integral part of the highland dress carried by civilians and clan members in the style of European gentlemen of the early 17th century. Early types of dirks had their blades made from broken sword blades but, by the 18th century, a typical blade shape had been adopted with a single cutting edge, a flat back tapering to an edge on the bottom few inches. (Plates 206 and 207). One cannot be dogmatic about this blade form as double edged dirks and dirks with even triangular or diamond sectioned blades are known and documented.

Following the 1715 rebellion, the Disarming Act was passed in the following year when peace was restored to the Highlands, and made it a penal offence to have, use or wear 'Broadsword or target (*shield*), poignard, whinger or dirk, side pistol, gun or other warlike weapon'. In the enforcement of this Act of 1716, the Government paid for each item surrendered leading to General Wade complaining that £13000 had been paid out for useless and broken arms. One can only draw the conclusion from this that the canny Scot had lived up to his legendary reputation! In 1725, the Act was again enforced but without repayment for the weapons relinquished and, as a result, a great number of dirks, broadswords and pistols were broken up and melted down by local smiths to be remade into agricultural implements rather than be handed in. In the 1725 enforcement, only 2685 weapons were collected and these deposited in Edinburgh Castle. Following the 1745 uprising, the Act was again enforced and supplemented by the passing of a new Act 'The Abolition and Proscription of the Highland Dress' in 1746.

Since the early part of the 18th century, companies of soldiers had been raised for service in the Highlands; these troops were permitted to wear Highland dress and to use Scottish weapons, and in 1739, when the first regular Scottish regiment, the Black Watch, was formed, the Government issued muskets, bayonets and broad swords, but dirks, highland pistols and targets (shields) were either supplied by the Colonel or the men themselves. This seems to have been the case until such time as the dirk ceased to be carried by the ordinary soldier, so it is very doubtful whether a uniform pattern existed. The rarity of dirks and other Scottish weapons from the first half of the 18th century is undoubtedly due to the Disarming Act of 1716 and the Abolition and Proscription Act of 1746, and those weapons that have been found are either those hidden by the owners or worn by the military.

In 1782, the Disarming Act and the Abolition and Proscription Act were repealed and the dirk came back into use. The civilian version now assumed a different style with a slightly exaggerated carved hilt and the mounts of both knife and scabbard more elaborate, with thistle or Celtic interlaced engraving. The companion knife and fork now became a more

common feature of the dirk, matching the larger knife.

The military dirk seems to have undergone little change with officers still wearing a pattern of their choice or clan and a fairly plain type being worn by sergeants. The men apparently gave up wearing the dirk when they stopped carrying the broad sword in 1767 and only sergeants continued to use both these items, their dirk having a carved bog oak grip surmounted by a flat pommel on which was engraved the Crown. Drummers also carried a dirk and this was probably the same pattern as used by sergeants, but pipers, who until 1854 were not officially sanctioned, were maintained and equipped at the expense of the officers, and so various patterns were worn.

In 1881 each Highland regiment was allowed five pipers charged to public funds and three years later Lowland regiments were accorded the same number provided that these pipers were not charged to the public. A dirk formed part of the equipment of pipers, bandsmen and drummers of Highland regiments and a suitable pattern was approved by the authorities for issue to these men. Lowland regiments either provided their own patterns or were able to buy the regulation dirks from Ordnance. The pattern worn was very similar to the dirk described above worn by sergeants and pipers in the late part of the 18th century. The grip was of carved ebony (later because of cost changed to black dermatine) with Celtic interlacing and topped with a flat pommel which bore a raised crown. The blade was plain and single edged and carried in a plain black leather scabbard with four mounts, each one embossed with thistles. There was no knife and fork. In 1918, all Scottish regiments were allowed one Pipe Major and six pipers paid for and equipped by the Government.

Pipe Majors were issued with the same pattern of dirk as used by the officers, but there

Fig. 9 42nd Highland Regiment Officers dirk. From the Pattern Book of Wilkinson Sword Ltd. *Circa* 1858.

were exceptions to this when a more decorative weapon was supplied at the expense of the officers. The only Scottish regiment which did not carry the regulation pipers dirk was the Scots Guards, their pipers wearing a weapon with companion knife and fork with small chains fitted to the knife and fork and attached to the scabbard mounts. The pommel of the dirk was tilted forward slightly and bore the regimental badge. This pattern with appropriate change in badge was adopted by pipers of the Canadian Guards.

Many of the dirks available today to the collector are those worn by officers. These weapons and their civilian counterparts were solely decorative and are well preserved because they were not subject to the rough usage of a sword or other normal service weapon. For the various descriptions of the dirks worn in each regiment we must look to another source than Dress Regulations for the Army which provides much of our information on officers' dress in the 19th century. The first Dress Regulations of 1822 gives the only description of dirks and this rather vaguely, as it states: 'Dirks — Plain gilt mountings; black ebony grip, plain steel blade, scabbard fitted with knife and fork. Scabbard in black leather worn on right side'. Subsequent regulations issued in 1831 and 1834 only repeat this description while those of 1846 simply state 'Of established Regimental pattern'. The regulations of the late 19th century are not helpful, either, stating as they do much the same information as 1846 but adding: 'The dirk is not to exceed 17¼ins overall from extreme end of dirk handle to the point of the sheath. The blade should not be more than 1⅜ins in breadth at the broadest part'.

The way that we can identify the dirks worn by officers during the 19th century is by examining surviving examples and drawings in manufacturers' pattern books. Each regiment had its own design with special engraving and embossing on the hilt and mounts and with, before 1881 the regimental number on the top mount of the scabbard. (Plates 209, 211 and 212). After 1881, the number was replaced by a badge, although new patterns were not approved until 1883. (Plates 211 and 212). Not all regiments followed the 1822 regulations directing

Fig. 10 Design for a dirk blade. From the Pattern Book of Wilkinson Sword Ltd. *Circa* 1850.

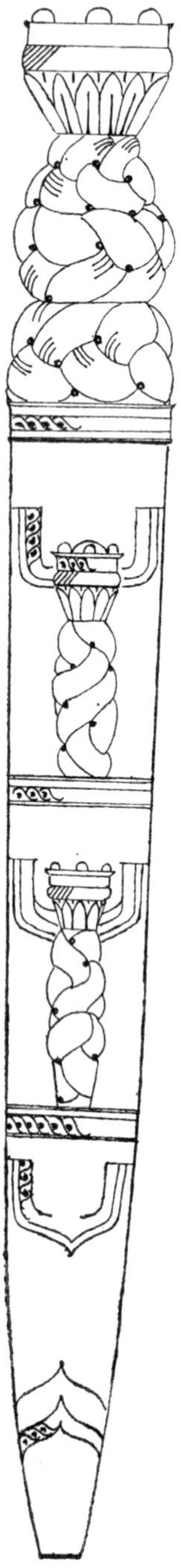

that the dirk be gilt mounted and, during the 19th century, the style changed. The early patterns have the flat pommel to the grip which was changed to a tilting forward pommel on all except the dirk worn by the Gordon Highlanders in the 1860s. The pommel was decorated with an inset stone, usually a cairngorm, and the ebony grip was elaborately carved and studded with small nails. The companion knife and fork followed the style of the dirk. The blade was not left plain as stated in the regulations, but decorated by etching showing the regimental number and badge, if entitled, and later the badge only together with battle honours and thistle designs. Not all regiments stuck to the regulations concerning dirks; the Black Watch (42nd & 73rd), (fig 9), the Highland Light Infantry (71st & 74th), (Plate 209), the Seaforth Highlanders (72nd & 78th), (Plate 212), and the Cameron Highlanders (79th), (Plate 212), had gilt mounts to their dirks while the Gordon Highlanders (75th & 92nd) and the Argyll and Sutherland Highlanders (91st & 93rd), (Plate 213), had silver mounted dirks. Volunteers tended to have silver mounted dirks, (Plate 209 and fig 11), that of the London Scottish being a particularly attractive example with carved grip and elaborate silver mounts. (Plate 209).

Besides the regimental pattern of dirks, there were many other civilian varieties. (Plates 208 and 210). As with swords, presentation dirks are known, a most elaborate one with its grip studded with sea pearls was presented to Sir Colin Campbell after the Crimean War. (Plate 214).

Another small but not very old item of Highland dress was the *skean dhu*, worn in the right stocking. These skean dhu's, the name deriving from the Gaelic word *sgian* meaning knife and *dubh* meaning black, have a short single edged blade with carved wooden handle decorated in the same manner as the dirk. The military weapons for pipers are plain with metal mounts, while those for officers have a cairngorm in the pommel and have the grip decorated with either a badge or Celtic lacing and nails to match the dirk; usually the blade is etched with the regimental badge and honours. (Plate 215).

Fig. 11 **Design for Argyllshire Rifle Volunteers dirk *circa* 1880. From the Pattern Book of Wilkinson Sword Ltd.**

Naval Dirks

The naval dirk originated in the last half of the 18th century, although daggers and short hunting swords had been carried for many years before by Naval officers. The wearing of dirks was fairly universal and they were carried by various ranks of officer as a convenient alternative to a sword when on board ship. It was only in the 19th century that the dirk became regulation wear and its design and use stipulated.

Early patterns of naval dirk are not easy to identify; very few bear any mark or motif to connect them with that service. The most popular type, used by a number of navies, had a turned ivory grip, a simple cross guard and a straight double edged blade. The scabbard was in black leather with gilt brass mounts which had rings for attachment to the belt. Some examples of this style encountered are so small in blade length and grip that they appear to be scaled down versions made for boys, which is perhaps more than likely considering the age at which boys went to sea as midshipmen in the early 19th century. (Plate 217). France, Denmark and Holland favoured the curved blade, which was also used in the Royal Navy after about 1806, probably copied from that of Denmark against whom they fought in that year.

Another style of dirk used in the Royal Navy at this period was similar to the so-called '5 ball' sword which had been adopted by the Navy and Military in the 1780s and which is more correctly termed as a bead hilt spadroon. This pattern had a double edged blade with a single fuller each side extending to the point. The cross guard was 'S' shaped and incorporated a side ring containing five balls or beads. The grip, rectangular in section, was in ivory and decorated with vertical fluting and a gilt metal band bisecting the grip on which was an oval cartouche engraved with an anchor badge. The pommel was what was termed as cushion shaped and had a ring fitted to which the dirk knot was tied.

The curved bladed dirk had a different style of hilt, with a carved ivory grip, gilt pommel and backpiece and small 'S' shaped cross guard. In the British pattern, the pommel was in the form of a lion's head, (Plate 216), although this was also used on a number of foreign patterns.

In the Royal Navy, the dirk has always been associated with Midshipmen, but this was not always so. In 1825, Midshipmen, Volunteers and Masters Assistants were ordered swords and forbidden to wear dirks, which were, however, restored to Volunteers in 1827 and worn by them up to 1846 when the sword took its place. The pattern carried by Volunteers is thought to have been of the curved variety with an ivory or horn grip and a lion head pommel and backpiece. No knot was worn but instead the weapon was provided with a chain knuckle guard connected between the lion head and the cross piece. In 1856, Midshipmen, Naval Cadets and Masters Assistants were ordered a dirk in place of the sword and the new weapon, described in Uniform Regulations on April 4th 1856, as 'according to pattern' had a single edged blade and an 'S' shaped cross piece terminating in acorn ends. (Plate 218). The grip was bound in white fish skin and wound at intervals with gilt wire and was fitted with a backpiece with a lion head top. The scabbard was in black leather with two mounts, the locket having a frog stud. A variation of this pattern had a much wider blade 12ins long and a straight cross guard. (Plate 218). At a later date, the blade length of dirks was increased to 17¾ins and two rings were added to the locket for sling suspension. A new pattern was approved in 1879, (Plate 218), which, although similar to the previous weapon, had an oval medallion bearing the Crown and anchor in the centre of the cross piece, and regulations described the blade as being 'blue and gold' but this type of decoration was abandoned around 1890 although regulations up to 1939 continued to mention this form of blade etching. In 1936, Paymaster Midshipmen and Paymaster Cadets were ordered the dirk but, with the outbreak of war in 1939, regulations for its wear ceased to be enforced.

The dirk adopted by the *Deutsche Marine*, created under the German Federation in 1849, had a straight double edged blade, a cross piece with button quillons having a central tablet on which was a raised anchor badge, and a round or global pommel decorated with flame-like engraving. The grip was in ivory and the scabbard was of gilt metal with two bands and rings. This weapon was worn by all ranks of officer, seniority being distinguished by the wearing or the absence of a dirk knot (*portepee*). Sometime in the early 1860s, officer's dirks were abolished and in 1872, Midshipmen and cadets were ordered to replace the dirk with a brass hilted side arm.

The side arm, which was ordered in 1872, had a cast brass hilt with a small shell guard and cross piece with, on the shell guard, the foul anchor and on the cross piece, the Imperial Crown. In 1890, when the dirk was once more ordered for Midshipmen, the *Marine Applikanten* or Engineer cadets retained the side arm. Some variations of this weapon have an Imperial Crown on the pommel as well as the cross piece. (Plate 220).

The restored dirk was based on the 1849 pattern except that the global pommel was replaced by an Imperial Crown. (Plate 219). In 1901, officers were ordered to wear the dirk as worn by Midshipmen. The scabbards of German Naval dirks were many and varied ranging from gilt brass with hammer finish to examples with superb engraving. The blades also differed, some being plain while others had etching and even blue and gilt work on them. There were many small variations in German 'regulation' weapons which were allowed, most of these differences being dictated by the cost of the item rather than the rank of the officer. The Carl Eickhorn catalogue of 1908, *Musterbuch der Waffenfabrik* illustrates 18 different types of scabbard for the naval dirk.

On 28th November 1919, following the issue of regulations for the new German Navy, a further pattern of dirk was introduced. This had the same type of blade and cross piece but a black grip and a global pommel of the pattern used up to 1873. The scabbard was also black with a single band and ring. Complaints concerning the chipping of the black paint led to the restoration of the old pattern scabbard in 1921 and in 1929, the white grip replaced the black one. (Plate 219).

In 1938, the global pommel was replaced by the *Wehrmacht* eagle and a dateline of April 20th was given for this change to be carried out (Plate 241); however, officers who had received their commissions before November 1st 1918, were still permitted to retain the Imperial Naval dirk. In 1943, by order of the Reich-Minister for Armament and Munitions, the manufacture of swords and daggers was discontinued. All officers who did not possess dirks were ordered to wear pistols, but those with dirks were still allowed to wear them.

Although a number of other countries prescribed dirks for Naval war, France was a notable exception. Denmark who first ordered the dirk in 1822 favoured the curved blade up to the 1860s when a straight bladed weapon with a turned ivory grip carried in an embossed scabbard was introduced for both the army and navy. The embossing on the scabbard incorporated the arms of the country and the same pattern was copied by the Greek Navy. Holland introduced the dirk in 1806, but it appears that the pattern and even the blade shape was optional, this also being true of the dirk introduced in Spain for Midshipmen.

Turkey introduced a dirk modelled on the British pattern of 1879 but with the cypher of Abdul Hamid II in place of the crown and anchor on the medallion. In 1890, the dirk was changed to the German style but with an 'S' shaped cross piece and a turban in place of the Imperial Crown. Russia ordered Officers and Midshipmen to wear dirks in 1803 but withdrew this for all except officers of the flag rank in 1828. In 1855 a straight bladed weapon with small cross piece, rectangular sectioned ivory grip with cap pommel and top nut was introduced. In some cases the Imperial cypher was engraved on the blade or pommel. There also existed in Russia the honour dirk which bore the enamel badge of the order of St George or St Anne conferred on an officer for gallantry.

The United States of America never authorised a dirk, although many unofficial patterns were worn at the beginning of the 19th century. South American countries tended to copy either the German or British patterns because of influence of that country or because of source of supply. The Columbian naval dirk was a copy of the British pattern of 1879, but with the Columbian arms instead of the British Crown. The Mexican dirk was also styled on the British pattern, but with an oval medallion bearing; for the navy, a Condor with outspread wings holding a snake surmounting two crossed foul anchors; for the army, the Condor and the words 'Republica Mexicana' above and 'Colegia Milita' beneath, and in place of the lion head on the back piece was the head of a Condor. (Plate 221). A number of other South American countries had their dirks based on the

German pattern, some having black grips and the global pommel with an anchor on it while others utilised a faithful copy of the German weapon. (Plate 222).

Both China and Japan had naval dirks, the former based on the British pattern but with an anchor within a wreath of corn in place of the Crown and anchor while the latter had a dirk based loosely on their national style of dagger. There is also reason to believe that a dirk modelled on the British style was worn in Japan, but with a cherry blossom device substituted for the Crown on the medallion. This design appears on a British style naval sword supplied by Wilkinson's in January 1872, when samples of sword, lace, button, belts and buckles were submitted and approved.

The Siamese navy also copied the British and had a dirk based on the 1879 pattern, but with an elephant head on the backpiece and a plain foul anchor on the medallion. The embossing on the blade was altered to include the arms of Siam.

The Belgian Navy, formed in 1831 after independence did not adopt a dirk until 1883, and then not exclusively for the navy. The *poignard d'officer* closely resembles the British dirk of 1856 except that it had a single edged blade with no fullers and a false edge at the point, a straight cross guard and black grip. (Plate 171). In 1893, the blade shape was changed to one having a single edge and a fuller. The scabbard was in black leather with two mounts decorated in the British style.

Other Daggers and Knives

In this section are listed the main features of a number of native and other daggers and knives which are commonly available to the collector and with each heading, a short description is given. Space does not permit the following of the evolution of native weapons, many of which, it is almost impossible to place in the evolution of daggers and knives because so little is known about their history. The list together with the illustrations which show a number of the more common varieties will aid the collector in identifying the weapon under consideration.

BOWIE KNIFE

This weapon had a large, straight single edged blade with a clipped back and was used for both fighting and hunting. It was named after the legendary Colonel James Bowie who was said to have visited a blacksmith in the 1830s and asked him to make a knife to his own design. A very large number were made by well-known Sheffield cutlery firms and many have etched blades bearing loyal mottoes and scenes. The grips were originally in bone or staghorn, but elaborate models of this knife with silver hilt were made in the last quarter of the 19th century. (Plates 224, 225 and 240).

COMMANDO KNIFE

This was a double edged bladed weapon with a small cross piece and a knurled brass grip. It was designed by Captains Fairbairn and Sykes at the beginning of World War II. Later patterns differed in having die cast grips with concentric ridges on them. The leather scabbard was adapted to enable the wearer to sew it to the leg of the battle dress so as to eliminate any noise the sheath might make banging up and down while the man was running. (Plate 226).

DHAS

This Burmese weapon was essentially a sword which had a plain round grip, no cross guard and a slightly curved single edged blade. Smaller versions the size of daggers were known. The overall appearance was like the Japanese sword.

HUNTING KNIFE

This is a general term for the many varieties of knife with a short single or double edged blade with stag horn or bone grip that were turned out during the last half of the 19th century and are still made today by cutlers in Solingen and Sheffield for sportsmen and general outdoor use. The illustrations show some of the styles available at the turn of the century and today. (Plates 223 and 227).

JAPANESE DAGGERS AND KNIVES

Besides the small utility knife about 6ins long carried in the scabbards of the *Wakizashi* and the *Tanto*, the other form of dagger was the *Aikutchi*, which although similar to the *Tanto* had no hand guard. Most of the Japanese knives had a single edged slightly curved blade and were scaled down versions of the larger swords, the *Katana* and the *Wakizashi*. The knives normally had a lacquered wood scabbard decorated with small motifs in a contrasting colour and had the grip bound in sharkskin and overwound with braid. The cross piece or hand guard was usually round and decorated with chiselling and other hand work. The styles of furniture changed according to the prevailing fashion. (Plates 224, 228, 231, 232 and 233).

JAMBIYA

This type is one of the most common of native knives available and can be found in varying styles. It was used by both Arabs, Indians and Persians, the Arab and Persian models having the curved blade almost at right angles whilst the Indian weapon had a more gentle curve to the double edged blade. The grip of the Arab version swelled out towards the pommel whilst the Indian version had a more gentle sweep to the grip. (Plates 230, 233 and 239).

KARD

This knife was similar to the Kyber knife mentioned on page 57 and had a tapering blade sharpened on one side only and normally a thickened point for armour piercing. (Plate 231).

KATAR

This knife was designed to deliver a thrust like a boxer's punch. The sharp double edged blade tapered quickly to a point and was very thick. The grip consisted of steel in an 'H' shape with the bottom legs of the 'H' joining the blade and it was held with the hand gripping the cross bar of the letter. (Plate 224).

KINDJHAL

This knife had a long straight double edged blade with a central fuller. The hilt consisted of two sides of wood or horn which decreased from the shoulder of the blade and broadened out at the pommel. Examples came from Persia, the Balkans and Russia where it was one of the weapons of the Caucasian Cossacks. Besides the ordinary knife, the Cossack version can be found with very decorative furniture to both knife and scabbard. (Plates 234 and 236).

KRIS

This knife was peculiar to the countries of Malaya and Indonesia, although it seems to have originated in Java in the 14th century. The wavy blade was made from steel and iron in the Malayan version but a straight blade was used in Java. The blade widened towards the top and formed a guard to the grip which was either round and straight or slightly cocked back. Another version of the weapon with a polished blade, which was a larger variety of the same style, was called a *Sundang*. A notable feature of the *kris* other than its blade was the all wood sheath shaped to accommodate it. Whether for the straight or wavy blade, the scabbard remained outwardly the same. Some very fine examples can be found with hand painted scabbards depicting animals and jungle scenes. (Plates 233 and 237).

KUKRI

The traditional weapon of the Gurkhas of Nepal was made in differing sizes from about a 14ins blade to a 24ins one. The blade was curved and broadened out from the hilt with the cutting edge on the inner curve. It was usually carried in a leather covered wood scabbard with a small knife and sharpening tool made as small replicas of the larger knife. Although the Government issue weapon in its plain scabbard does not command a very high price, some more decorative silver mounted versions can be fairly expensive. (Plates 194 and 229).

KYBER KNIFE

A similar knife to the *Pesh Kabz* (see page 59) which had a 'T' sectioned blade of greatly varying lengths which tapered to a point. The scabbards for these knives were unusual in that they also accommodated most of the grip leaving about 2ins only showing.

NAVAJA KNIFE

This was the large 19th century Spanish folding knife which had a locking mechanism to hold the blade in the open position. The grips were normally in bone, inset with brass panels and motifs. Small replicas are now sold in Spain in the souvenir market.

NAZI DAGGERS

Whilst it would need a complete book to describe and illustrate the variations of dagger that were worn under Nazi rule in Germany between 1933 and 1945, this short section gives a brief introduction plus details of some of the varieties that may be encountered. (Plates 241, 242 and 243). Nazi daggers maintain a high value and many patterns command prices well above those of fine 19th century swords and daggers. A large number of reproductions have been made in recent times from the original tools and therefore they are impossible to tell from the originals except with expert knowledge or advice. The story of the Nazi dagger started during the trade depression that Solingen suffered after the First World War which, despite efforts to break into more foreign markets, mainly South America, failed to give jobs to the large number of unemployed who had no other trade to fall back on. Many of the smaller knife manufacturers in Germany went out of business while others attempted to keep going by changing over to razors, penknives and cutlery. In 1933 when Hitler came to power, a deputation of local leaders from the Rühr travelled to Berlin to pay their respects to the *Führer* and Krupp presented him with a knife. It was suggested that it would help unemployment in Solingen if the *Führer* would agree to party officials wearing some form of dagger. The idea was wholeheartedly received and various designs were prepared. The final design selected was a copy of a 16th century Swiss dagger. (Plate 199). Three differing types were introduced on 15th December 1933. The first had a brown wood grip with an inset eagle and enamel SA (*Sturm Abteilungen*) badge and was carried in a brown metal sheath with plated fittings. (Plate 241). The second version, for the NSKK (*Nationalsozialistisshes Kraftfahr-Korps*) was the same as the SA dagger except that the scabbard was in black and there was a naval version with gilt fittings.

The last model was that issued to the SS (*Schutzstaffeln*) which had a black wood grip with an inset eagle and SS badge (two lightening flashes called 'Runes' each in the shape of an 'S'). A simplified version without badges inset in the grip was carried in a plain metal sheath and utilised by students of the National Political Education Institute and a further pattern was issued to their instructors. There were also more decorative daggers of this type which were either presentation pieces or honour weapons.

A different form of dagger was authorised to the Army in May 1935, having a blade and scabbard not unlike the Imperial naval dirk but in white metal. The grip was in horn or plastic with a cross piece incorporating the eagle. In the same year, the Air Force were ordered a dagger which had a long double edged blade carried in a sheath covered in blue leather. (Plate 241). The grip was also covered in blue leather and the cross piece had two down drooping quillons with, in the centre, an enamel *swastika*. The round pommel was also decorated with an enamel *swastika* in the centre. The Navy, as was mentioned in the section on Naval Dirks, received their new dagger in April 1938. A new model for the Air Force was introduced in 1937, which brought the design more in line with the Army version having a scabbard and blade of the same shape and the cross piece in the form of an eagle, the down drooping wings forming the quillons. The grip was in horn or plastic and the pommel was round with a *swastika* in the centre.

With the use by the armed forces and the political party, the dagger started to spread into every section of the administration of the Third Reich. The Labour Service dagger was introduced in 1936 having a stag horn grip and a blade with an abrupt clipped point. Daggers in Germany were carried by Firemen, Water Police (who had a dagger like the Navy dagger of 1919 with an inset badge), Air Raid Protection, Technical Emergency Corps, Water Customs, Land Customs, Railway Protection Service, Railway Leaders, Postal Protection Service, German Red Cross, Fishery Control and State Officials and Diplomats. All had slightly differing designs some of which are extremely rare. Another form carried by the State Forestry Service, German Hunters' Association and German Rifle Association was akin to the hunting dagger that had been carried during the 19th century in Germany. The design usually had a straight long blade with hunting scenes etched upon it and a stag horn or white plastic grip with a cross piece and down pointing shell guard. The Forestry and German Hunters' Association also had a knuckle bow to their dagger. This style of dagger or dirk is still being made in Germany today and as very few of the originals bear any Nazi emblem, it is often difficult to distinguish between a Nazi era dagger and a post war one.

This dagger had a curved blade which was ribbed and thickened at the point and the grip was usually of jade or bone. The blade had the distinct feature of a step at the shoulder and a 'T' section. The scabbard was made

PESH KABZ

to accommodate the entire knife leaving perhaps only an inch or so of the hilt showing. (Plate 239).

These are only a few of the many types of daggers and knives available to the collector. India, Asia and many African and South American countries have individualistic styles which are sometimes found in the collector's market but which are not easily identifiable as belonging to any one particular country or century.

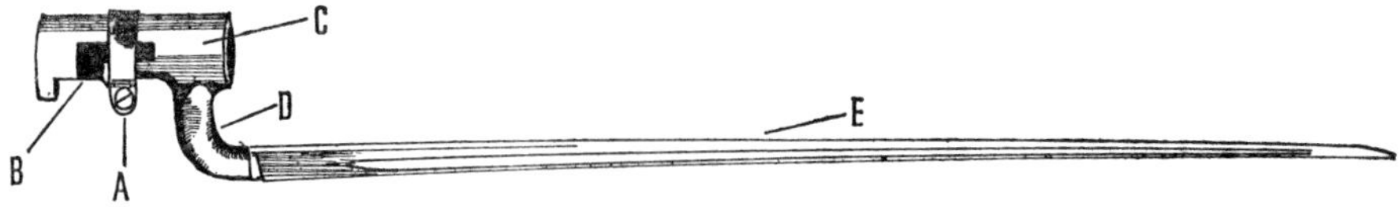

Fig. 12 Parts of a socket bayonet. A. Locking ring; B. Zigzag slot; C. Socket; D. Neck; E. Blade.

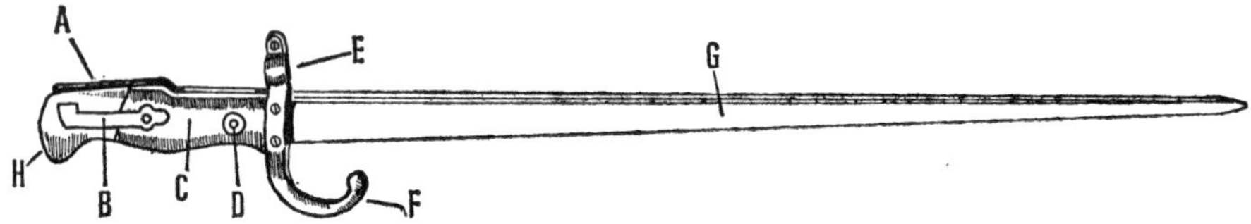

Fig. 13 Parts of a sword bayonet. A. Groove in pommel to fit on bar on firearm; B. Spring (leaf); C. Grip; D. Grip rivet on screw; E. Muzzle ring; F. Hooked quillon; G. Blade; H. Pommel.

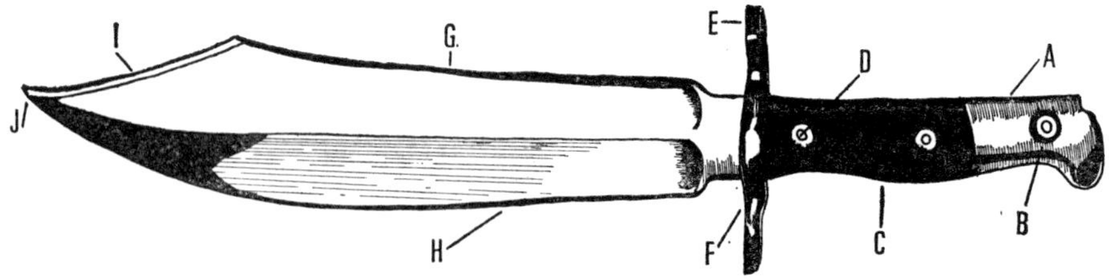

Fig. 14 Parts of a knife bayonet. A. Pommel; B. Press stud activating locking mechanism; C. Grip; D. Grip rivet or screw; E. Muzzle ring; F. Cross piece; G. Back of blade; H. Cutting edge; I. False edge; J. Point.

3: BAYONETS

Evolution and History up to 1750

Of all the weapons discussed in this book, the bayonet is perhaps the 'youngest', originating as it does with the expansion in the use of firearms in the world's armies during the 17th century. With the realisation of the capabilities of firearms in the hands of the foot soldier, the musketeer, as he became known, took his place in the ranks of the armies of Europe, which up until then had their infantry composed of pikemen.

The vulnerability of this new type of soldier was his defencelessness during the long loading procedure when having discharged his musket he was at the mercy of the enemy's cavalry whose lances far outreached the sword he carried. The main defensive system employed by most armies was having the musketeers grouped with pikemen so that having discharged their pieces, they could retire behind the protective hedge of 16ft long pikes during re-loading. This system meant that pikemen and musketeers had to be used together and no tactical advantage could be taken by using musketeers separately in a surprise attack or skirmish.

Various ways were tried to enable musketeers to be self sufficient such as outward projecting blades on the musket rest or the carrying of stakes which were planted in the ground in front of the line of troops, but these methods met with very little success and any idea of using the musketeer without the pikeman was abandoned. Even when the bayonet was in widespread use in various regiments in the British Army, pikes and muskets were used together and the drill or 'Exercise of the Pike and Match-Lock Musket together' in *An Abridgement of the English Military Discipline* published in 1686 gives this drill as if the bayonet was not in existence. Even many years later when the pike had been discarded in favour of the musket and bayonet, troops were still drawn up in lines before battles and the tactical use of firearms was not fully exploited until the American War of Independence, when the American backwoodsmen used firearms to their full advantage with skirmishing and disregard of formation fighting.

How the knife or dagger came to be used as a bayonet is impossible to establish. Many theories have been put forward over the years as to the place of origin, the inventor or discoverer of this weapon. It may be true to say that the bayonet came into being by chance, when perhaps in a tight spot in a battle, a musketeer found himself cut off from the protective shield of pikemen and, in order to give himself sufficient reach to be able to combat the enemy cavalry, either put his dagger in the muzzle of his musket or perhaps picked up an end of a lance or cross bow bolt and inserted or tied that to his musket. This theory does not, however, explain the reason why the weapon is called a bayonet.

Early mention in drill manuals calls the weapon a dagger, because indeed the weapon was just that, although the memoires of a French officer refers to his men being equipped in the 1642 campaign with 'bayonettes with handles one foot long and the blades of the bayonettes were as long as the handles, the ends of which were adapted (*ie. either tapered or fitted with spring, see plate* 246) for putting into the barrel of the fusils, to defend themselves, when attacked, after having fired.' A 1611 French dictionary gives '*Bayonnier*' as a cross bowman, who could have hardly anything to do with musketeers, although the first bayonet might have been a bolt inserted into the muzzle of the gun. Another theory was that the cross bowmen were renowned for their short sword from which the bayonet developed when these bowmen were equipped with muskets. Another possible claimant is the town of Bayonne, which was well-known for its iron works and cutlery trade and a French dictionary of 1694 describes '*bayonette*' as 'a type of dagger, called thus from the town of Bayonne'.

The French and a number of other European countries employed bayonets some years before their introduction into England and in 1660, Louis XIV issued a proclamation forbidding the use of the bayonet because of accidents. The proclamation stated (*translation*) 'The frequency of accidents which happen almost daily by the use of bayonets and knives in the form of daggers which are placed in the muzzle of sporting guns or which are carried in the pocket. . . .'. It is not surprising to find the French using the bayonet at this date, because at this time they were the foremost military power in Europe with perhaps the best organised army. In 1671, *Le Régiment Royal D'Artillerie* was raised to protect the artillery train and was armed with fusils and bayonets which were carried in scabbards in the same frog as the sword.

The use of the plug bayonet in sporting guns seems to predate the use in any armies in Europe and it is interesting to note that the plug bayonet continued to be employed with sporting weapons many years after the military had abandoned it. Examples of plug bayonets some quite ornate with ivory grips and chiselled fittings were still being made and used, especially in Spain as late as the middle of the 19th century.

The introduction of the plug bayonet into the English Army cannot be accurately dated, but what was thought to be the first issue of bayonets was to the Tangier Regiment (later the Queen's Royal West Surrey Regiment). In 1662, Charles II sold Dunkirk to the French and the three battalions who had formed the garrison were sent to Tangiers. It is possible that if these troops were armed with bayonets, they were of French manufacture. An order in the Public Record Office, dated 14th

March 1662, states that 'the French pikes and short swords or bayonettes that lately were received from Dunkirk be surveyed and an account presented to this office of their defects to the end a contract be made for their speedy repair'. On 17th March, it was ordered that 'the bayonettes lately received from Dunkirk be issued to persons to be made by them clean and repaired within ten days space at 14p a piece. Joseph Awdeley 200, Samuel Law 200, Robert Steadman 100'.

By Royal Warrant of 2nd April 1672, Charles II ordered that '12 troops of the new regiment of Dragoons shall carry matchlock musket . . . also to have and carry one bayonet or great knife', and in June of the same year, Joseph Awdeley delivered a quantity of bayonets, some of which were issued to Prince Rupert's Regiment of Dragoons. (Plate 244). It appears that the plug bayonet was used by cavalry and infantry in 1673 but fell into disuse with all but grenadiers, a specially trained body of men skilled in the art of grenade throwing introduced in 1686, a few years later.

An Abridgement of the English Military Discipline of 1686 mentions bayonet drill only for grenadiers although the Foot Guards received bayonets in that year. (Plate 244). In 1685, when the Ordnance Regiment or Royal Fusiliers were raised, James II's orders for arming the Regiment stated 'Our Royal Regiment to have snaphance muskets strapt (*with slings*) with bright barrels of three feet eight inches long, with good swords, cartouche boxes, and bionette'. The Royal Artillery is recorded as having been issued with bayonets as early as 1683.

The plug bayonet had its obvious drawbacks including the inability to fire when the bayonet was fixed and if the bayonet was broken off in the muzzle the musketeer was without musket or musket and bayonet. This problem had been considered by the French as early as 1678 when Marêchal de Puysegur recorded in *Art de la Guerre*, 'that he had seen a regiment armed with swords, without guards, but in lieu thereof a brass ring and another at the pommel. Through these, the barrel of the fusil passed'. General Mackay, in England, stated that after the battle of Killicrankie in 1689, when the highlanders charged too fast for his men to fit their bayonets, he had invented the ring bayonet. The Swedish Army had a pattern of musket in about 1685 which had two rings fitted to the side of the barrel at the muzzle into which the plug bayonet was fitted leaving the muzzle free. (Plate 245).

The ring bayonet from its construction alone appears to be less sturdy in its fittings than the plug bayonet but presumably the advantage of being able to fire with fixed bayonets outweighed this fact. Although ring bayonets are not mentioned in contemporary drill manuals, they are mentioned as being used in the reign of Queen Anne (1702–1714) by Horse Grenadiers that escorted her coach, but contemporary paintings of the period show the plug bayonet.

The natural progression from the ring bayonet was to replace the two rings with something more solid and with a firmer fit to the barrel. The obvious answer was a metal tube or socket, but there was a drawback to this method. The muskets used by the soldiers at this period were far from standard and the external diameters of the barrels differed so that a tube could not be used unless it was specially made for each musket. The problem was solved by having a split tube which could be opened up or closed depending on the size of the barrel. (Plates 250 and 232). This invention was short lived as standard size musket barrels soon became a feature of the regulation musket of the armies of Europe.

In the adoption of the socket bayonet, the French lagged behind, although Louis XIV had tried socket bayonets as early as 1688 with a view to discontinuing the pike and it was not until 1704 that they were adopted by the French Army. In England, the situation was somewhat different and although socket bayonets are mentioned in the Ordnance records as early as the 1680s, they do not appear to have been issued on any scale, socket bayonets coming into use in the British Army in about 1702. Not every regiment used them, as the following extract from the correspondence between Lord Mark Kerr and the Ordnance concerning bayonets, shows. Lord Kerr wrote requesting bayonets for the muskets he had received to replace pikes, but the Ordnance replied that 'all regiments raised since the disuse of pikes have provided Byonets as they do swords and belts at their own Charge. . . . Few of the Officers agree to the sort of Byonets fit to be used or in the manner of fitting them to the Musquets as may appear by the various sorts that are of them in ye Army'. From this one can presume that plug, ring, and split socket bayonets were all in use at the same time.

This state of affairs continued for a number of years although by 1720, a socket bayonet of roughly uniform pattern had been adopted. (Plate 252). Colonels were still responsible for providing the soldiers' musket and bayonets and so considerable variety of both were in use, although of a standard bore, but by 1722 the Ordnance in a minute of July 28th stated that 'all Colonells who have any new Arms made shall be obliged to make them according to the said Pattern and proved and viewed by the Proper Officers of the Ordnance.'

Other countries soon followed the lead of Britain and France and the socket bayonet became a feature in many continental armies. Designs were, however, by no means uniform, some countries having triangular sec ton blades while others favoured a flat double edged blade. Some sockets had a plain slot while others had curved slots with elementary locking rings or screws. (Plates 248 and 249). One of the main problems with the socket bayonet was its liability to fall off and many methods were tried to keep it firmly in place. Some countries favoured springs, others screws and others locking rings but Britain persisted long after others had adopted a locking device in retaining a plain socket with a zigzag slot.

Bayonets of Europe 1750–1918

In this section, a brief look will be taken at some of the bayonets of the armies of Europe. Not every variation can be discussed and the bayonets described are mainly those that were universal issue.

BRITAIN

With the introduction of a regulation musket, an uniform pattern of bayonet was adopted. This had a 17ins triangular sectioned blade fitted by a short curved neck to a socket with a plain zigzag slot. Early types of this pattern of bayonet had a plain tube socket but by the 1760 period a small reinforcing collar had been added. (Plate 252). The scabbard was in black leather with a brass chape and locket with the frog stud fitted just below the locket. There was a pattern with a shorter blade for Sergeants which was also used with the addition of a spring clip in the top of the blade for the Irish Constabulary. (Plates 250 and 239). This pattern of bayonet was used until 1839 when a similar one but with a shorter socket was introduced. In 1842, another variation of this pattern was produced. In the 1839 version, the socket collar was thick so that a small spring fitted in the nose cap of the musket stock could clip over it, while that of 1842 has a small 'ear' which engaged the spring, of different design, on the 1842 musket.

The majority of this type of bayonet had no locking device on the bayonet itself except for the bayonet used by the forces of the East India Company which had a spring screwed to the socket which kept the foresight in position at the end of the slot. A spring clip on the shortened socket was introduced with the New Land Pattern series of Arms, but it never became an universal issue. The first bayonet of this type with a locking ring was adopted in 1853 with the Enfield rifle and continued in service for the rank and file until the 1880s, being 'bushed', the term used for reducing the inside diameter of the socket, for the smaller Martini Henry barrel in 1871. (Plate 258). In 1876, a bayonet of similar design but with a longer blade was adopted, but the shorter bladed weapon continued in service with volunteers and Colonial troops for a number of years after that date. With the introduction in 1888 of a magazine rifle for the British Army the socket bayonet disappeared, except for a revival with the Martini Enfield in 1895, from the British Service, being replaced by the more popular type of bayonet, the sword bayonet. (Plate 264).

Sword bayonets first made their appearance in the British Army with the Baker Rifle, which like the Jaeger rifle of a number of the Continental armies it was copied from, was equipped with a short sword adapted as a bayonet. (Plate 253). Prior to this a number of volunteer units that were formed during the Napoleonic War period equipped themselves with long socket bayonets, into which a sword hilt could be fitted when not used on the musket, or swords adapted with rings and short socket to fit on their muskets. (Plate 255). The Baker bayonet, of which there are at least five varieties, have a brass hilt with on two of the types a knuckle bow and long blade. Other varieties have triangular blades of the socket bayonet type. The Brunswick Rifle, which replaced the Baker in 1836, also had a brass hilted sword bayonet with a double edged blade which was leaf shaped at the end. (Plate 257). This style was also used on a number of Irish Constabulary carbines during the period. Perhaps the commonest type of sword bayonet, encountered in many of the world's armies at this period was that with a yatagan blade. Introduced in the British Army in 1852, but with a brass hilt like the French pattern, the bayonet soon adopted a steel hilt with chequered leather grips. (Plate 259). The blade was single edged with a double curve and was carried in a steel mounted black leather scabbard. This pattern with slight variations was used by the Royal Artillery, Sergeants of Infantry regiments and all rifle regiments. During this period, it became popular for each arm of the service to have a bayonet peculiar to itself and so we find the Naval Cutlass bayonet, (Plate 261), the saw back bayonet for the Artillery, (Plate 263), the brass hilted bayonet for the Lancaster carbine adopted by the Engineers and a great number of variations either experimental or limited trial issue weapons.

In 1888, a short double edged sword bayonet was introduced which was issued with the Lee Metford Rifle and soon replaced the variety of other bayonets in use. (Plate 266). In 1903, with the adoption of the SMLE or Short Magazine Lee Enfield, the pommel design was altered to fit the new pattern of rifle. (Plate 266). In 1907, when the need was felt for a longer bayonet, the famous pattern 07 bayonet with its 17inch blade replaced the 12inch bladed pattern 1903. (Plate 267). This bayonet, introduced in 1907, had until 1913 a hooked quillon with which to catch the opponent's blade in bayonet fighting; however, in that year it was removed although contemporary photographs of the First World War show it in use, especially by Australian troops as late as 1916. (Plate 267).

British bayonets will also be found bearing marks which show they were used by Empire and Dominion troops as they were all, with one exception armed with British weapons. Canada, the exception, found itself in 1900 with a shortage of modern arms which could not be supplied from the Mother country because of the needs of troops in the South African War of 1899–1902. After much discussion, Sir Charles Ross, set up a plant in Canada for the manufacture of a rifle of his own design. The weapon was not a great success and was modified a great many times before being abandoned in 1916 in favour of the SMLE. The Ross bayonet was styled on the British pattern of 1903 but with a square pommel and a wide single edged blade with a rounded point. (Plate 267). By 1918, and the end of the First World War, all British, Empire and Dominion troops were armed with the SMLE and the long bladed 1907 bayonet.

FRANCE

The early socket bayonet used in the French army of about 1750 differed very little from the types used by other troops which makes the identification of early bayonets something of a problem for collectors. In 1763, France adopted a socket bayonet with a locking ring which blocked the channel behind the foresight once the bayonet was in position. This type was eventually adopted by nearly every other nation at a later date. In 1774 with the issue of a new pattern of musket, a bayonet was supplied without the locking ring and which was held in place by a spring catch on the top band of the musket. In 1777 a return was made to the bayonet with locking ring but this time with the locking ring situated in the middle of the socket and not at the end as the pattern of 1763 had been. This bayonet underwent an increase in blade length in year IX of the Republican Calendar (Sept. 1800–1801) and was used by the Infantry throughout the Napoleonic War from that date onwards. In 1822, the blade of a new pattern was increased again by a few inches from the length of which had been used on the year IX weapon.

With the advent of percussion arms the bayonet adopted in 1822 was used until 1847 when the last socket bayonet used by the French army, except for a special bayonet made in 1874 for the *Gendarmerie*, was adopted. This differed very little from its predecessors except that it had an oval section neck whereas the others had had a round sectioned one. It is interesting to note that all French bayonets from the pattern 1777 onwards fitted on a stud under the barrel rather than on the foresight as in the British pattern weapons.

From 1866 onwards when the Chasspot breach loading rifle was adopted by the French army, the socket bayonet was discarded as this new pattern arm took only a sword bayonet, unlike some rifles namely the Martini Henry of Britain which could take either sword or socket bayonet. The 1866, (Plate 272), brass hilted sword bayonet with yatagan blade was loosely based on the 1842 pattern that had been adopted for use on the carbine of that year. (Plate 272). The 1866 bayonet had an all brass hilt with a cross guard with forward sweeping quillon and adjustable muzzle ring. The blade, with a wide fuller was 22½ins long and the weapon was carried in an all steel scabbard. This style of bayonet was widely copied and its influence can be seen in the British sword bayonet of 1853, and 1856, the Danish and Swedish patterns of 1867 for the Remington rifle, the 1859 pattern for the Norwegian Remington rifle, the Austrian pattern bayonet for the Werndl rifle, (Plate 289), the Belgian bayonet of 1880 for the Comblain rifle and a number of American bayonets to name a few.

In 1874, the French adopted the Gras rifle and with it a new pattern of bayonet which had a 'T' sectioned blade with a single edge that tapered to a point. (Plate 271). The distinctive hilt, with its slight step, had a brass pommel and a forward sweeping cross guard which had an adjustable muzzle ring. This bayonet, but with a flat back and no step was used on the Kropatschek rifle issued to the navy in 1878. The dating of French bayonets of the sword bayonet variety mentioned up to now is no problem for the collector as on the back of each blade, in script, will be found the place and year of manufacture. This marking was discontinued with the adoption of the quadrangular sectioned blade on the bayonet used with the Lebel rifle of 1886. (Plate 274). This bayonet has an all metal hilt in German silver or brass and with a forward sweeping quillon, which was removed in 1916, and the fixing catch situated in the cross guard and not at the pommel. There are a number of variations of this bayonet, namely the Gendarmerie pattern of 1890 which has a groove in the side and the fixing catch in the pommel. Another bayonet encountered is the knife bayonet adopted in 1892 for the Berthier carbine which has a cross guard like the Lebel pattern but without the catch, a steel pommel with catch and black composition grips. (Plate 271). The fuller of the blade has a cut out which engages with a catch in the scabbard. A straight bladed bayonet with wood grips was used on the remington rolling block rifle used on a limited scale in 1914.

GERMANY

Prior to the unification of Germany in 1871 with Prussia as the dominant power, there was a Confederation of states which dated from 1816. For this reason, a single style of bayonet was carried by a number of the member states of the Confederation, but with slight variety in the bayonets issued to special troops such as pioneers and those worn when walking out which are termed as dress bayonets.

The early pattern of socket bayonet used by the Prussians was very similar in style to those used by many other armies at the period and it was not until the end of the 18th century that a distinctive pattern was adopted. The bayonet used with the model 1805 musket had a plain socket without any collar and a long triangular sectioned blade, although a shorter bladed bayonet with the distinctive 'Kyhls' locking spring had been adopted in the 1790s. This spring which was mounted on the socket had two ears that were lifted which allowed the stud under the barrel to engage the slot in the socket. Once in position, the spring was lowered which blocked the slot and kept the bayonet firmly in place. This spring was used for many years by the Prussians and features on a number of various patterns of socket bayonet. It was also copied by Denmark on their 1794 pattern, (Plate 281), and used until about 1848 when a locking ring was adopted.

The Prussians, however, were not great users of socket bayonets, preferring instead the sword bayonet. On the Jaeger rifle from which the British Baker rifle was copied, a large all brass hilted sword bayonet or *Hirschfanger* was carried. (Plate 275). The hilt, which except for the knuckle bow, was cast in one piece had an oval section grip which broadened out towards the top. The knuckle bow, which was an inverted stirrup guard had a small down pointing shell guard on which is usually found engraved numbers and letters referring to the regiment to whom it was issued. A variety of hilt designs were used with this style of bayonet but nearly all have the slot for the bayonet bar in a separate 'box' brazed to the grip. Along the top edge of this 'box' is a steel spring with a catch which locked the bayonet in position on the bar on the barrel.

When Prussia introduced its revolutionary 'needle gun' or Von Dreyse pattern as it is termed, a socket bayonet was approved for the rank and file. This model had a 19inch blade and as is expected employed the Kyhls locking spring fitted to the socket. In 1849 a brass hilted bayonet with a steel cross guard was introduced for the Baden Jaeger regiments and Guard regiments. In 1860 a pattern of sword bayonet with brass hilt and steel cross guard was adopted for Fusilier Regiments and it was from this style of bayonet, with a falchion pattern blade that the better known model of 1871 was copied for use on the Mauser rifle of 1871. (Plate 276). In 1865 another sword bayonet was introduced which although in appearance is styled similarly to the pattern of 1860 had a steel pommel and cross guard and chequered leather grips like many other types of sword bayonets of the period.

In 1871, when Prussia adopted the Mauser magazine breech loading rifle a brass hilted bayonet was used with it. The grip had an engraved panel in which was fitted the leaf spring and the panel engraved with lines at about 40 degrees. (Plate 276). The scabbard which took the falchion shaped blade was in black leather with brass mounts. A variety of this pattern of bayonet exists, some with saw backed blades being pioneer weapons while others with slim blades which are engraved being dress models which in some cases have no fitment for the bayonet and the leaf spring engraved in the grip. The pattern for Jaeger regiments had a chequered leather grip, while the standard infantry pattern had a slim blade with a central fuller and that of NCOs having in addition a saw back. The cross guard of this pattern has a distinctive 'S' shape. There were also slight differences in blade shape and design between the various German States. In 1884 a short knife bayonet with a 10inch blade was adopted. (Plate 280). This bayonet was an all steel construction with wood grips. The first pattern can be distinguished by the shaping to the top of the grips and tang and the pronounced beak on the pommel. In 1888 a Commission for the trials of Small Arms recommended various improvements to the pattern 1871 rifle which changed its designation to Infantry Rifle Model 1871/84. In 1888 a new pattern rifle was adopted which took the 1871/84 bayonet, (Plate 276), and also the brass hilted 1871 bayonet.

In 1898, the famous *Gewehr* 1898 (Gew 98) rifle was adopted and with it a new pattern of bayonet. A number of the 1884 bayonets were adapted for use on the new rifle and were designated 1884/98. One variety was a conversion of the old knife bayonet having the muzzle ring removed while the newly manufactured model had no muzzle ring, an oil drain slot above the cross guard and no beak to the pommel. The later model had a flat back to the grips and tang and with a shaped pommel, and a steel plate along the back of the hilt to protect the grips from muzzle blast.

With the new rifle, a variety of bayonets were used, the number and pattern increasing during the First World War to the staggering total of over 40 variations and patterns. (Plates 277 and 8). The original bayonets issued with the rifle were of three varieties, that with the long falchion shaped blade of 20¾in, that with the so called 'Butcher' blade which swelled at the point of 14in, with a pioneer variation with saw backed blade, and that with a short 10in blade. The hilt had the shaped pommel used on the 1884/98 bayonet and with a single sided cross guard and no muzzle ring. On the first two varieties mentioned the grips were linned but on the third they were plain. These three patterns formed the basis for the many variations found except for the all steel *Ersatz* or emergency models and the converted captured and obsolete bayonets. (Plate 278). The book, GEW 98 published in 1921 by Bannerman & Sons illustrates 31 bayonet variations for the Gew 98 rifle.

Space does not permit the detailed look at every bayonet of every country in Europe, but every effort has been made to include bayonets of all the European countries in the illustrations. A selection of bayonets, which are interesting because their size or method of fitment to the rifle are discussed beneath.

It is not surprising that a great many bayonets used in Europe during the 19th century bear a marked resemblance to those patterns described under Britain, France and Germany for it was these three powers that dictated the military fashion and thinking of Europe during that century. The Norwegians, having used socket bayonets up until 1859, (Plate 281), except for the brass *hirschfanger* bayonets on their Jaeger rifles which are almost identical to the Swedish and Danish patterns, adopted a yatagan bladed bayonet for their *kammerladingsgevaeror* chamber loading rifle in 1859. This pattern was followed by a further model with checked leather grips and yatagan blade used in 1867 on the Remington Rolling block rifle, similar models being adopted by Sweden and Denmark in the same year. (Plate 282). It is at this point that these Scandinavian countries went their own ways with the Danes adopting the Krag rifle and distinctive bayonet in 1889, (Plate 282), the Swedes adopting the Mauser, again with its most unusual bayonet in 1894 and the Norwegians using the Krag Pettersons rifle with yatagan bayonet from 1871 to 1876 and then using the Jarmann rifle again with yatagan bayonet until 1894 when they used the Krag rifle with a slightly different bayonet to the Danes. (Plate 283).

The great variety of socket bayonets used in Europe have either a locking ring or leaf spring attached to the socket and little else to distinguish or identify them, except for Austrian weapons which have a distinctive curved slot in the socket as opposed to a straight or zigzag one. (Plate 289). The Austrians also favoured the broad double edged blade to the socket bayonet with a blade length of about 23 inches. The Austrians too adopted a sword bayonet with yatagan blade in 1867 for the Wenndl rifle, (Plate 289), and in 1870 introduced a variation which had a stepped pommel and adjustable muzzle ring. In 1885, the well known Mannlicher rifle was adopted and with it a short bladed bayonet, which was used during the First World War. A number of variations of this pattern of bayonet exist, some with loops fitted to the pommel to take the sword knots worn by NCOs, and another variety without the down sweeping quillon to the cross guard. The bayonet had a steel pommel and cross guard, which in the 1895 version has two rivets in it, and a $9\frac{3}{4}$ins blade. (Plate 289).

The bayonets used in the Belgian army had always been styled on the French patterns and the bayonets for the Comblain rifle have the brass hilt of the French 1866 pattern but can be found with a variety of blades including a saw backed version. (Plate 288). In 1889, the Belgians adopted the Mauser rifle and with it a typical short bladed bayonet of $9\frac{3}{4}$ins blade length, steel pommel, wood grips and a French pattern of cross guard found on the 1874 Gras bayonet. In 1916, a long double edged blade model was issued which measured $17\frac{1}{2}$ins but still retained the same style of hilt but minus the curved quillon.

Portugal had from 1885 to 1898 used the Guedes rifle which was made by Steyr in Austria and was a close copy of the Martini-Henry pattern used by the British Army but in 1898 they adopted the Mauser rifle with a short bladed bayonet. The Guedes bayonet, had a yatagan blade with steel pommel and cross guard. The grips were made from chequered leather and a distinctive feature of the bayonet was a small finial attached to the muzzle ring which was removed when a number of these bayonets were shortened. Spain, who had for a number of years used the Remington Rolling block rifle with socket and sword bayonet of the yatagan shape adopted the Mauser in 1893 which in fact served as the forerunner for the famed Gew 98. (Plate 290). The blade was 10ins long and deeply fullered with a single cutting edge. The hilt had a steel pommel and cross guard with an extended muzzle ring and typical in appearance to a number of other bayonets used on the Mauser rifle. The Artillery had a similar styled bayonet but with a $15\frac{1}{2}$ins blade and chequered wood grips. (Plate 290). All Spanish bayonets of this type were carried in black leather scabbards with steel mounts. Turkey who up to the 1880s used the Martini Peabody as its breech loading military arm adopted the Mauser rifle in 1887 with a long bladed bayonet of $18\frac{1}{4}$ins, a steel pommel and cross guard with down sweeping quillon and wood grips. A differing version was adopted in

1890 which is exactly the same except for the distance of the muzzle ring from the back of the grip, that of the 1887 being $1\frac{1}{16}$ins and that of 1890 being $1\frac{1}{2}$ins. In 1903 a short bladed bayonet of 10ins was introduced and some of the longer pattern were cut down to this size. There was also a long bladed model of 1903 measuring 20ins and falchion shaped.

It will be seen from the illustrations that many of the bayonets used in Europe in the late 19th century bear a resemblance to German or Spanish types. The main reason for this is the widespread use of the Mauser and Mannlicher rifles in Europe at this period which is also evident in many South American countries (see Bayonets of America 1770–1918, page 77). Greece and Serbia adopted the Mannlicher while Serbia adopted the Mauser, Holland, however, preferring the Mannlicher with a special pattern of bayonet which was adopted in 1895. The hilt of the bayonet was similar to the British pattern 1888 but had a 'T' sectioned blade like that of the French Gras 1874 bayonet. The length of the blade was 14ins but a shorter model with $9\frac{3}{4}$ins blade which was double edged was used on the cavalry carbine.

Switzerland, which had for many years been a neutral country has had a variety of bayonets both socket and sword. (Plate 290). In 1878, the Vetterli rifle was adopted although a rifle of this name had been in use previously. This older pattern was in percussion and employed both socket and sword bayonets. The Federal rifle, the Milbank-Amsler was adopted in the 1850s with a socket bayonet. (Plate 287). The socket bayonet was most unusual as it did not have a socket but a short projection with flanges that fitted to a bar on the right ride of the barrel. The sword bayonet issued with the Vetterli had a saw back on the pioneer version and a spatulate quillon which is found also on the British Elcho pattern and Artillery pattern 1875. This rifle was made obsolete by the introduction of the Schmidt Rubin in 1889 which had a short bladed sword bayonet with steel pommel and cross guard. (Plate 289). Four types of blade were used with this hilt, all measuring $11\frac{3}{4}$ins but differing in the way they were kept in the scabbard. The first had a ridge in the fuller, the second a domed rivet and the third a weld. The fourth had a plain blade but springs in the scabbard. In 1900 when a short version of the rifle was adopted a long bayonet was approved. This was a most curious pattern having a long cruciform sectioned blade which continued through the cross guard which was brazed in place to the pommel. There were no grips. In 1911, a large saw backed bayonet was introduced for engineers which had an enlarged version of the 1889 hilt and an $18\frac{3}{4}$ins blade which swelled out slightly at the point. The scabbard was all metal or steel mounted leather.

The Italian army had adopted the Vetterli Vitali rifle in 1870 and with it a long bladed sword bayonet with composition grips, and the tang running through the hilt and secured at the pommel with a nut much in the same way as a sword would be mounted. (Plate 291). The push button catch activated an outside leaf spring, a type used on many sword bayonets of this period, and the cross guard had a down sweeping quillon terminating in a ball. There was also a version of this bayonet with all brass fittings and another issued to special troops which had the blade of triangular cross section. The Vetterli carbine was issued with a socket bayonet which had a locking ring and extremely small inside diameter. In 1887 the leaf spring on the sword bayonet was shortened and eventually made obsolete by the introduction of the Mannlicher-Carcano rifle in 1891. Vetterli bayonets were shortened in 1916 and with the quillon removed were issued to reserve troops. The bayonet for the Carcano was a short knife bladed weapon of $11\frac{3}{4}$ins and a single cutting edge but with the top edge sharpened at the point of the blade. (Plate 291). The pommel and cross guard were in steel, the latter terminating in a small ball on the lower half. The scabbard was in leather with a central raised rib and brass mouth piece and chape. A feature of Italian bayonet scabbards was the shoe to the chape and the frog stud which was screwed to the top mount. The Carcano bayonet of 1891 was used throughout the First and Second Wars. A further pattern of bayonet existed for the carbine which can be found in three varieties; folding blade, folding blade altered to non-folding and non-folding. These bayonets have a short $6\frac{7}{8}$ins blade with a single cutting edge. There were also a variety of triangular bladed bayonets which were permanently attached to the carbine and which folded under the barrel when not required to be fixed. These were mainly used on the Carcano carbine 1891/1905 and 1891/38 Moschetto. (*An Italian term for a firearm, a cross between a rifle and carbine.*)

Bayonets of America 1770–1918

UNITED STATES

It was not until the late 1790s that the United States adopted a musket designed and manufactured by the US armouries at Springfield and Harpers Ferry. Up until that time a variety of muskets had been used during and after the revolution. The main pattern in use either captured British weapons or French made arms supplied when French troops arrived in North America in 1778. German muskets and bayonets also featured in the new army, these being mainly weapons captured from German mercenaries employed by the British. After the revolution, the American army was supplied with 1763 and 1777 muskets and bayonets but in 1795, the American made musket and bayonet was adopted. For the first few years, the bayonet was a permanent fixture to the barrel but in 1801, they were removed and replaced with a socket bayonet with zigzag slot and 15ins triangular sectioned blade. This style of bayonet, with minor variations in blade length continued until 1812, when a bridge at the end of the socket was introduced to strengthen it. This pattern, again with variations, remained standard issue until 1840, when a socket bayonet with 18ins blade of triangular section and a locking ring on the socket was adopted. This pattern with a slight change in the shape of the top of the blade was retained with the 1855 musket until 1873, when the socket was bushed and the bayonet redesignated the Pattern 1873 to fit the breech loading Springfield rifle adopted in that year. In 1884, experiments were tried with a ramrod bayonet, which when not in use was pushed back in a channel in the stock like a ramrod but was withdrawn and locked into place when required. This pattern ousted the socket bayonet but was itself made obsolete by the adoption of a knife bayonet with the Krag-Jorgensen rifle approved in 1892. (Plate 293).

Another type of bayonet which employed a socket was the trowel bayonet adopted on a limited scale for the 1873 Springfield. The bayonet combined entrenching tool and socket bayonet in one. The socket had an internal groove in the top half which swung over to one side to allow the barrel to be put in, then closed to lock the bayonet in position. Less than 10000 were made and it is doubtful whether very many were ever issued.

As in a number of armies, there were a great many variations in sword bayonets, a large proportion of which were experimental or only trial issues. The first pattern of sword bayonet adopted was that to fit the 1841 musket. As this musket was not originally issued with any form of bayonet, various modifications were made to adapt it to take a socket and a sword bayonet. Two types of bayonet were decided upon by the Ordnance, one for rifles already made and another for those being manufactured, and where a bar could be fitted to the barrel. Other than fit a bar, a special band with stud was designed to clamp on the barrel but this method was less common. The first bayonet had two rings to the hilt, one on the normal muzzle ring position and another at the pommel end which could be folded down when the bayonet was used as a short sword. The muzzle ring, which was oval in outside shape, was fitted with a spring loaded catch that held it in position on the barrel. The grips of the bayonet was in brass and ribbed with the cross piece being 'S' shaped and cast as an integral part. The blade was yatagan in form and the scabbard black leather with two brass mounts. The sword bayonet for the new rifles with band and rifles fitted with the adaptor had a brass hilt with large muzzle ring and forward curving quillon. The blade was again yatagan in form and the scabbard the same as the previous bayonet.

Another sword bayonet with a strange fitting arrangement was the Sappers and Miners model of 1841 whose overall appearance was like a Roman short sword with brass hilt engraved with scales and a leaf shaped blade similar in form to the Brunswick rifle bayonet blade. The grip had a slot in the pommel to take the sword bar on the musketoon but also had a muzzle ring on the cross piece which had a locking ring incorporated into it. The bayonet locked on the barrel in two places, the slot in the pommel and the muzzle ring.

In 1855 a further pattern of sword bayonet was adopted for the rifle approved in that year. The bayonets overall appearance was similar to the bayonet just described except that the slot in the pommel of the hilt was shorter. The bayonets used on the 1861 Navy rifle were a sword bayonet similar to the 1855 model but without the finial on the top of the muzzle ring and the Dahlgren knife bayonet. Admiral Dahlgren described the sword bayonet as 'similar to that of the French' (*French pattern 1842*) and the knife bayonet as 'a short, broad and stout knife of the well-known bowie pattern'. The hilt had a cross piece, which was 'S' shaped, a back piece and flat pommel cast in one which enclosed a wood grip. The spring was fitted to the right side of the back piece worked by a stud on the opposite side. The blade was 12ins long with spear point and single cutting edge.

During the American Civil war period a large number of sword bayonets were adopted by the Confederate States; some to the design of American manufacturers as the bayonets which fitted the Boyle Gamble and Macfee rifle, which had brass hilts and various blade forms, which fitted to the rifle and various others it seems by using an adaptor band as mentioned above. (Plate 294). Another type was the bayonet for the Fayette Armoury rifle which except for the scaled grip looked like the French pattern of 1842. Various European arms and bayonets were imported by both sides, the most popular being the British Enfield of 1853 with socket and sword bayonets.

In 1862 a sword bayonet very similar again in style to the French pattern of 1842 was adopted on the Remington 'Zouave' rifle but with a straightish blade with only a gentle curve. In 1870, the Remington breech loader was adopted which for the Navy was issued with a sword bayonet, which had a curious brass hilt, with a raised section at the top which took the bayonet bar and incorporated the spring. The grip was scaled and the pommel decorated with the badge of the Navy Bureau of Ordnance. The blades found on various examples were either yatagan or straight.

In 1892, the American Army adopted the Krag rifle and with it a short knife bayonet similar in appearance to the Swiss Schmidt Rubin bayonet of 1889. (Plate 293). It had a blade length of 11¾ins with a single cutting edge and deep fuller. The pommel and cross piece were steel and the grips, wood held by rivets to the tang. The scabbard was blued steel with a metal belt attachment fitted to it. A shorter bayonet was issued with the cadet rifle and another version with a wide bowie blade with a clipped point which could be used as a knife for clearing brush. (Plate 239 and fig 14).

In 1895, the Navy adopted on a limited scale the Lee rifle with a bayonet nearly the same as the Mannlicher 1895 adopted by Austria but without the rivets in the cross piece. This pattern of bayonet, but with a down sweeping quillon was used on the Remington rifle sold to Mexico in 1899, the reason being that both patterns were made by the Remington Arms Company.

1905 was the year when the sword bayonet was adopted for the 1903 Springfield rifle had for two years been equipped with a ramrod bayonet. The new bayonet had a 16ins blade with single cutting edge and deep central fuller. The cross piece and pommel were in steel with the locking catch in a slot in the pommel but activated by a catch just behind the cross guard. The grips were wood held to the tang with a single screw and nut. (Plate 295). This bayonet was used throughout World War One together with the Pattern 1917 bayonet used on the American version of the P.14 rifle with which the British were experimenting when the War broke out. (Plate 295). The bayonet for this pattern is the same as the British version except for the oil drain hole in the pommel and American markings.

CANADA

Except for two instances, Canadian troops were equipped with British pattern bayonets. The first pattern peculiar to Canada was approved in 1893 for use on a special batch of Martini Metford rifles purchased in England in an attempt to find a suitable replacement for the Snider-Enfield. The bayonet, of which only 1000 were made were manufactured by Wilkinson's. The Martini Metford bought by Canada was basically a Martini Henry rifle but in .303 calibre instead of .45/577. The new Metford barrel fitted had the same outside dimensions as the Henry barrel and therefore could take a Martini Henry bayonet which was the case with those Martini Metford Mk VI manufactured. The majority of Martini Metfords, however, were fitted with the nose cap of the Lee Metford rifle and therefore took the 1888 bayonet. It is difficult to understand why Canada ordered a special pattern of bayonet when they could have had Martini Henry 1887 bayonets. The new bayonet had the pommel and shortened cross guard of the 1887 Mk III bayonet but the blade and grips of the pattern 1888. (Plate 265). Shortly after issue, the rifles were found to be too heavy and incorrectly sighted and so were withdrawn.

The second type of bayonet peculiar to Canada was the Ross. (Plate 267). The first batch of new rifles were received in 1905 but the bayonets were not issued until 1908. Modelled on the British pattern of 1903, the Ross bayonet had a wide blade with rounded point, a cross guard with slightly set back muzzle ring and a square pommel. In 1910, a new pattern was issued which differed in having no set back muzzle ring and a larger diameter to the ring to fit over the heavier barrel adopted in that year. On the outbreak of the First World War, the bayonets had the rounded points ground to give them more of a spear point with increased penetration. In 1916, the Ross rifle which had had numerous troubles since the beginning of its life was withdrawn from service as it was totally unsuitable in the mud of the trenches. It was replaced by the SMLE with pattern 1907 bayonet.

SOUTH AMERICA

Besides the Remington rolling block rifle, which was adopted by Mexico, Argentine in 1871, and a number of other South American countries, the Mauser rifle, introduced at the time when German influence on South American uniforms and tactics became noticeable, was the favoured weapon. Mexico, after having abandoned the Swiss made Mondragon rifle used both the Remington and the Mauser 98, (Plate 296), the latter eventually replacing the American made arm. The bayonet for the Mexican Mauser was similar in design to the Spanish pattern of 1893 with a single edged blade of 11ins and steel pommel and cross piece. Peru also adopted the Mauser in the 1890s using the pattern 91 then the 98 with standard long bladed German pattern used on the Kar 98. Costa Rica used the Gew 98 rifle but with 95 Mauser fore-end fitting so as not to have to change bayonet patterns, which was the same design as the Spanish Mauser pattern of 1893. Argentine, having used a sword bayonet with brass hilt and 'S' shaped guard on the Remington rifle adopted the Mauser in 1891. The bayonet used with this rifle was unusual in having brass or white metal grips. The pommel and cross piece with down sweeping quillon were in steel and the blade, which was straight and single edged with a deep fuller measured 15¾ins. All these bayonets were made in Germany and some can be found with the Argentine Coat of Arms on although these are normally removed by the authorities prior to disposal. (Plate 297). In 1909, the bayonet lost the metal grips which were replaced by ones in wood held by two screws and rivets. Again, these were German made and the scabbard for both patterns was all steel.

The Mauser and bayonet are still in use today in many South American countries.

Bayonets of Asia Including Russia 1800–1918

Except for the Army of the Honourable East India Company, there were no armies organised along the Western style in Asia except Russia, until the latter part of the 19th century when Japan and China formed European styled and trained armies.

RUSSIA

The Russian army of the early 1800s was equipped with a socket bayonet similar in design and construction to the pattern used by Prussia. When percussion muskets and conversions of flint muskets started to be issued, a socket bayonet with a locking ring and cruciform sectioned blade was introduced. Sword bayonets were not used to a great extent by the Russians presumably because of the cost in arming so many thousands of men, but they did have sword bayonets for certain types of troops before 1850. The earlier versions were brass hilted and similar in appearance to the Prussian *hirschfanger* and used on a flintlock Jaeger style rifle. This pattern gave way to a Russian copy of the Brunswick rifle which employed an exact copy of the British Brunswick bayonet except that the blade is marked in Russian and the scabbard has an extra tube built on to the front face. In 1866 Russia started to convert her percussion muskets to breech loaders and two years later started to import from the United States 30000 Berdan I rifles. The Berdan rifle had the breech mechanism designed by Colonel Hiram Berdan and patented by him in 1866. The mechanism was essentially designed to convert the American Springfield musket to breech loading, but was adopted by the Russians and made to their own specification concerning the stock, furniture and barrel dimension. In 1871, an improved version incorporating the Mauser turning bolt was designed and manufactured in Russia being designated the Berdan II. The bayonet for this rifle had a short 3ins socket with a locking ring and a 23ins cruciform sectioned blade which was designed to fit to a stud on the side of the barrel. (Plate 298). This feature of the side bayonet stud was used on both models of Berdan rifle. Between 1887 and 1889 the Russian Government experimented with the Krnka rifle which had a socket bayonet with an unusually long socket of 4½ins and the blade fitted almost directly to the socket with no elbow. The length of the blade was 20¾ins and it was a symmetrical diamond in cross section. The bayonets for both the Berdan and the Krnka were not issued with scabbards as they were meant to be kept permanently fixed to the rifle.

In 1891, the Imperial Government adopted the Mosin Nagent rifle in 7.62mm with a 17ins long blade on the socket bayonet. The blade, as in the case of the Krnka, was fitted almost directly on to the socket which had a locking ring and fitted on to the top side of the barrel on the foresight. The blade was again a cruciformed section and had a chisel point which could be utilised as a stripping tool. (Plate 298). No scabbards were issued to the Infantry but the cavalry had special fitments on the top and middle band of the sword scabbard to take the bayonet. (Plate 149). Scabbards can be found for the Mosin Nagent, those in leather being Finnish while those in metal are either German or Austrian. The German scabbards are steel while those of Austrian manufacture are zinc.

During the First World War, the United States Government purchased 280000 Mosin Nagent rifles from US manufacturers after the outbreak of the 1917 revolution and used them for training purposes. In the early part of the War, Russia had been forced to import arms and to order arms abroad to augment her supplies of rifles. American Winchester Arms Company supplied a number of the Winchester 1895 pattern magazine rifle and bayonet. These bayonets have a straight blade, single edged and deeply fullered, with a plain steel pommel and cross guard with muzzle ring. Russia also purchased a large number of Arisaka pattern 1907 rifles from Japan complete with bayonets.

JAPAN

Japan only emerged as a western styled military power in the 1870s, her army being equipped on the French style, later abandoned in favour of the Prussian style. In 1887 the Murati 8mm rifle was adopted and with it a sword bayonet with a long single edged blade with a down sweeping quillon to the cross guard. In 1897, the Arisaka rifle of 6.5mm replaced the heavy larger calibre Murata. The new rifle, like its predecessor, had a sword bayonet. The pattern for the Arisaka, similar in appearance to the British pattern 1907, had a 15⅝ins single edged blade with a fuller on each side. (Plate 299). The cross piece, with extended muzzle ring, had a down sweeping quillon and the pommel was all steel with the locking catch and press stud. The grips, of wood, were riveted to the tang and the bayonet carried in an all steel scabbard which were blued. The 1897 rifle and bayonet are also referred to as 'year 38' patterns. The same pattern bayonet, but with a slight change in design of the pommel shape, was used on the 1905 Arisaka rifle, introduced as a result of the Russo Jap War of 1904–05. A folding bayonet with cruciform sectioned blade was introduced with the 1911 carbine. (Plate 300). The blade fitted to a block attachment which was secured to the rifle by two bolts passing through the stock at the fore-end and a tube which passed over the muzzle. An unusual feature of this bayonet was the hooked quillon fitted to the right side of the block. The blade length was 14ins and like the Russian Mosin Nagent bayonet had a chisel point which could be used as a screwdriver.

CHINA

After the Boxer Rebellion of 1900–01, attempts were made to organise the army along western lines, but it was not until 1911 that this had been entirely accomplished. The rifle adopted by the Chinese was the Mauser 1888 pattern with a sword bayonet. These were at first exported from Germany but later manufactured by the Chinese themselves. The bayonet was the standard German pattern used on this type of rifle.

APPENDIX

Various makers and other marks found on edged weapons.

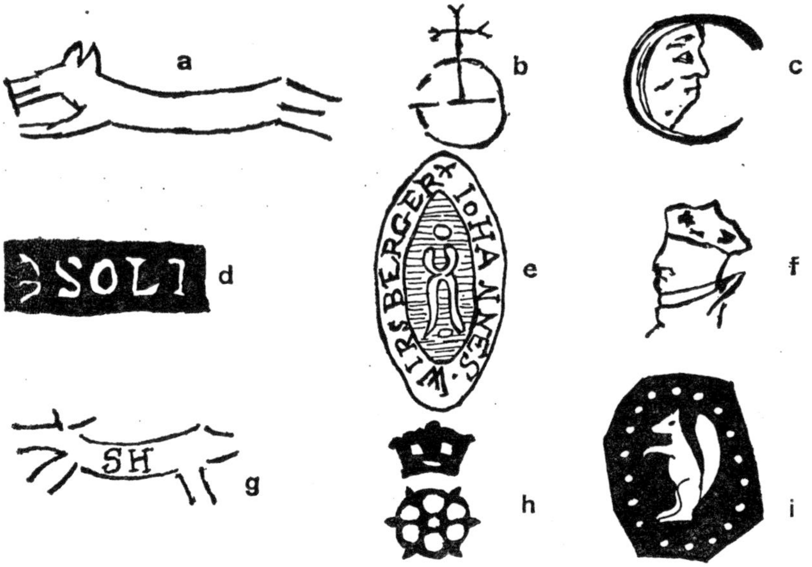

Fig. 15 a. Running Wolf mark of Solingen and Passau.
b. Orb and cross mark.
c. Half Moon mark.
d. Solingen mark *circa* 1630.
e. Iohannes Wirsberger, Solingen *circa* 1620.
f. Johannes Wudnes, Solingen *circa* 1560–1610.
g. Samuel Harvey, Birmingham 1748.
h. Crown and Rose mark of James II.
i. Squirrel sign of Frierich Eickhorn, Solingen.

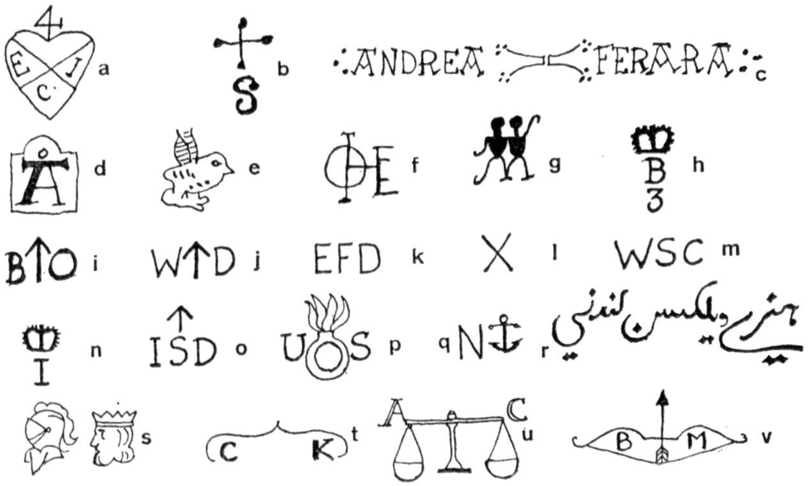

Fig. 16 a. Honourable East India Company.
b. Anthonio Picino, Italy *circa* 1613.
c. Andrea Ferara, Italy *circa* 1555–1593.
d. Anthonio de Baena, Spain.
e. Toledo mark. Spain
f. Juan Martin, Spain.
g. Peter Henkel, Solingen *circa* 1620.
h. British inspectors mark.
i. Board of Ordnance mark to 1855, British.
j. War Department mark after 1855, British.
k. Royal Small Arms Factory, Enfield, British.
l. Cross mark showing the convex side of a blade for future bending tests, British.
m. Mark of the Wilkinson Sword Company, British.
n. Inspectors mark of the India Stores Depot.
o. Acceptance mark for the India Stores Depot.
p. Acceptance mark, United States of America.
q. Mark on arms for the Royal Navy.
r. Henry Wilkinson, London. Inscription on a Persian sword.
s. Weyersburg Kirschbaum and Co. 1883. The King's head mark alone was used by Gebr. Weyersburg Solingen prior to 1883 and the Knight's head with WKC beneath was used by Weyersburg Kirchbaum and Co. *circa* 1930.
t. Carl Kaiser and Co., Solingen.
u. Alex Coppel, Solingen.
v. J. E. Bleckmann, Solingen.

ILLUSTRATION CREDITS

Author's Collection: 20, 21, 31, 163, 250, 253, 257, 258, 259, 260, 261, 262, 263, 264, 265.
C. Kennedy: (*Photos: Jack Blake*): 205, 206, 207, 208, 209, 210, 211, 212, 213, 214, 215.
Collection de la boutique d'Armes Anciennes 'La Dragonne' Cannes (*Dr Villanova*): 71, 74, 75, 76.
Derek Spalding: 216, 217.
Deutsches Klingenmuseum Solingen, Germany: 81, 82, 83, 84, 85, 86, 87, 88, 89.
Frederick Stephens: 241.
Heeresgeschichtlishes Museum, Austria: 108, 109, 110, 111, 112, 113, 114, 289.
Herman A. Maeurer: 271, 272, 276, 277, 278, 282, 287, 288, 290, 291, 293.
Historical Research Unit: 144, 145, 146, 147, 148, 149, 150.
Imperial War Museum, London: 266, 267, 268, 270 (*Photos: Jack Blake*).
Kungl. Aremuseum, Sweden: 33, 35, 36, 37, 101, 102, 103, 104, 105, 106, 107, 245, 246, 247, 248, 249, 284, 285.
Musée de l'Armée, France: 273.
Musée Royal de l'Armée et d'Histoire Militaire, Belgium: 78, 79, 80, 171.
National Maritime Museum, Greenwich: 50, 163, 165, 166, 167, 168, 172, 174, 218.
Pattern Room, Royal Small Arms Factory, Enfield: (*Photos: Jack Blake*): 64, 65, 66.
Peter White: 269, 274, 275, 279, 280, 283, 286, 292, 297, 299, 300.
Roy Butler: 244.
Tøjhusmuseet, Denmark: 92, 93, 94, 95, 96, 97, 98, 99, 100, 174, 281.
Tower of London, Armouries: 72, 115, 116, 117, 118, 119, 120, 122, 161, 173, 251, 252, 264, 255, 256.
Victoria and Albert Museum, London: 12, 17, 18, 22, 199.
Wallace Collection, London (by permission of the Trustees): 4, 5, 6, 7, 8, 9, 10, 11, 24, 25, 26, 28, 29, 198, 200, 201, 204.
Wallis and Wallis, Lewes: 16, 27, 38, 41, 46, 51, 57, 77, 121, 143, 158, 162, 175, 177, 184, 185, 187, 188, 189, 190, 191, 193, 196, 229, 231, 232, 236, 237, 242, 243.
Weller and Dufty, Birmingham: 23, 30, 32, 34, 39, 40, 53, 73, 157, 159, 160, 192, 194, 195, 197, 202, 203, 224, 225, 228, 230, 233, 234, 235, 238, 239, 240.
West Point Museum, USA: 123, 124, 125, 126, 127, 128, 129, 130, 131, 132.
J. Wilkinson-Latham: 1, 2, 13, 14, 15, 42, 43, 44, 45, 47, 48, 49, 52, 54, 55, 61, 62, 67, 154, 155, 156, 183, 186, 223, 226, 227.
Wilkinson Sword Ltd, London: 58, 59, 60, 63, 68, 69, 70, 90, 133, 134, 135, 136, 137, 138, 139, 140, 141, 142, 151, 152, 164, 169, 170, 176, 179, 180, 181, 182, 219, 220, 221, 222.

Line Drawings

Jack Cassin Scott: figs 1, 2, 3, 5, 8, 9, 12, 13, 14.
Christine Wilkinson-Latham: figs 4, 6, 7, 10, 11, 15.

BIBLIOGRAPHY

Archaeology of Weapons R. Ewart Oakeshott; Lutterworth 1960.

Armouries of the Tower of London Charles J. Ffoulkes FSA; HMSO 1916.

British Military Swords 1800 to present day J. Wilkinson-Latham; Hutchinson and Co. Ltd, 1966.

British Military Cut and Thrust Weapons J. Wilkinson-Latham; David and Charles 1971.

Cut and Thrust Weapons Eduard Wagner; Spring Books 1967.

Edged Weapons Frederick Wilkinson; Guinness Superlatives 1970.

European and American Arms C. Blair; Batsford 1962.

Gamle Danske Militaer Vaben Th. Møller; Høst & Søn 1963 and 1968.

Illustrated Catalogue of Military Goods Schuyler Hartley and Graham. *Reprint;* Norm Flayderman 1961.

Military Edged Weapons of the World Herman A. Maeurer 1967.

Naval Swords P. G. W. Annis; Arms and Armour Press 1970.

Rêvue Belge d'histoire Militaire, Articles on Belgian Military swords, June and September 1966. L. Leconte.

Russian Military Swords 1801–1917 Eugène Mollo. Historical Research Unit Publication 1969.

Regulation Military Swords J. Wilkinson-Latham. Collectors' Series 1970.

Swords in the Age of Chivalry R. Ewart Oakeshott; Lutterworth 1964.

Swords of Hitler's 3rd Reich Major J. Angolia; F. Stephens 1969.

Swords for Sea Service May and Annis; HMSO 1970.

Wallace Collection Catalogue Vols 1 & 2 Sir J. Mann KCVO, FSA, Hon V-PSA 1962.

British Military Bayonets R. J. Wilkinson-Latham. Hutchinson and Co. Ltd 1967.

Bayonets, The Collector's Pictorial Book of F. Stephens; Arms and Armour Press 1971.

The Canadian Bayonet R. Barrie Manarey; Century Press 1971.

Gew 98; Francis Bannerman & Sons 1921.

MUSEUM CATALOGUES

Kungl. Armemuseum, Stockholm.

Tøljhusmuseet, Copenhagen.

MANUSCRIPT AND ORIGINAL SOURCES

War Office Papers in the Public Record Office, London. Various Specifications of swords and bayonets issued by the War Office.

Pattern Books, Sketch Books, Contract Books. 1840–1918. of Wilkinson Sword Ltd, London.

VALUABLE INFORMATION WAS SUPPLIED IN CORRESPONDENCE WITH THE FOLLOWING:

Karin Oscarsson. Kungl Armemuseum, Stockholm.
W. Hofrat. Heeresgeschichtliches Museum, Vienna.
Dr Hanns-Ulrich Haedeke. Deutsches Klingenmuseum Solingen.
Robert W. Fisch. West Point Museum, New York.
J. R. Leconte. Musée Royal de l'Armée et D'histoire Militaire Brussels.
Colonel Wemaere. Musée de l'Armée. Paris.

INDEX

Note: Numbers in italic–Plates; numbers in brackets–figs; ordinary numbers–page.

1 *Japanese bladesmith checking the straightness of a pole arm blade. From an old print.*

2 *British bladesmith checking the straightness of a Household Cavalry trooper's blade. 1971.*

1

2

3 *Bronze Age swords. Left to right: With central rib; three with leaf shape blades.*

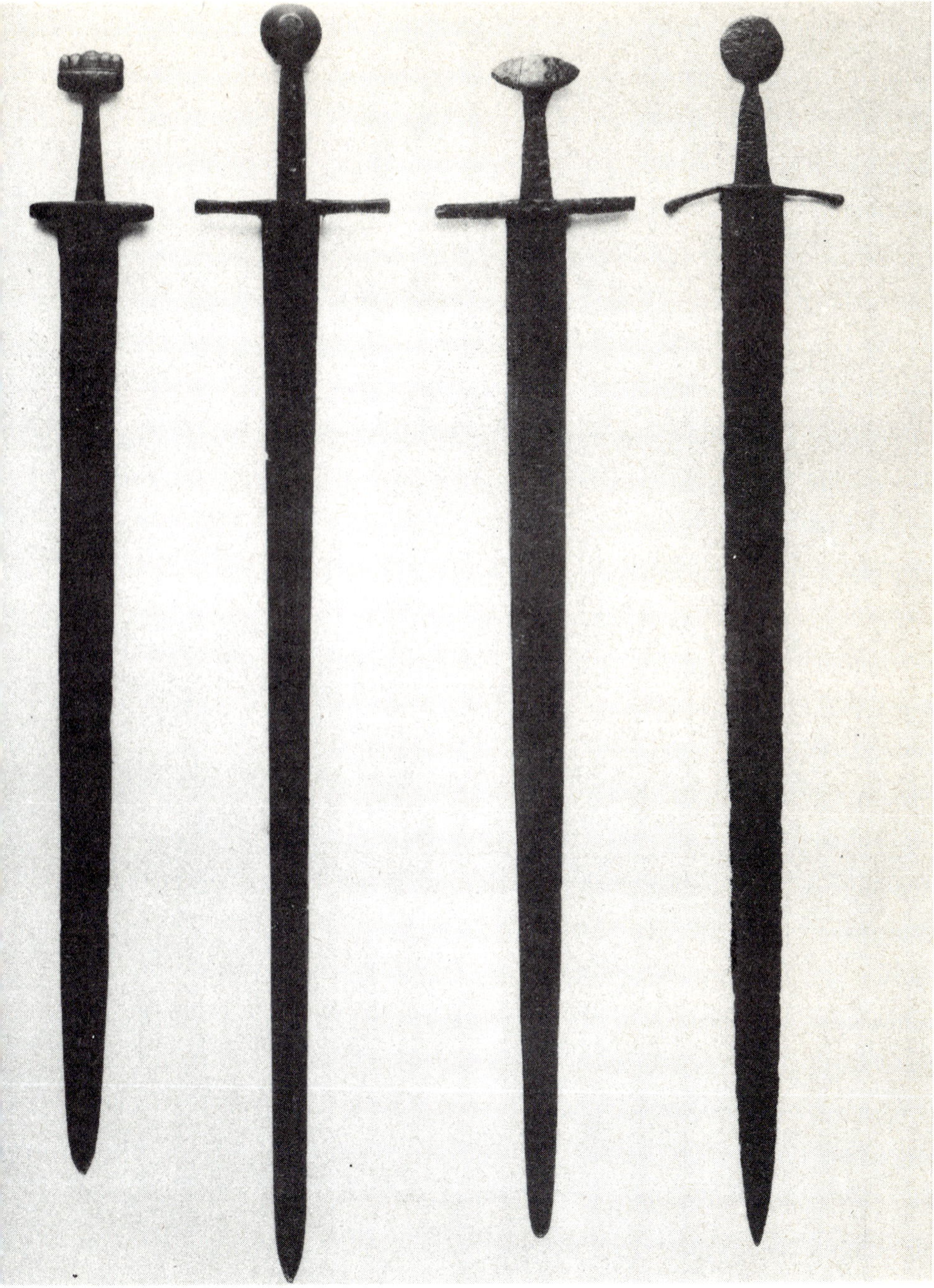

4 *Scandinavian sword 9th or 10th century; French sword* circa *1340; German sword 1150–1200; Sword, 13th century.*

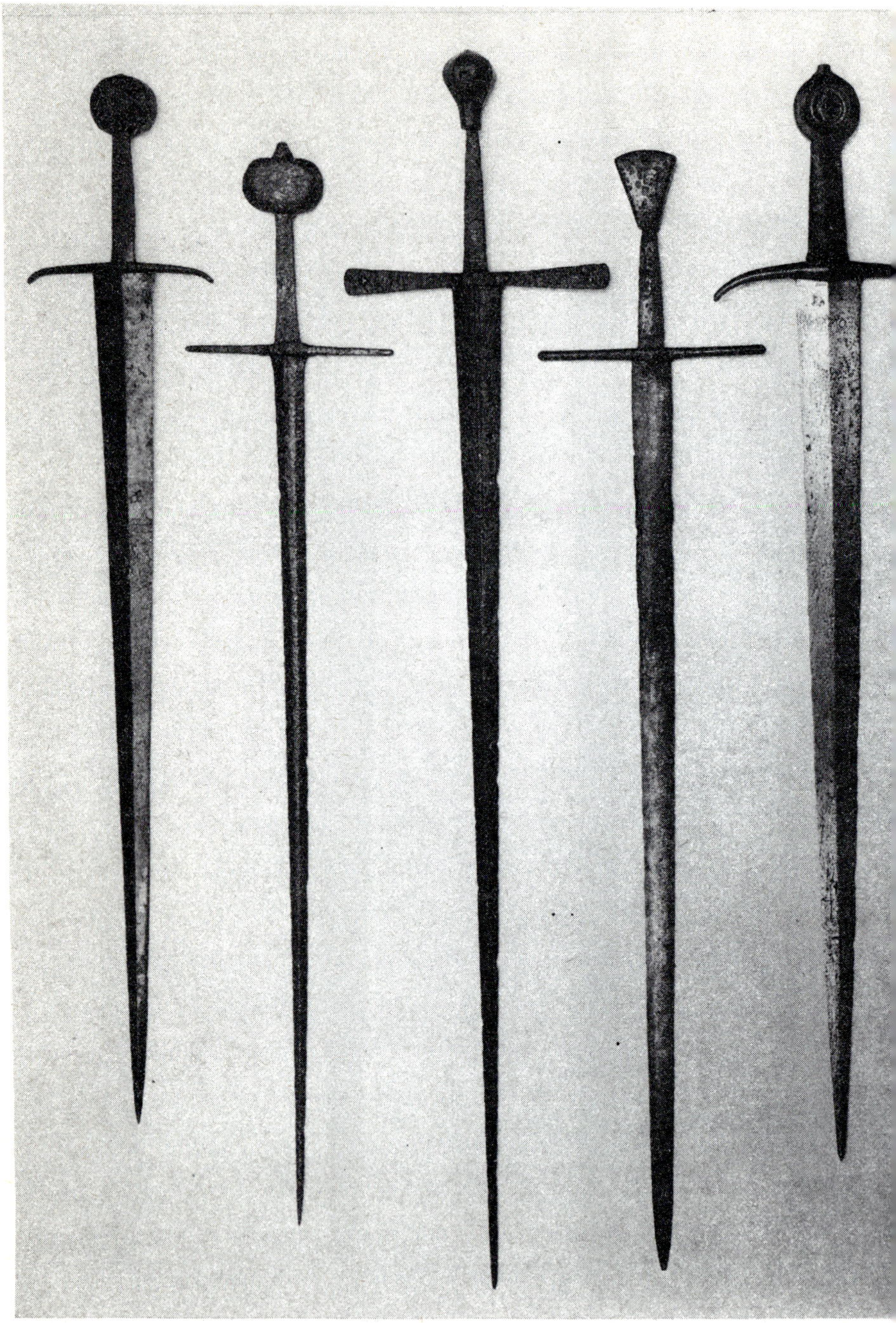

5 *French sword 1350–1400; Thrusting sword 14th century; Sword* circa *1400; Sword* circa *1380; French sword 1375–1400.*

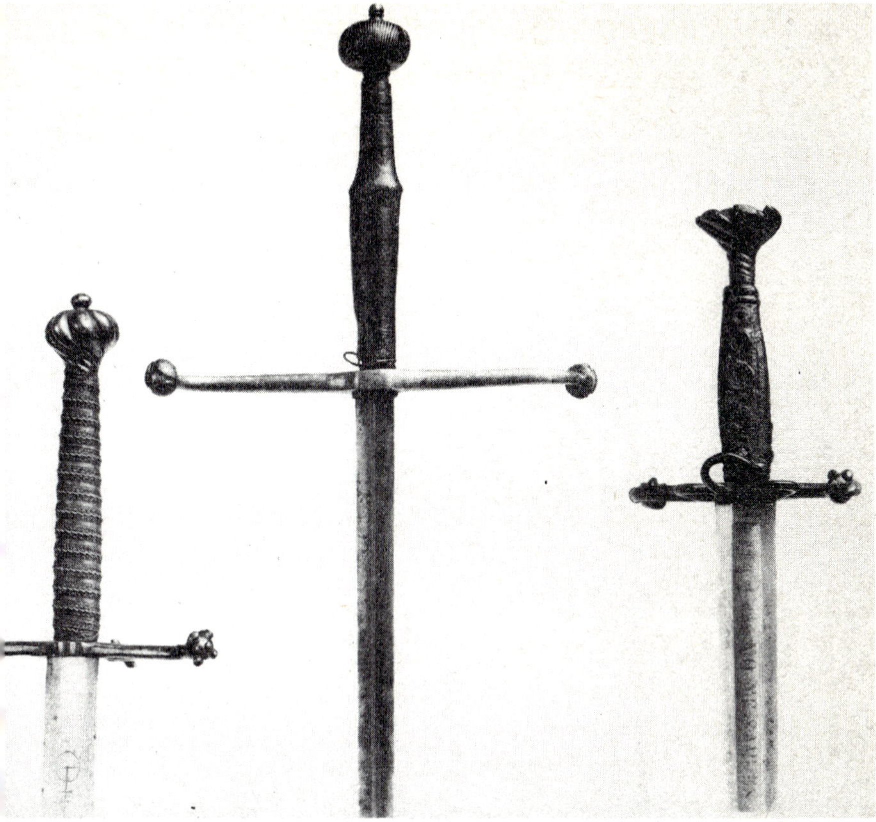

6

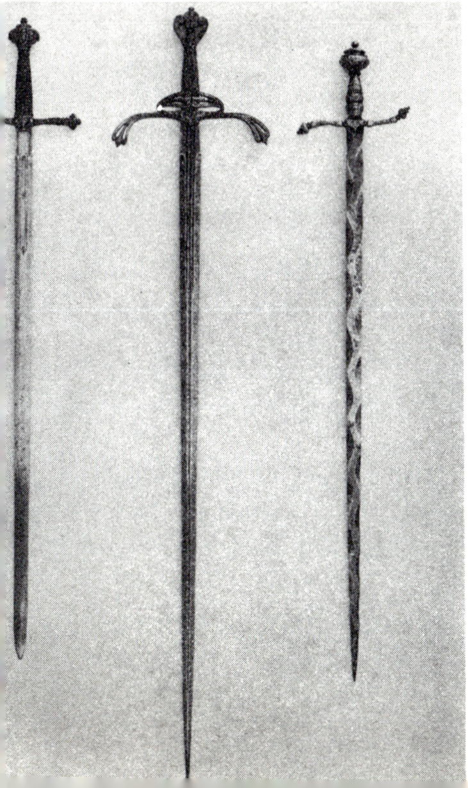

6 *German calendar sword 1550–1620; German estoc 1540; German sword with hilt* circa *1530 and blade* circa *1770.*

7 *German sword 1610; Spanish sword mid-16th century; Italian sword 1550.*

7

8

8 *Italian sword* circa *1460; Italian sword* circa *1490, the hilt appears to be modern; Swiss or German Baselard* circa *1530; German sword 16th century; Italian Falchion mid-16th century.*

9 *German (Saxon) sword late 16th century; German Bastard sword hand-and-a-half 1540-80.*

9

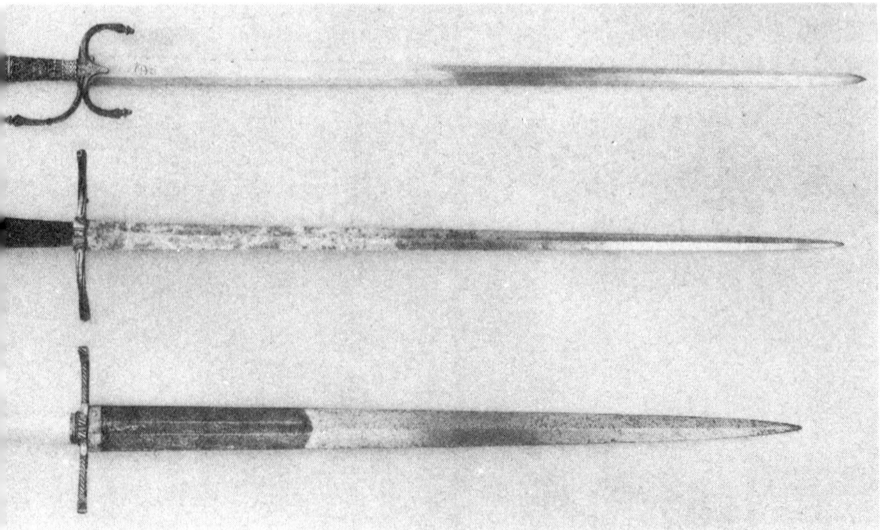

10 *German sword 16th century; Italian sword 1490–1520; Italian sword 1500.*

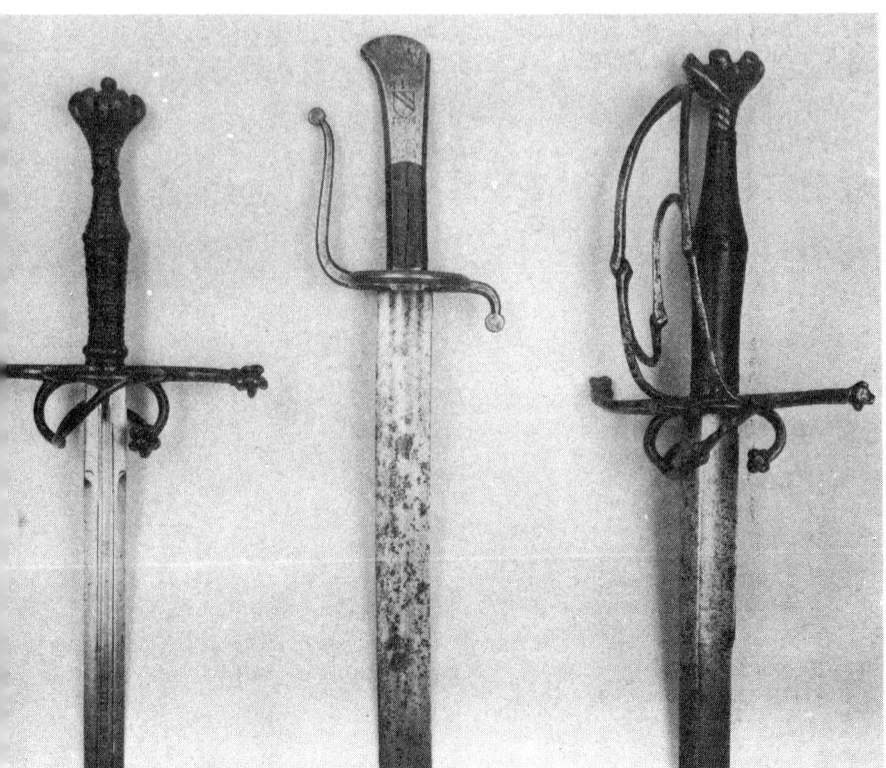

11 *German Bastard or hand-and-a-half sword* circa *1600; German sabre 16th century* (?); *German Bastard or hand-and-a-half sword* circa *1530.*

12

12 *Saxon swords of the second half of the 16th century.*

13 *German two handed swords.*

14 *German two handed swords.*

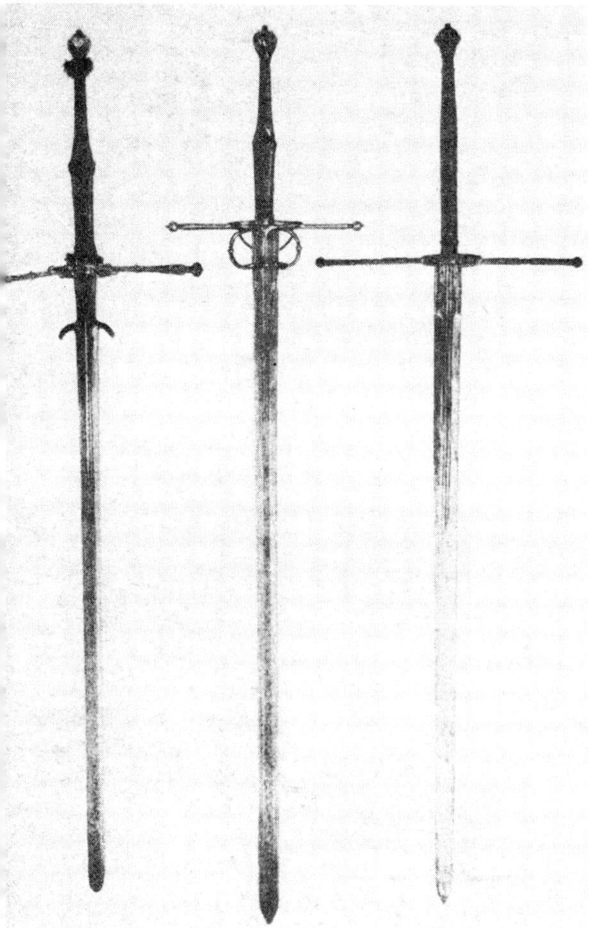

13 14

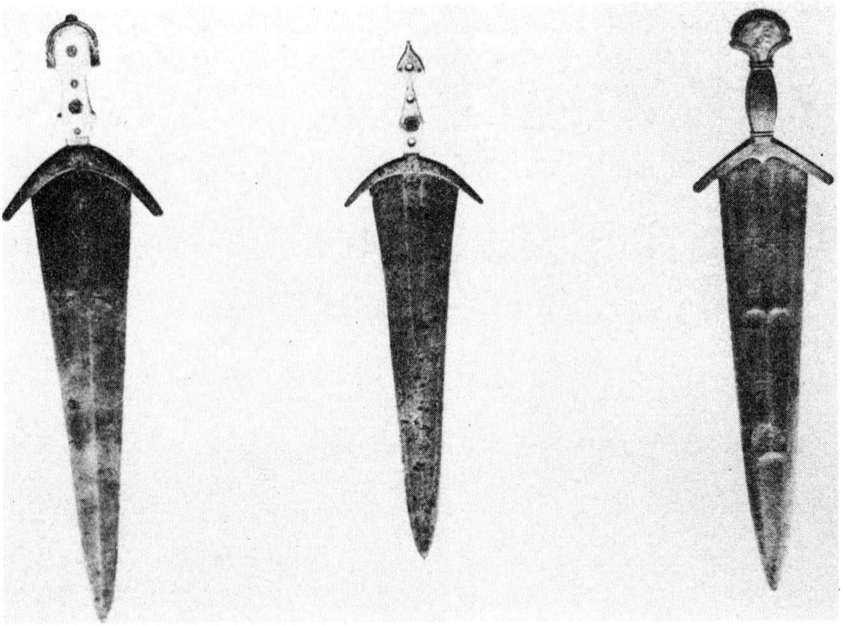

15 *Italian* cinquedeas.

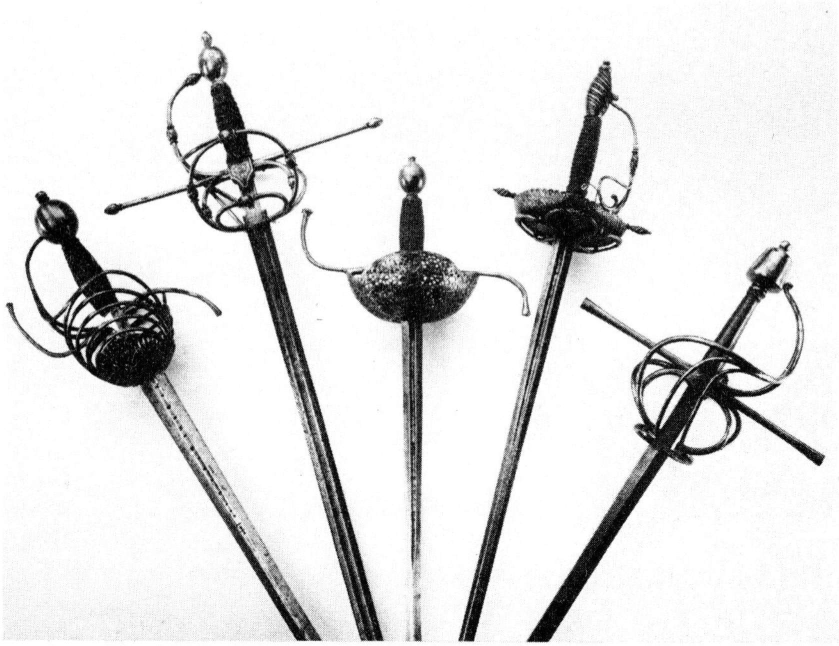

16 *German rapier* circa *1580; Spanish swept hilt rapier; Italian rapier; English rapier; German rapier* circa *1590.*

17

17 *Saxon rapier (?) about 1570–80; Spanish rapier late 16th century.*

18 *Saxon rapier with companion* main gauche, *end of 16th century.*

19 *Saxon swept hilt rapiers. Late 16th century.*

20 *Page from a pattern book of sword hilt designs. Antoine Jacquard of Poitiers. First half of 17th century.*

21 *Page from a pattern book of sword hilt designs. Antoine Jacquard of Poitiers. First half of 17th century.*

18

19

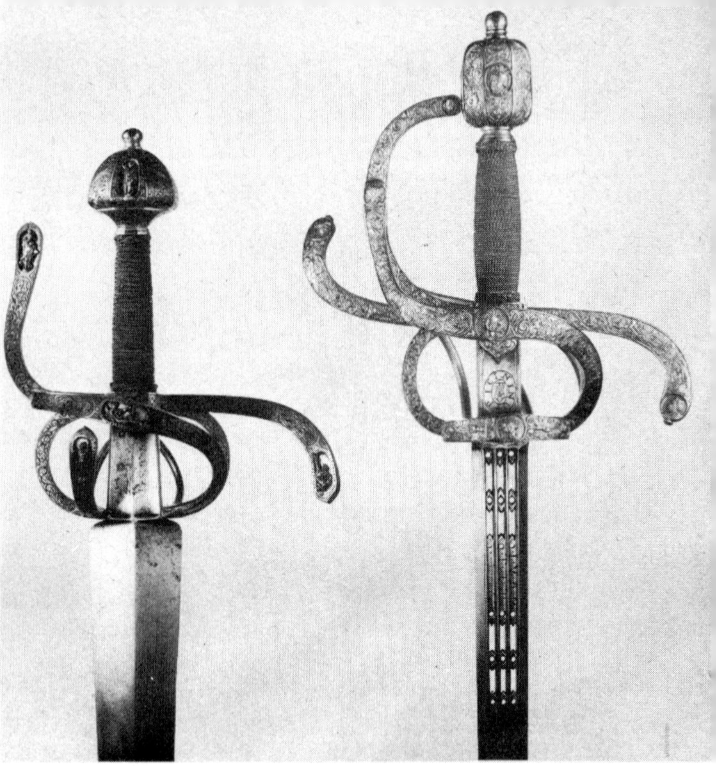

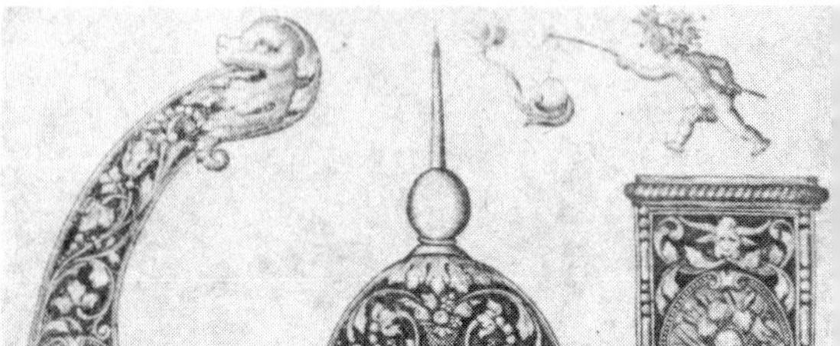

20 21

22

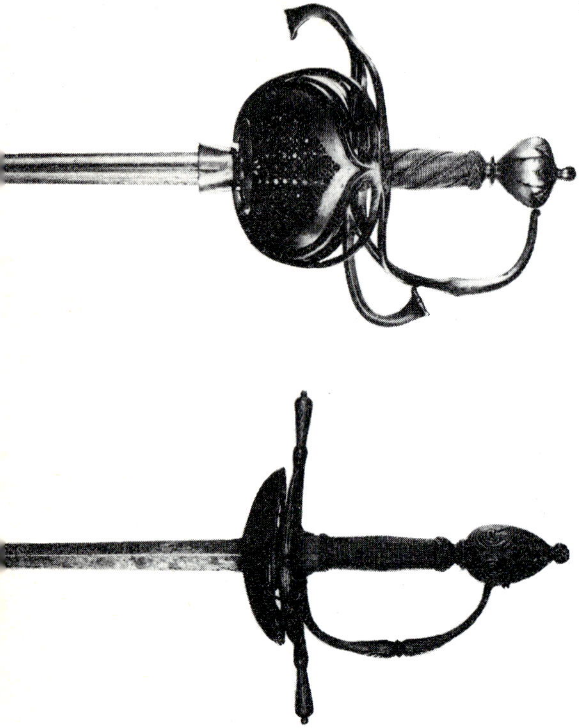

22 *Rapiers of the second quarter of the 17th century. Above: Flemish; Below: With blade signed Johannes Wudnes in Solingen.*

23 *Spanish cup hilt rapier* circa *1650; German half basket broadsword* circa *1650; Italian five ring rapier* circa *1625.*

24 *Cup hilt rapier* circa *1640; Cup hilt rapier and companion* main gauche circa *1660.*

25 *Spanish cup hilt rapier* circa *1680; Spanish cup hilt rapier* circa *1670; Spanish cup hilt rapier* circa *1670.*

23

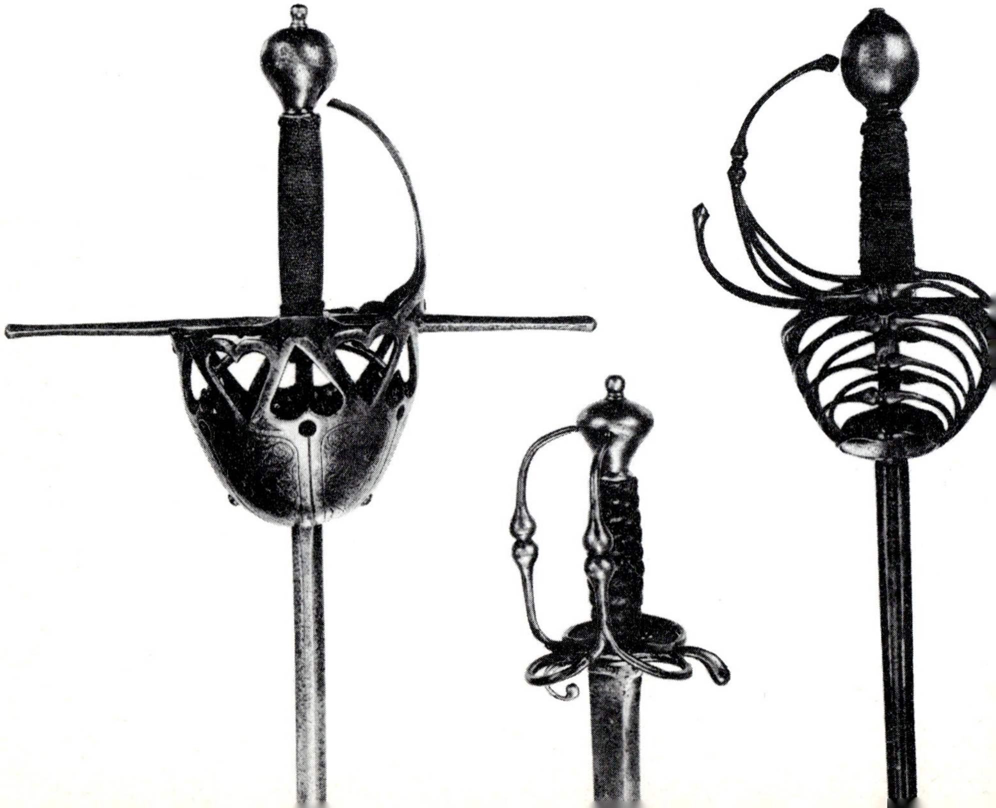

24

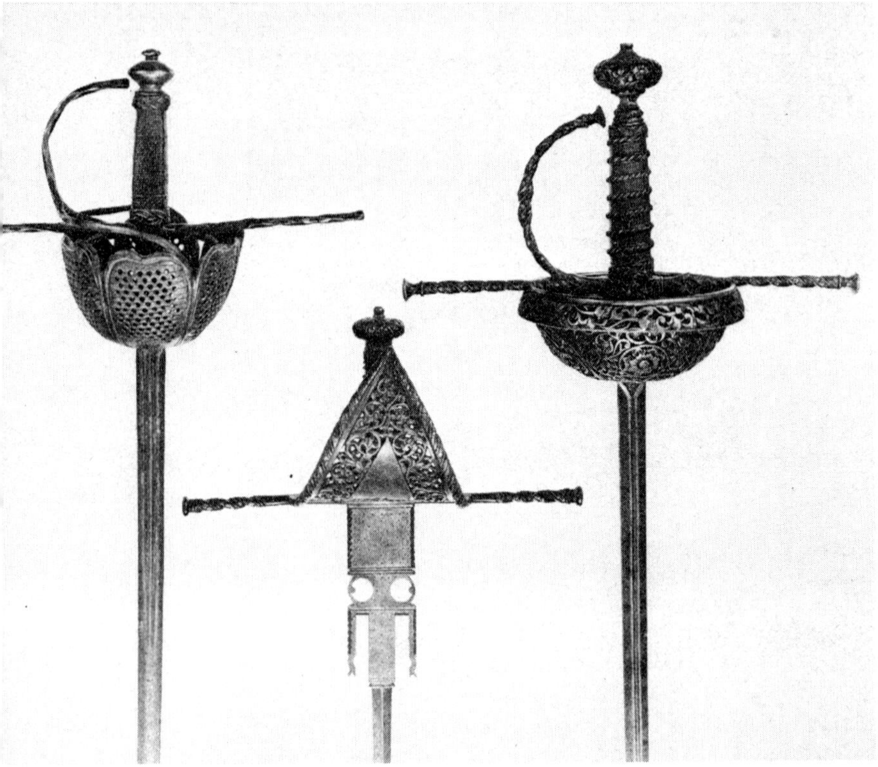

25

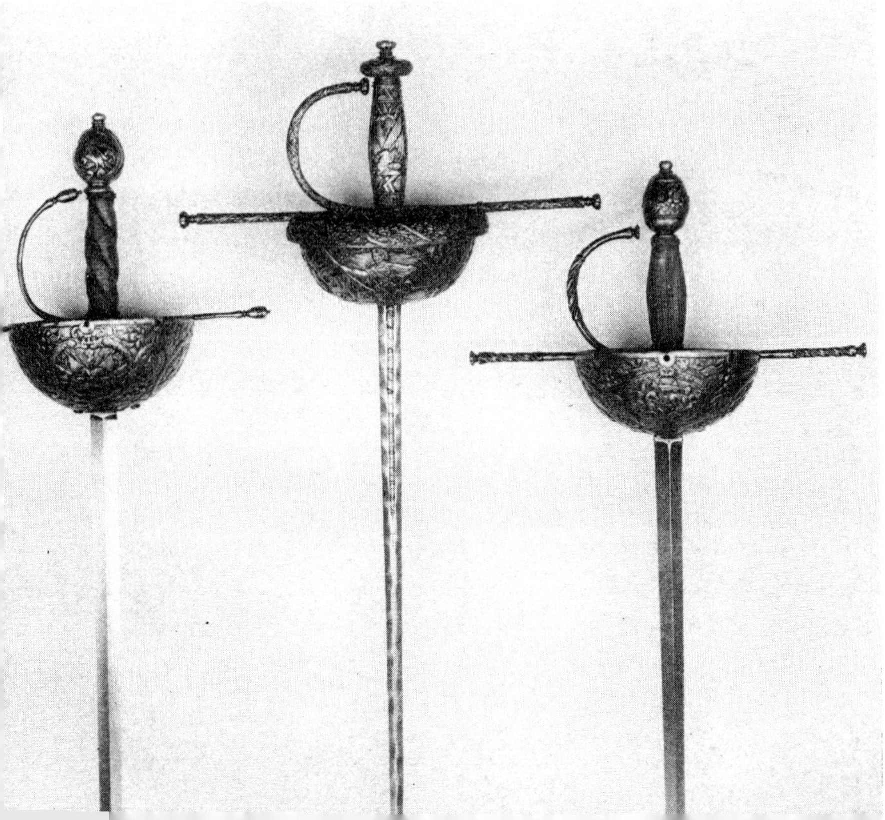

26 *French small sword 1660–80.*

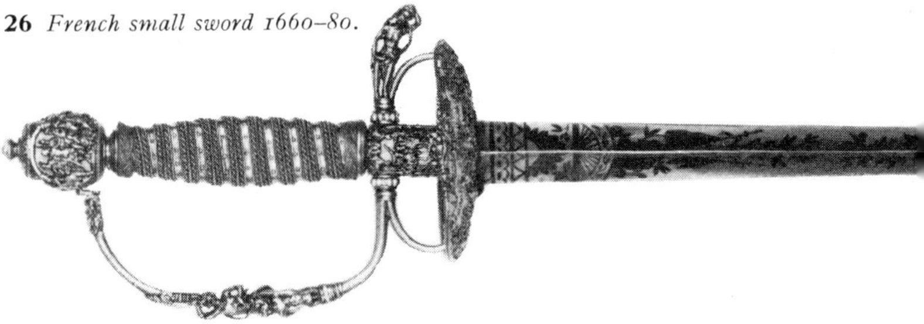

French small sword circa *1660.*

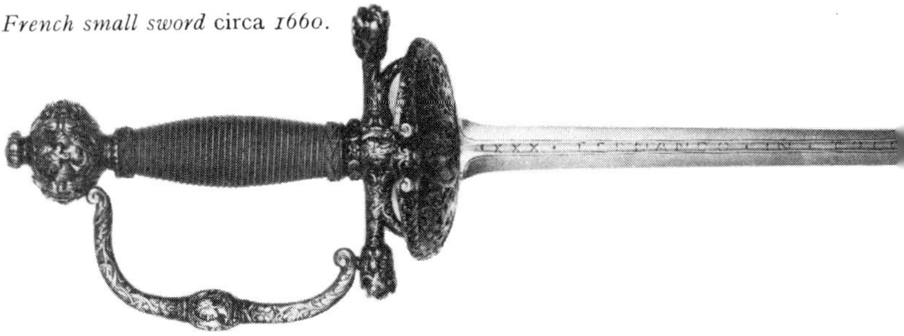

Italian or German small sword circa *1660.*

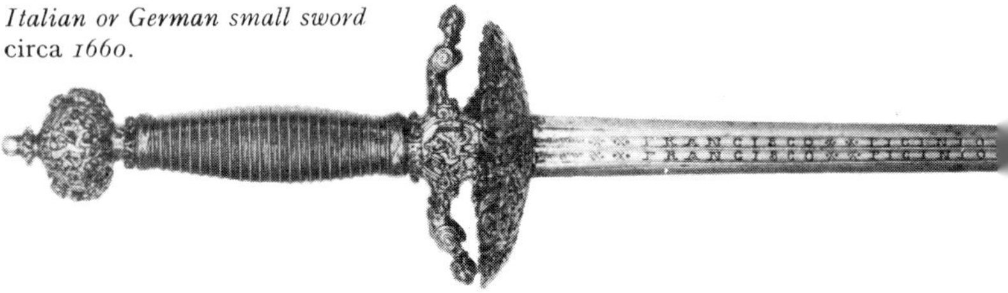

27 *French small sword with colimarche blade* circa *1680.*

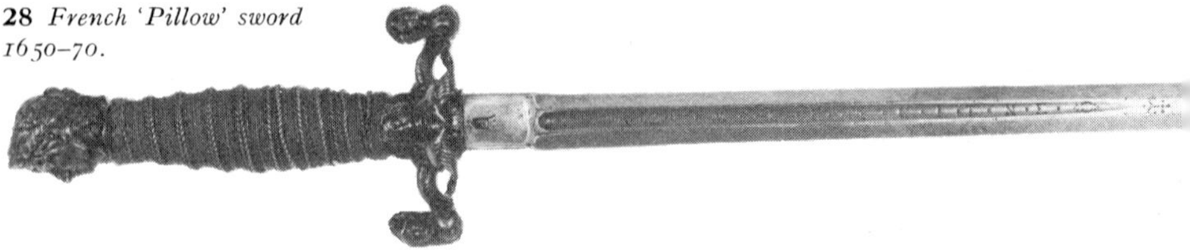

28 *French 'Pillow' sword 1650–70.*

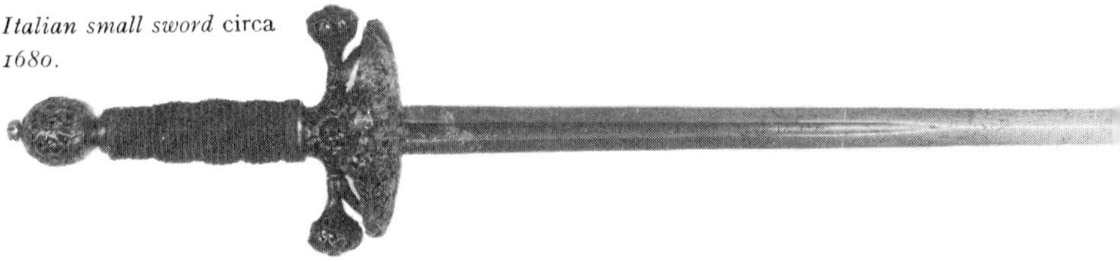

Italian small sword circa *1680.*

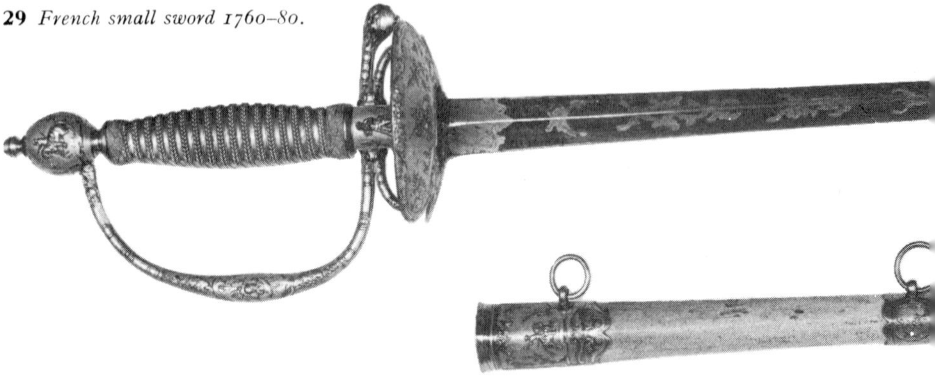

29 *French small sword 1760–80.*

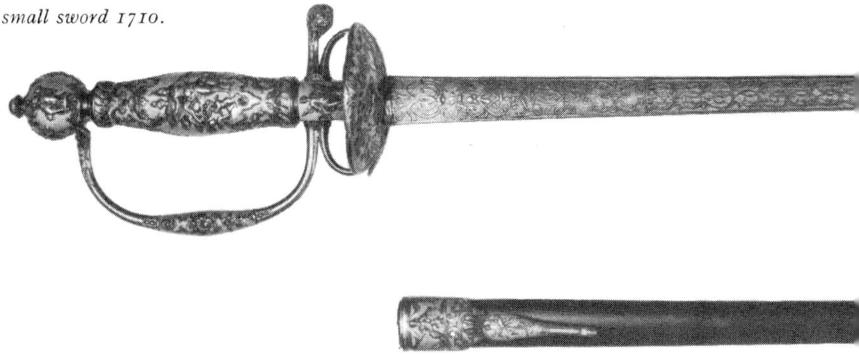

French small sword 1710.

30 *Various designs of late 18th century small swords.*

31 *Drawing of a presentation small sword* circa *1840.*

30

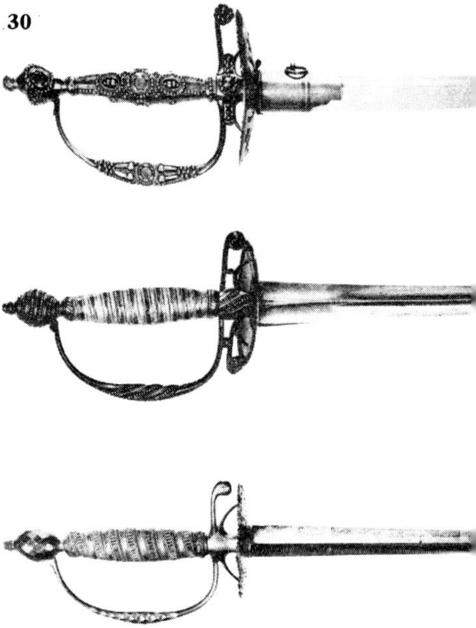

31

32 *Various styles of hunting sword 18th century.*

33 *Swedish officers sword 1620s.*

34 *Flemish 'Walloon' sword mid-17th century. Blade marked with the running wolf mark.*

35 *Swedish officers sword mid-17th century.*

32

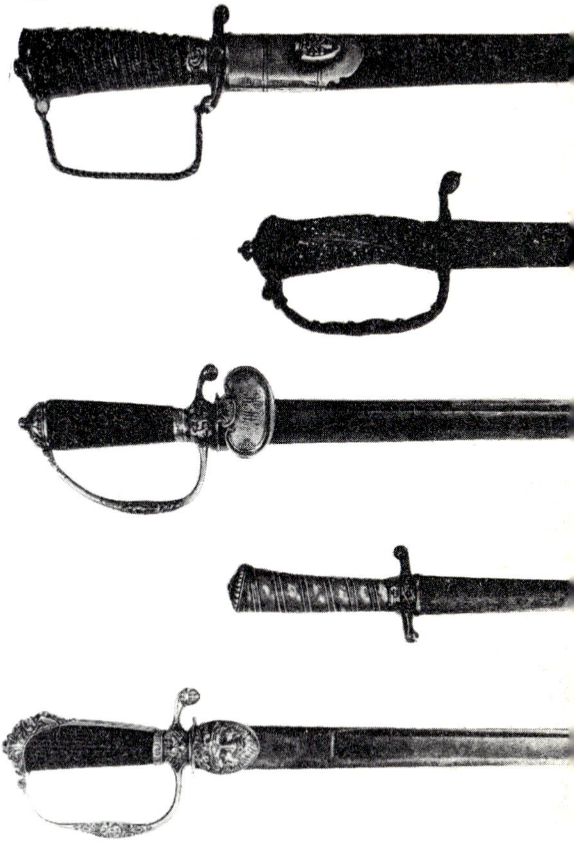

33

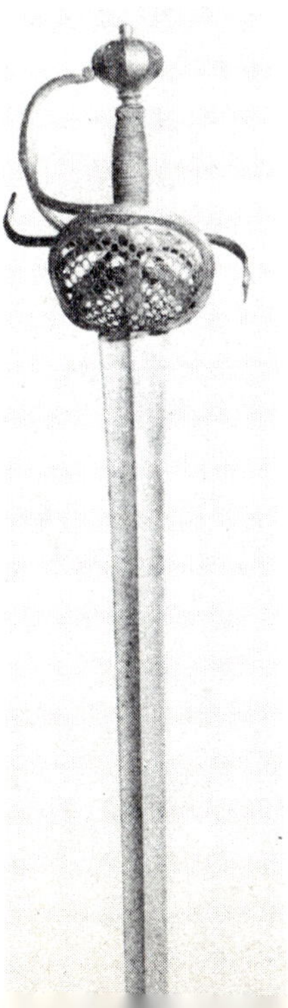

34

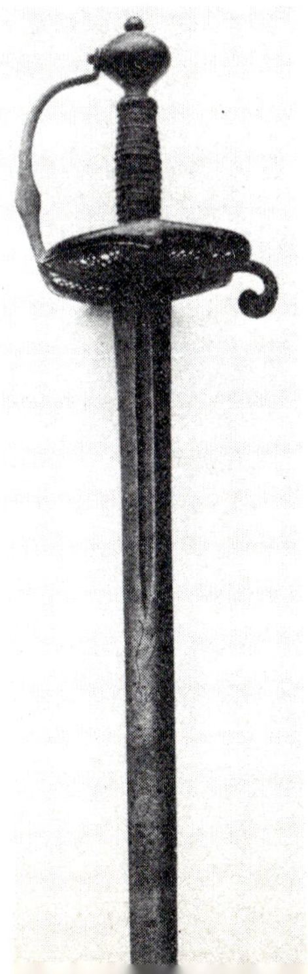

35

36

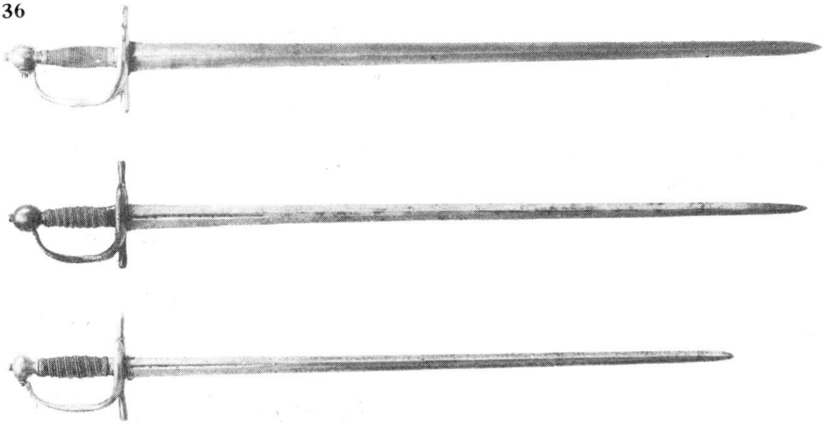

37

36 *Swedish cavalry swords; Troopers sword King's Own Horse 1701; Troopers sword King's Own Horse 1695; Officers sword* circa *1670.*

37 *Swedish officers sword, General Officer Charles XII period (1697–1718).*

38 *British. Basket hilt cavalry sword 1740; Basket hilted sword* circa *1740; Basket hilted broadsword* circa *1750; Heavy cavalry officers sword 1822 pattern.*

38

39 *Mortuary sword 17th century; Bilbao style sword* circa *1700; Venetian schiavona* circa *1700; Scottish broadsword early 18th century; Cavalry backsword* (*Mortuary*).

40 *Italian schiavona 18th century; British General officers spadroon late 18th century; steel hilted rapier with 'Walloon' style hilt* circa *1650; Hunting sword* circa *1700; Spanish cup hilt rapier late 17th century.*

39

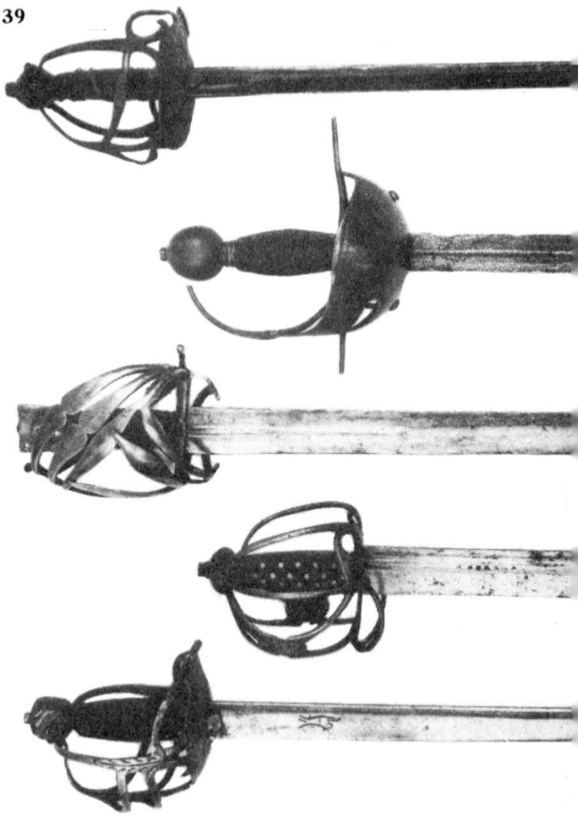

40

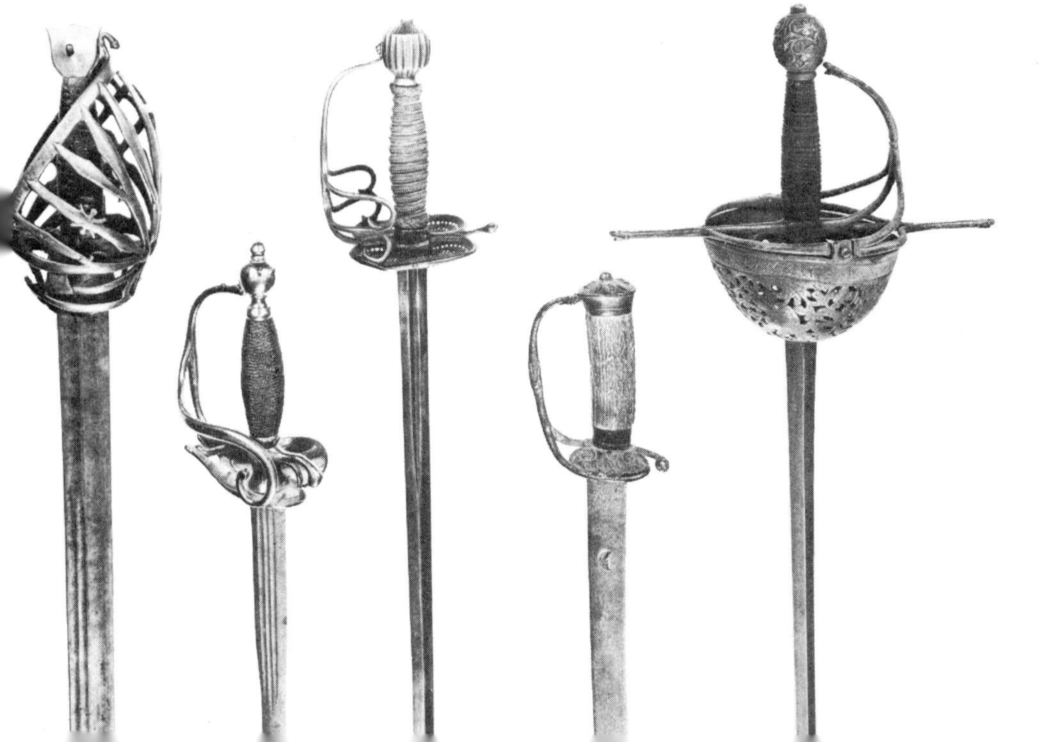

41 *British Infantry privates hanger* circa *1750. Also issued to Militia.*

42 *British Infantry Officers sword patt. 1786* (?).

43 *British Infantry privates hanger* circa *1750.*

44 *Scottish Infantry privates sword* circa *1750.*

41

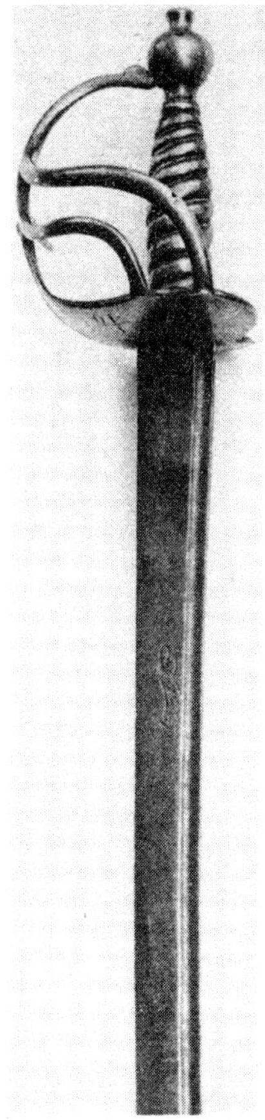

42

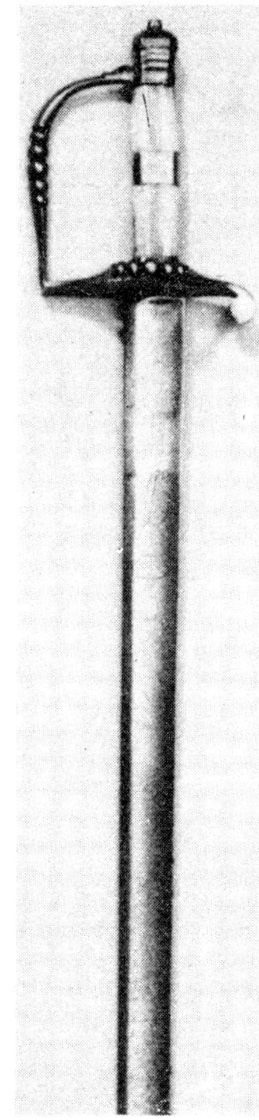

43

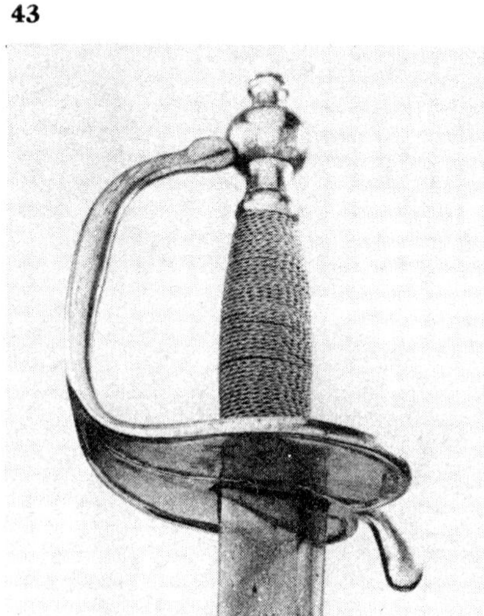

44

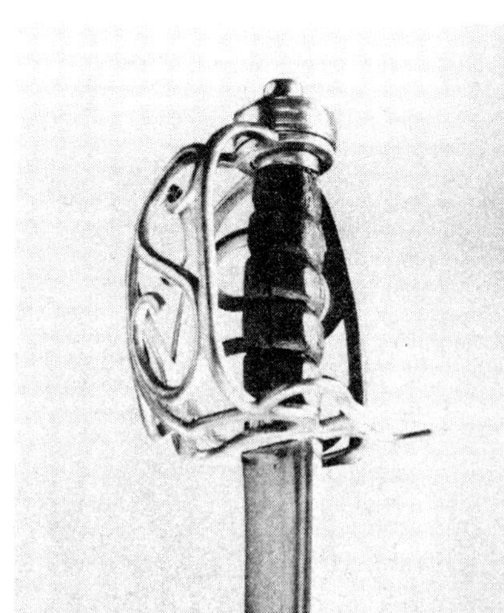

45 *British Volunteer Officers sword* circa *1790*.

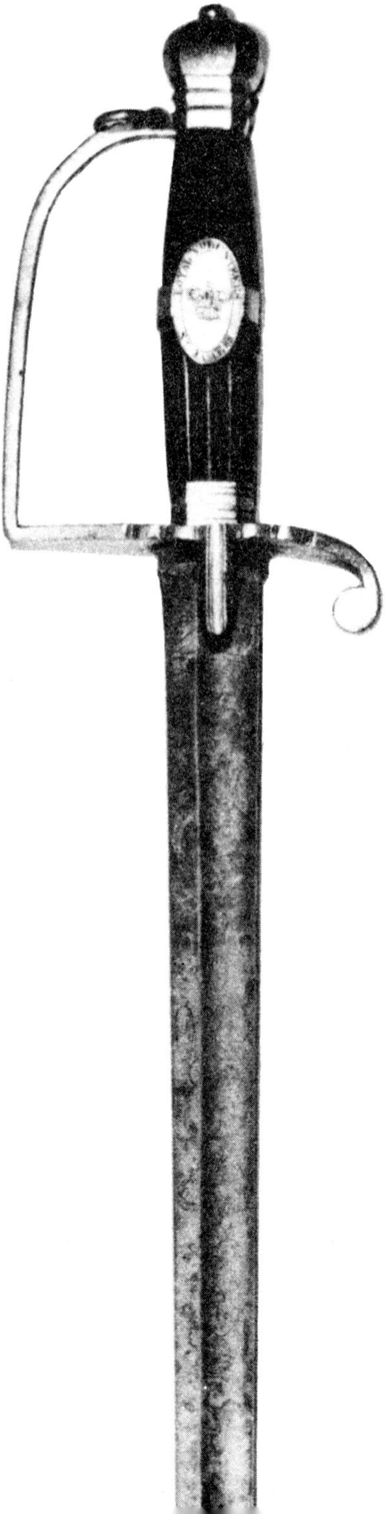

46 *British Officers sword* circa *1800*.

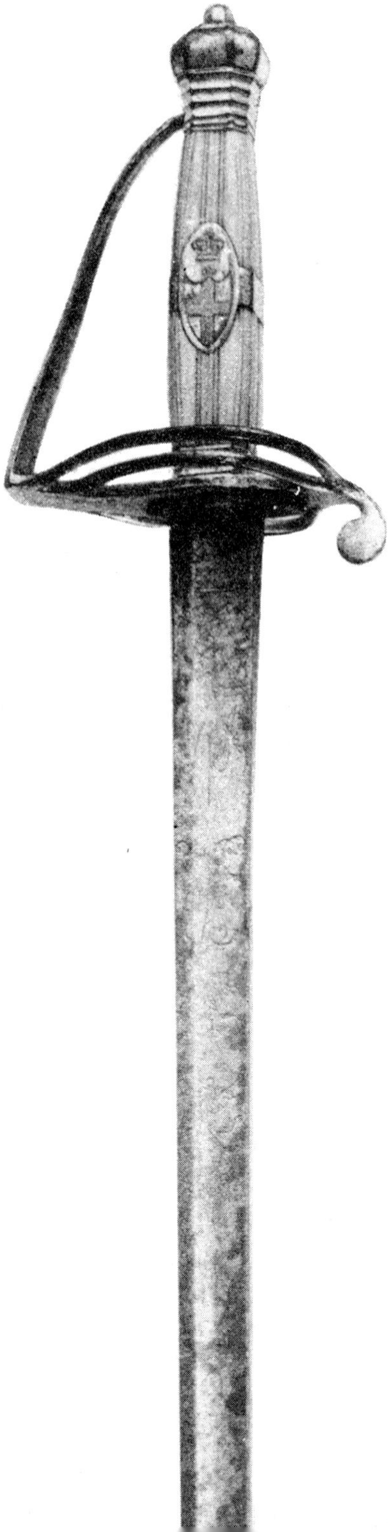

47 48

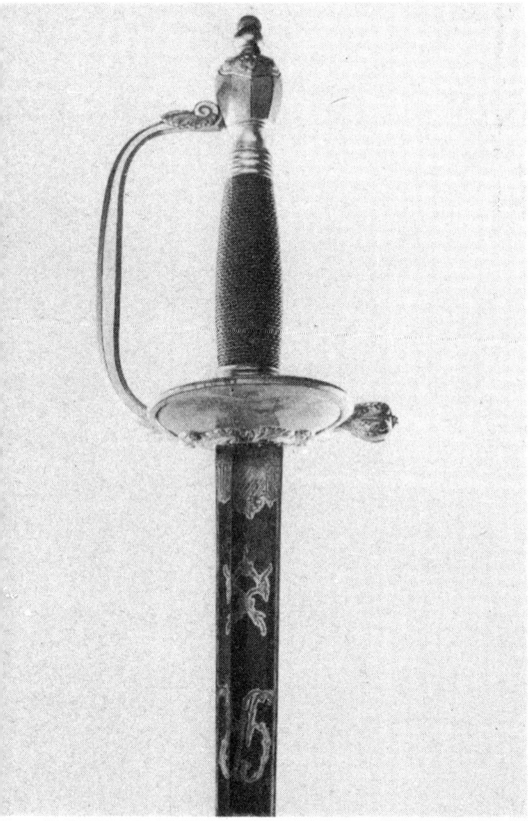

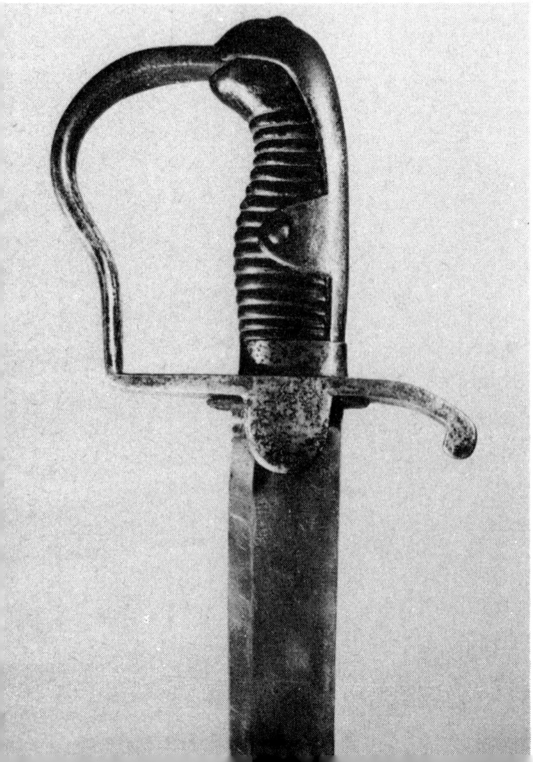

47 *British Infantry Officers sword patt. 1796.*

48 *British Dragoon Officers sword, last quarter of the 18th century.*

49 *British Light Cavalry troopers sword patt. 1796.*

50 *Heavy Cavalry troopers sword patt. 1822 (?) but not issued before 1830; British Heavy Cavalry troopers sword patt. 1796.*

51 *British Officers sword of the Royal Welsh Fusiliers* circa *1803.*

52 *British Officers sword of the 43rd Light Infantry* circa *1803.*

49

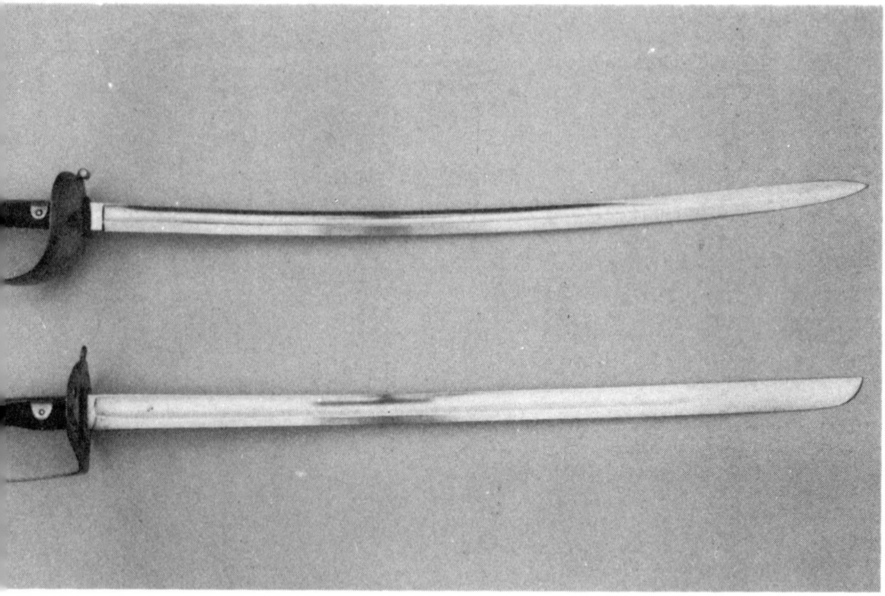
50

51

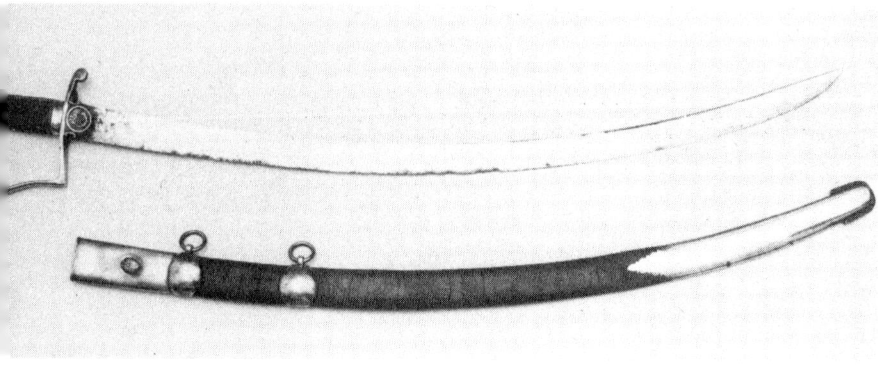
52

53 54

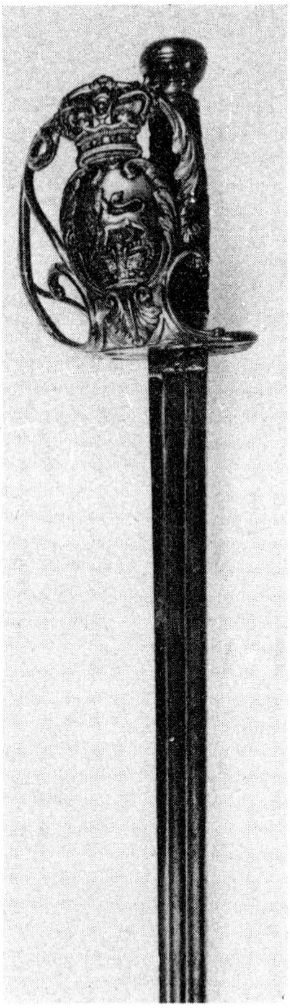

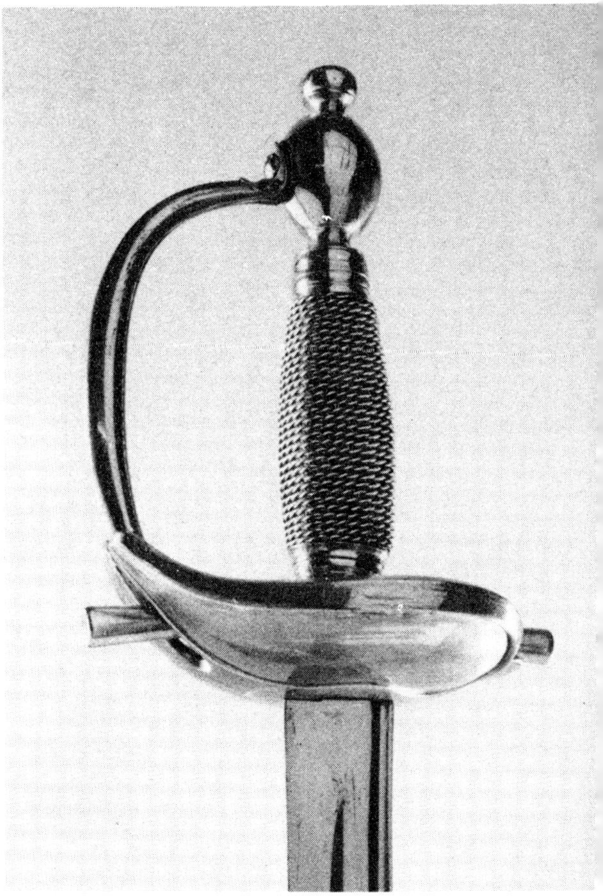

55

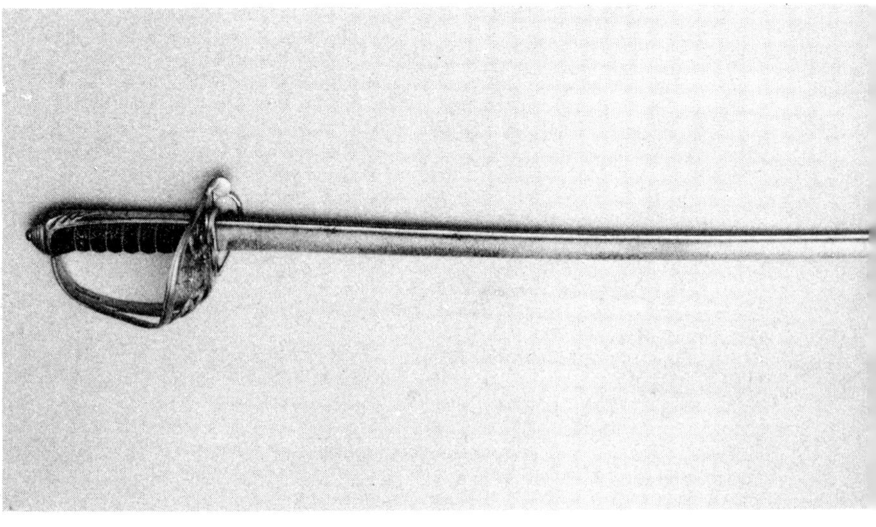

53 *British Household Cavalry Officers sword patt. 1815.*

54 *British Household Cavalry and Heavy Cavalry Officers sword patt. 1822.*

55 *British Infantry Officers sword patt. 1822 with pipe back blade (1822–46).*

56 *British Staff Officers sword patt. 1834. Used by General Officers from 1822–31.*

57 *British swords. Left to right: Scottish Officers broadsword; 1796 Light Cavalry Officers sword; 1st Life Guards Officers sword patt. 1834; Early 18th century cavalry sword; Heavy Cavalry Officers sword patt. 1834.*

56

57

58 *British. Drawing of the hilt of a regimental pattern sword of the 93rd Highlanders.*

59 *British. Scottish Officers broadsword first authorised in 1831 although worn before that date. Termed, incorrectly, in Dress Regulations as a 'claymore'.*

60 *British. Light Cavalry officers sword patt. 1822. Also worn by the Royal Horse Artillery, Royal Artillery (adopted 1855) and Royal Corps of Transport (late Royal Army Service Corps). Example illustrated is Royal Horse and Royal Artillery pattern with stepped pommel. All others have chequered pommel.*

58

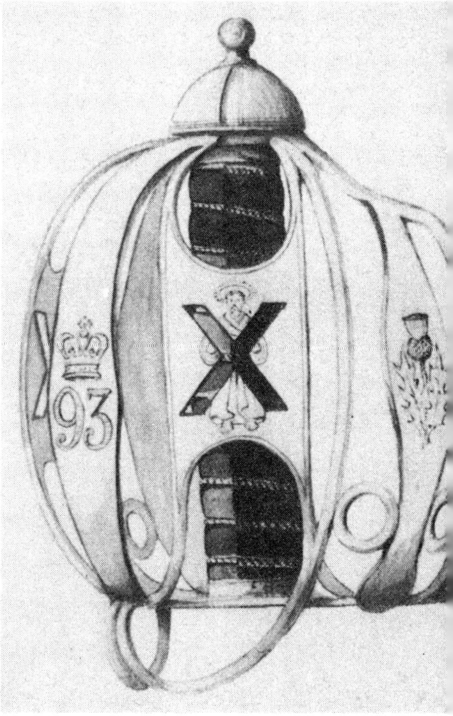

59 and **60**

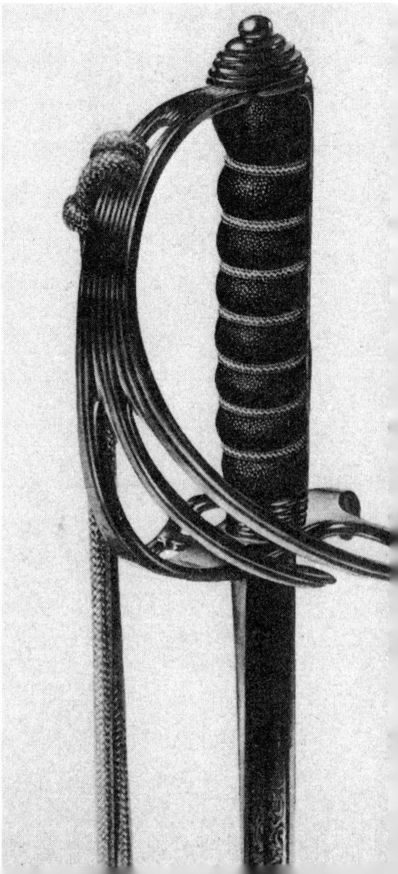

61

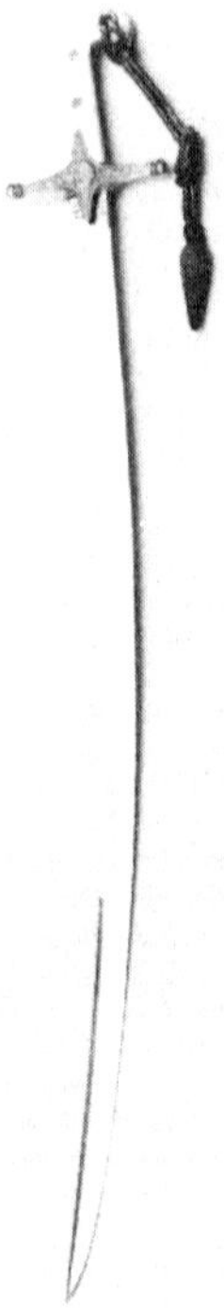

62

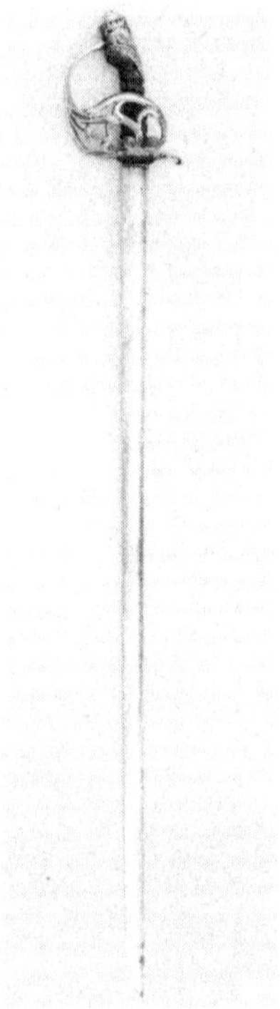

61 *British General Officers sword patt. 1831.*

62 *British Royal Horse Guards and 2nd Life Guards Officers sword patt. 1834.*

63 *British. Drawing of a heavy cavalry officers hilt patt. 1856. This particular hilt is for 6th Dragoon Guards and was approved in December 1877.*

63

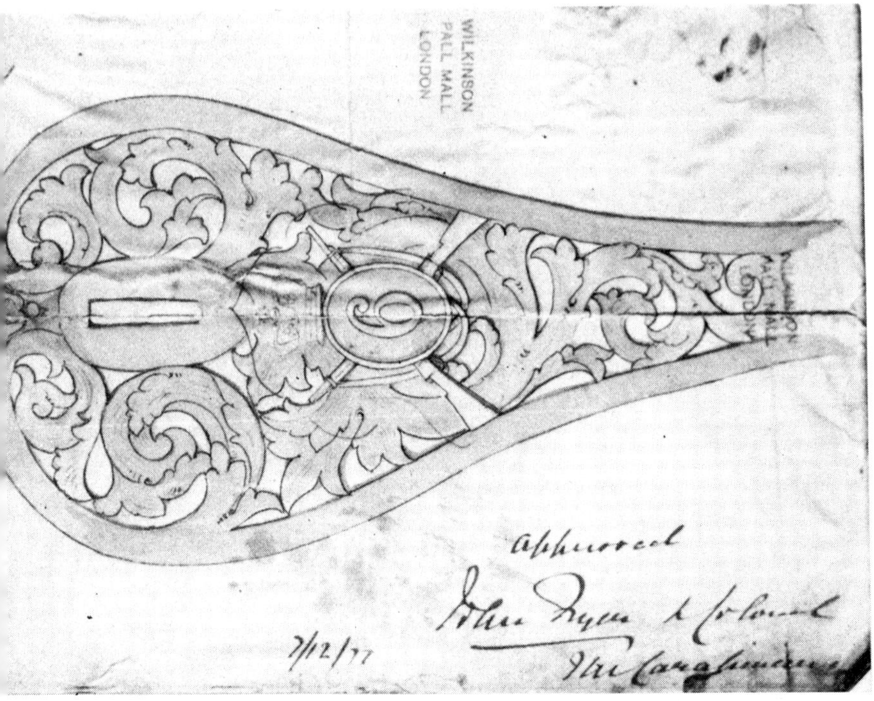

64

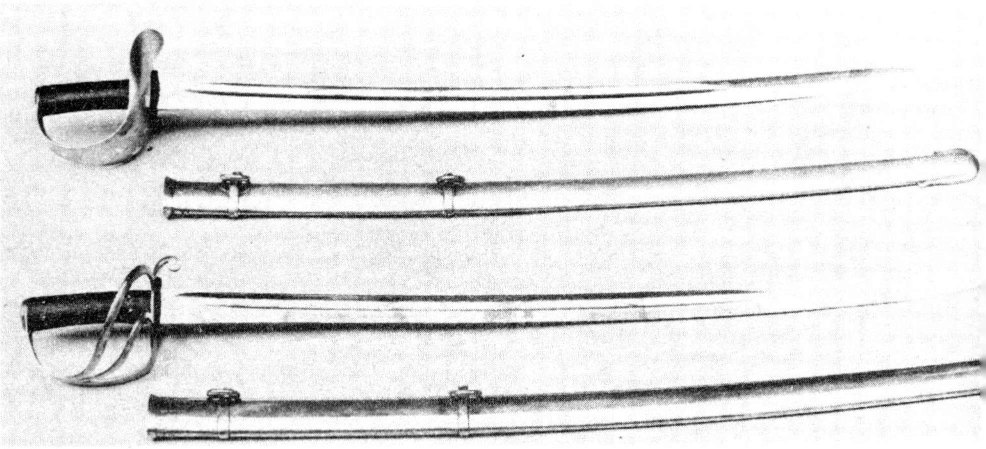

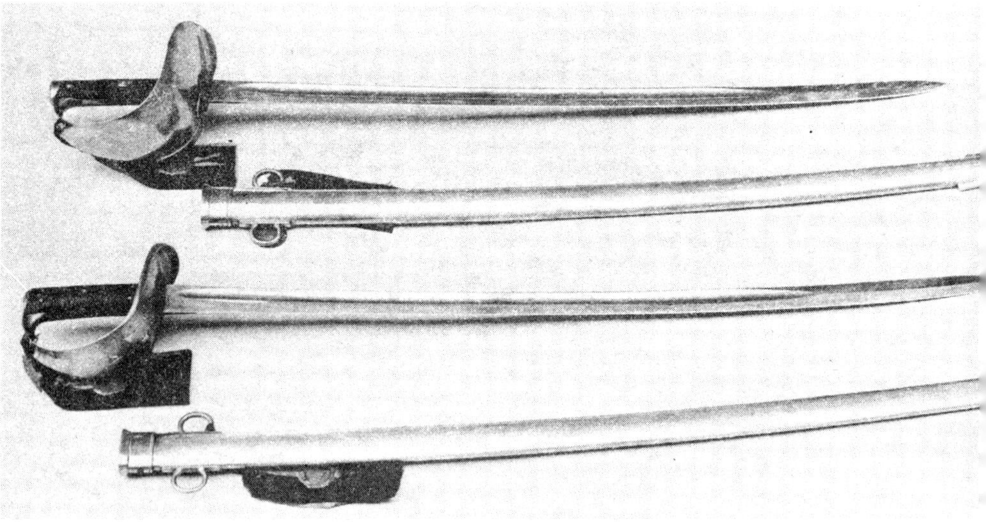

65

64 *British Cavalry troopers swords; Patt. 1864; Patt. 1853.*

65 *British Cavalry troopers swords; Patt. 1899; Patt. 1885.*

66 *British Household Cavalry troopers swords. Patt. 1882 Short; Patt. 1882 Long.*

67 *British Infantry bandsmans sword of a Light Infantry Regiment* circa *1850.*

68 *British Infantry Officers sword patt. 1895. patt. 1892 was similar but without the turn down on the inside of the guard.*

66

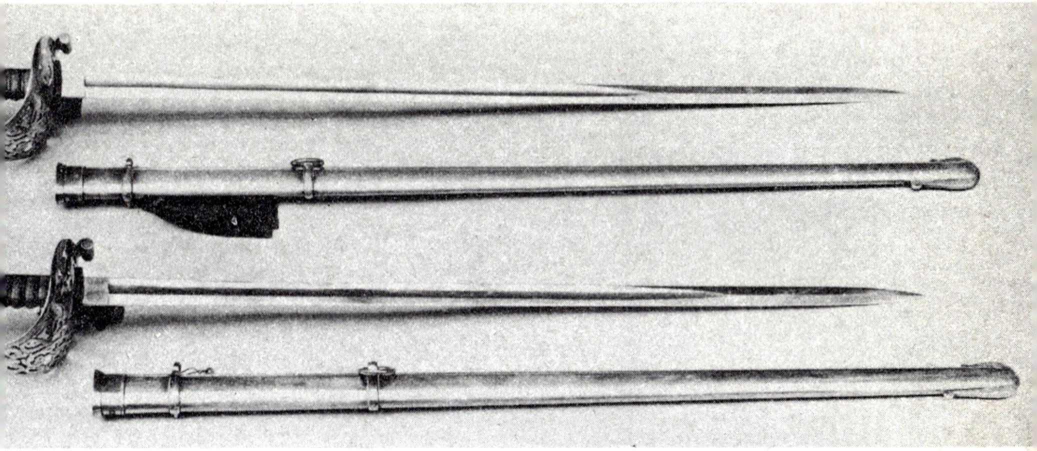

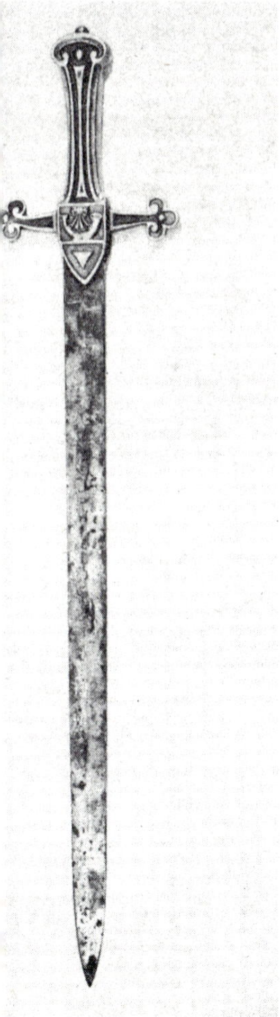

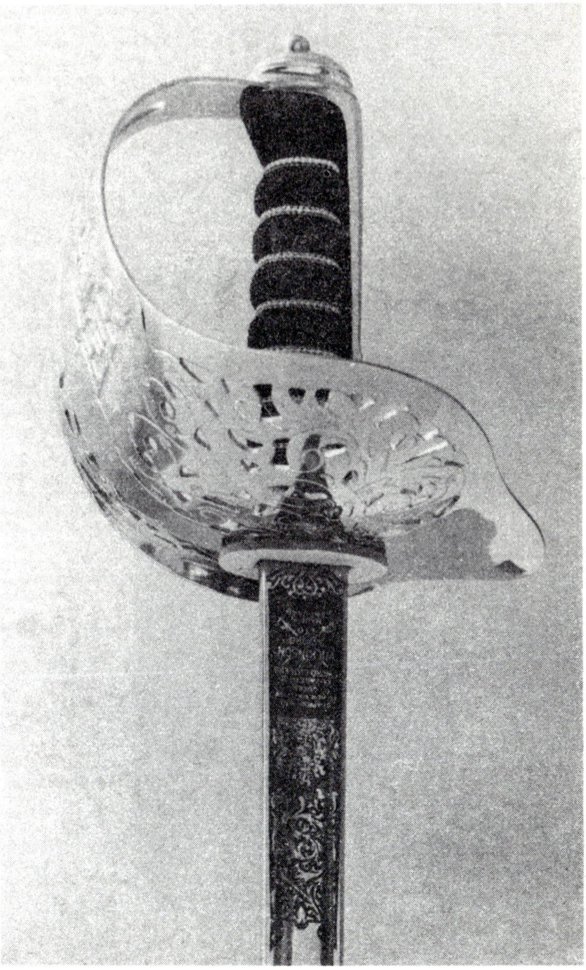

67 68

69

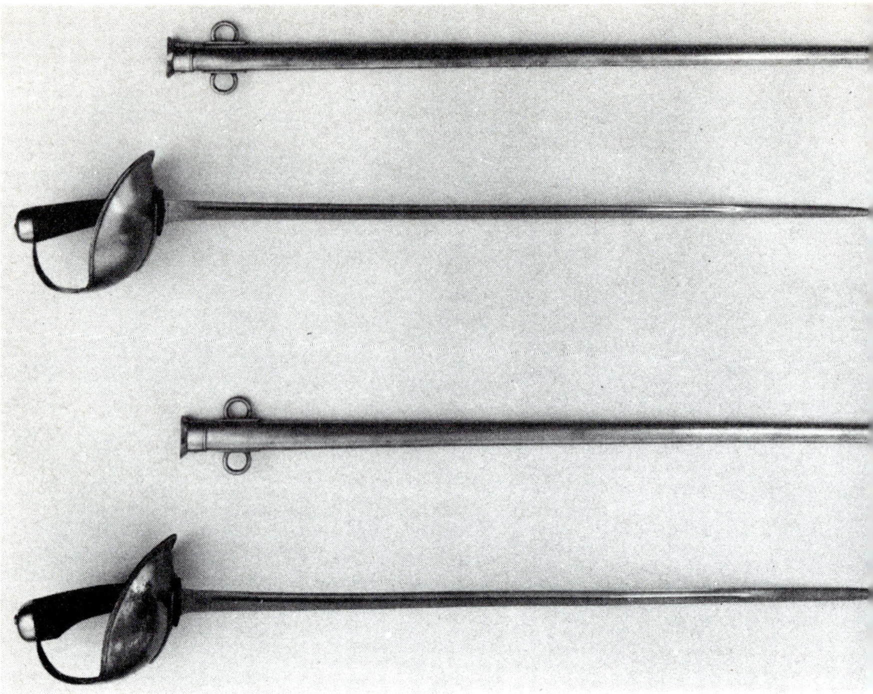

70

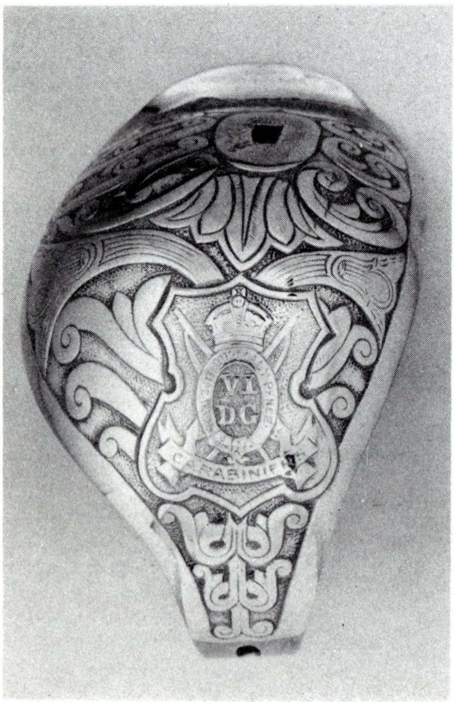

69 *British and Indian Cavalry troopers swords. Patt. 1908 Indian; Patt. 1908 British.*

70 *British Cavalry Officers hilt patt. 1912. This example is the regimental pattern of the 6th Dragoon Guards. The blade is the same as the troopers sword of 1908.*

71 *French Cavalry swords; Heavy Cavalry 1822; Dragoons 1790; 1790.*

72 *French Foot Artillery hanger.*

73 *French Infantry officers sword* circa *1800.*

71

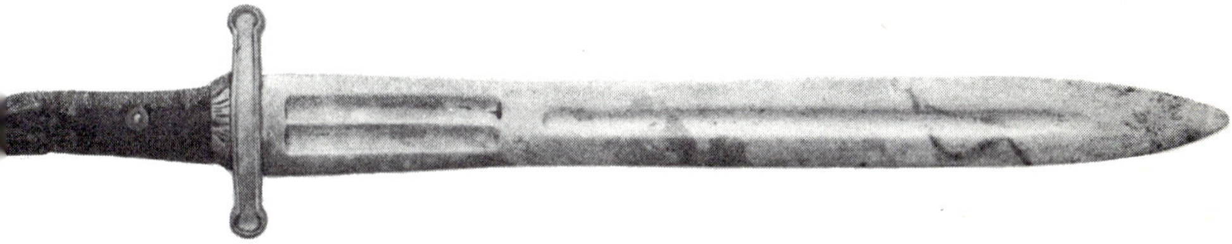

73

74 *French swords. Infantry Officer 1800; Infantry of the Guard 1802; Infantry hanger 1770–1800; Volunteer* Garde National Chasseur *hanger 1792; Infantry Officers sword 1854; Infantry Officers sword 1821 and* Garde National *1830–1848.*

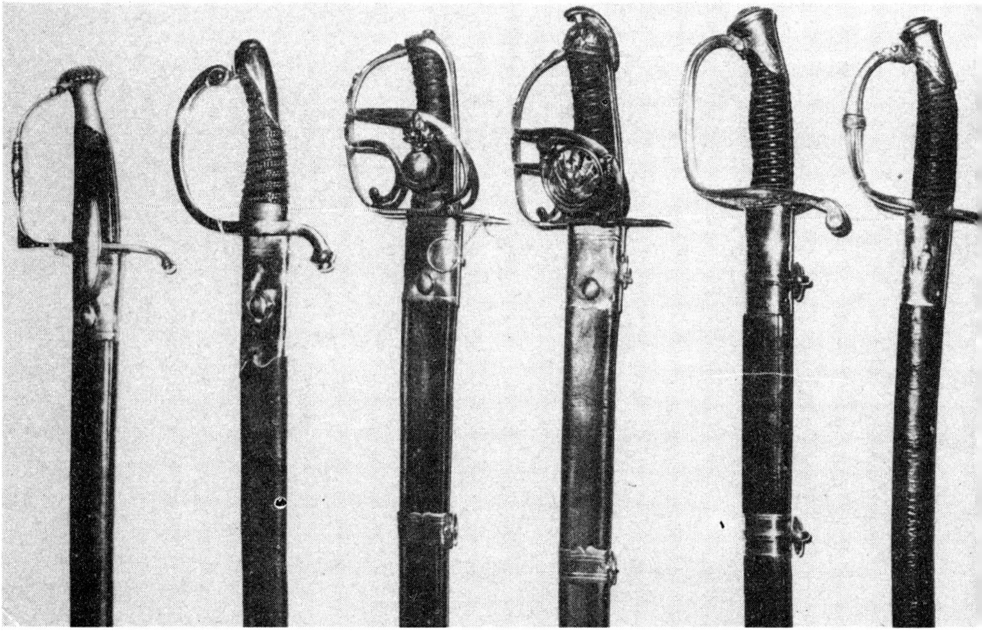

75 *French swords. Infantry hanger 1770–1801; Infantry hanger 1800; Infantry officers sword 1st Empire; Naval Cutlass* circa *1830; Infantry hanger 1790–1805; Artillery hanger 1830–1848; Infantry hanger with folding guard 1790–1805.*

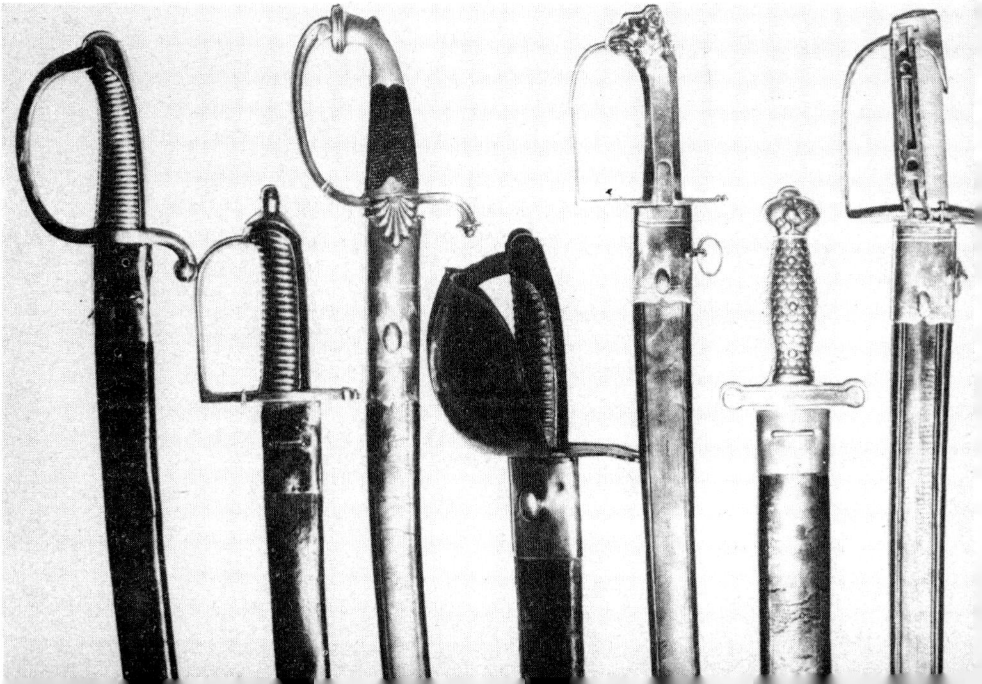

76 *French Infantry officers sword patt. 1882 with presentation inscription on the blade.*

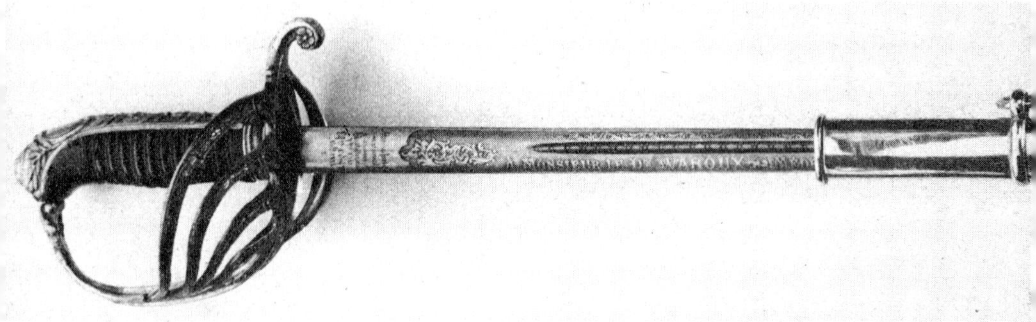

77 *French officers dress swords. Louis XVIII; Flag Officer Navy; Medical Officer Napoleon III; Three Star General 1845; Regimental pattern 1846.*

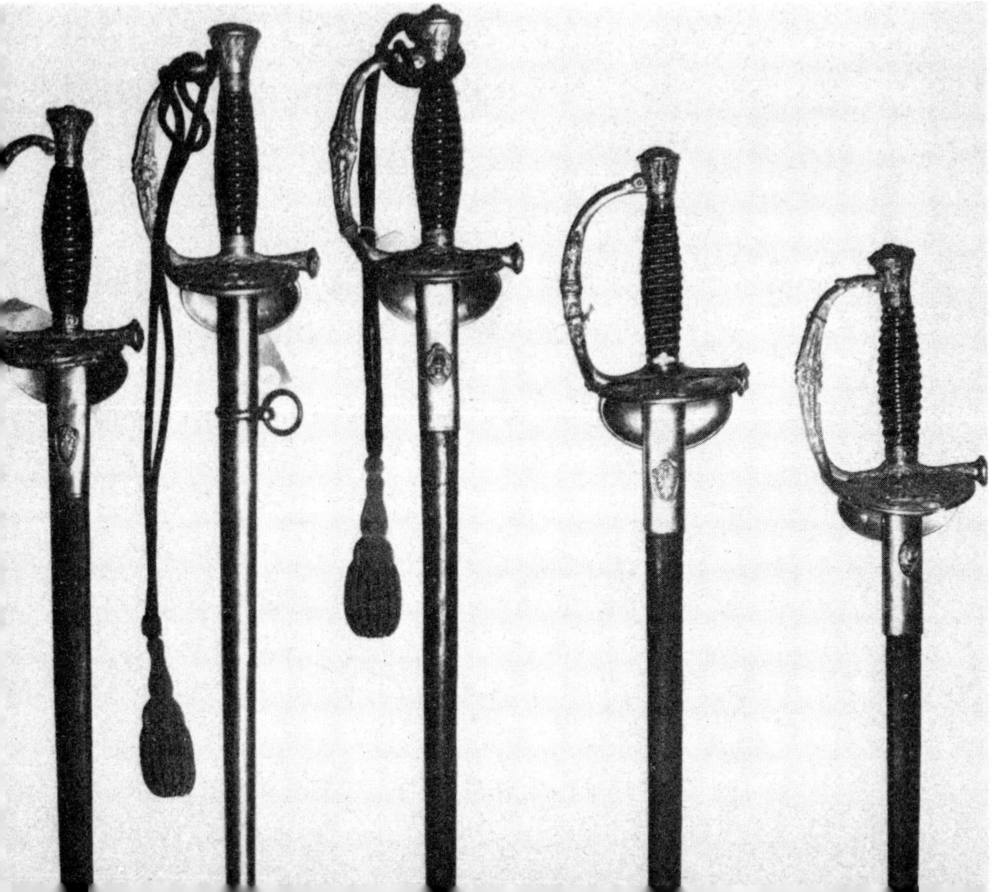

78

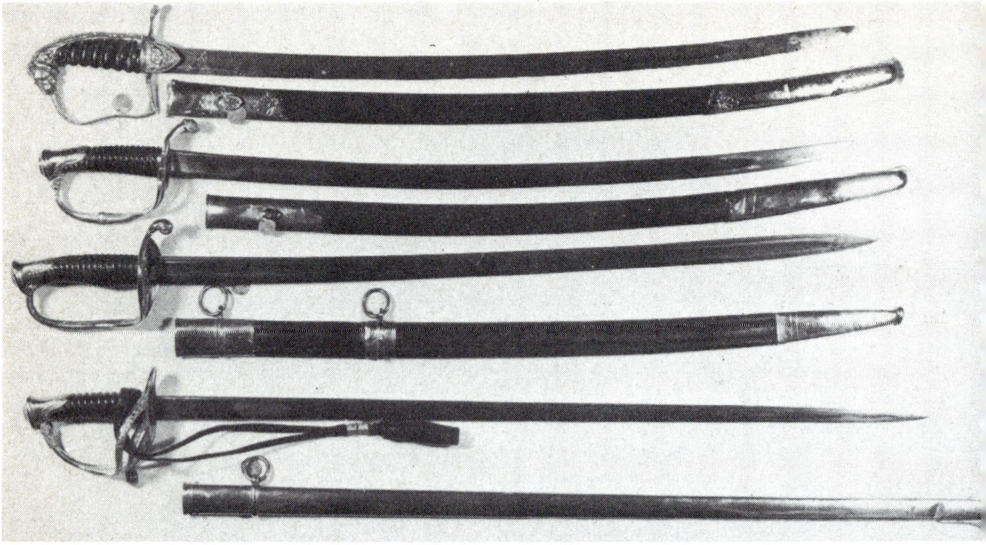

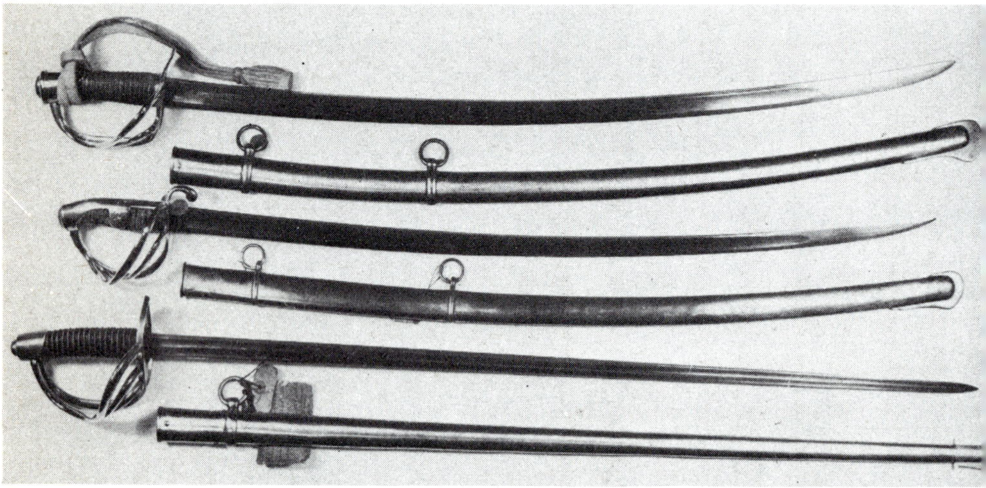

79

78 *Belgian swords. Officers sword 1st* Regiment Chasseurs à Pied *adopted in 1845; Subaltern officers sword adopted 1833; Infantry officers sword patt. 1850; Infantry officers sword patt. 1889.*

79 *Belgian swords. Light Cavalry troopers sword French patt. 1822; 'Montmorency' patt. sword 1802;* Gendarmerie *sword patt. 1852–73.*

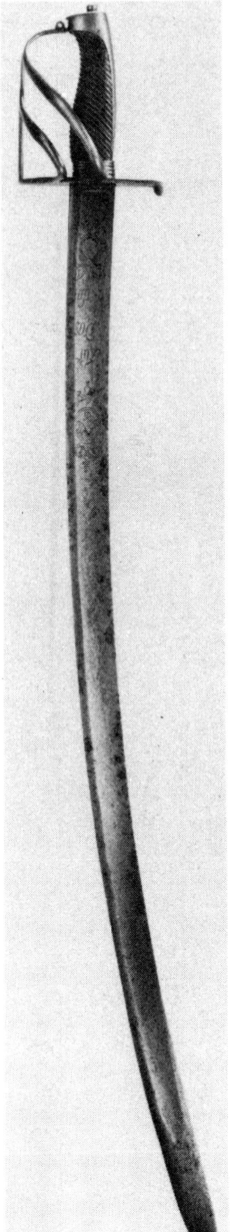

80

81

80 *Belgian swords. Infantry sappers hanger, Dutch patt.; Naval hanger, Dutch patt.*

81 *German sword. Light Cavalry officers sword* circa *1806.*

82 *German sword. Prussian Artillery sword, also used by other states after 1871.*

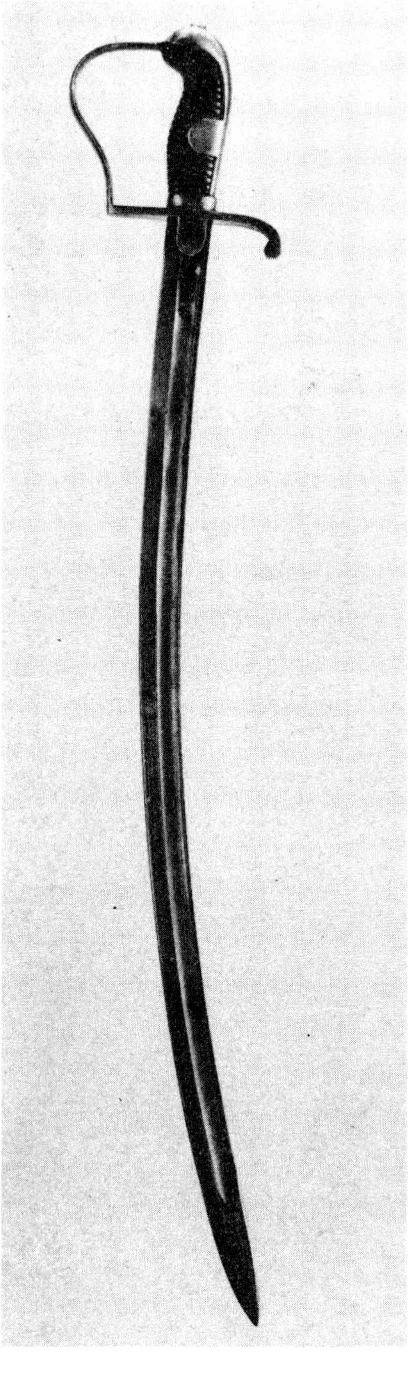

83 *German sword. Naval officers sword patt. 1889.*

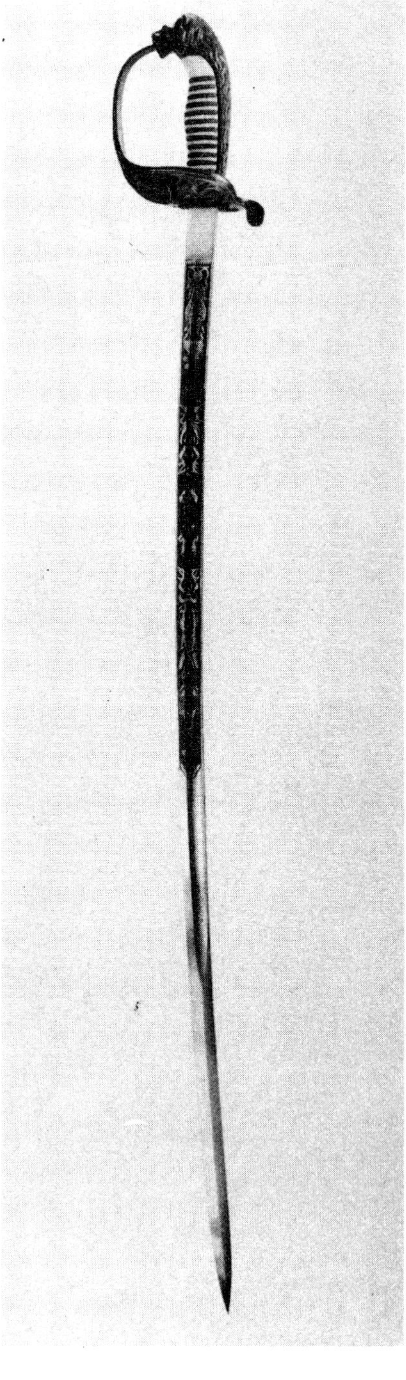

84 *German sword. Cavalry officers sword patt. 1889 with presentation inscription on blade.*

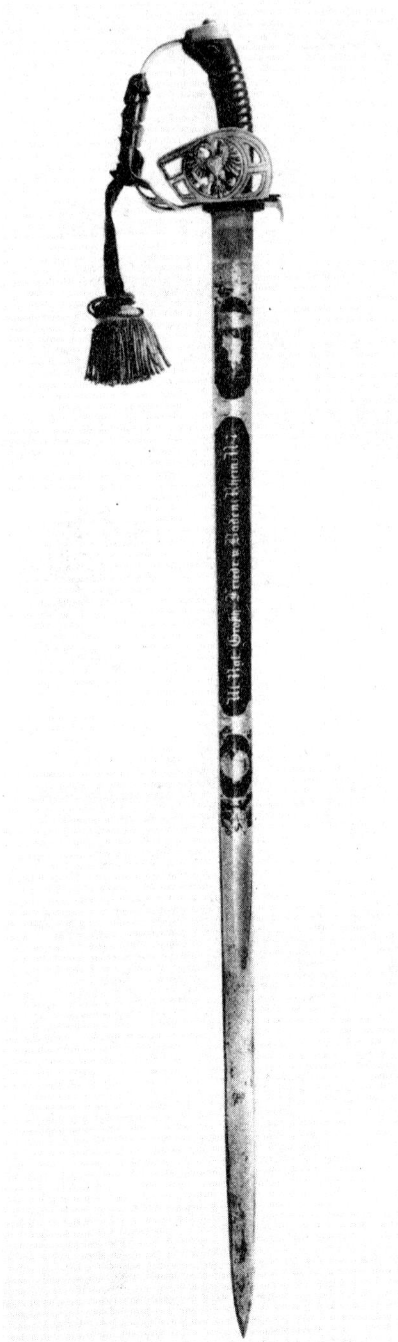

85 *German sword. Infantry officers dress sword 1881–1885.*

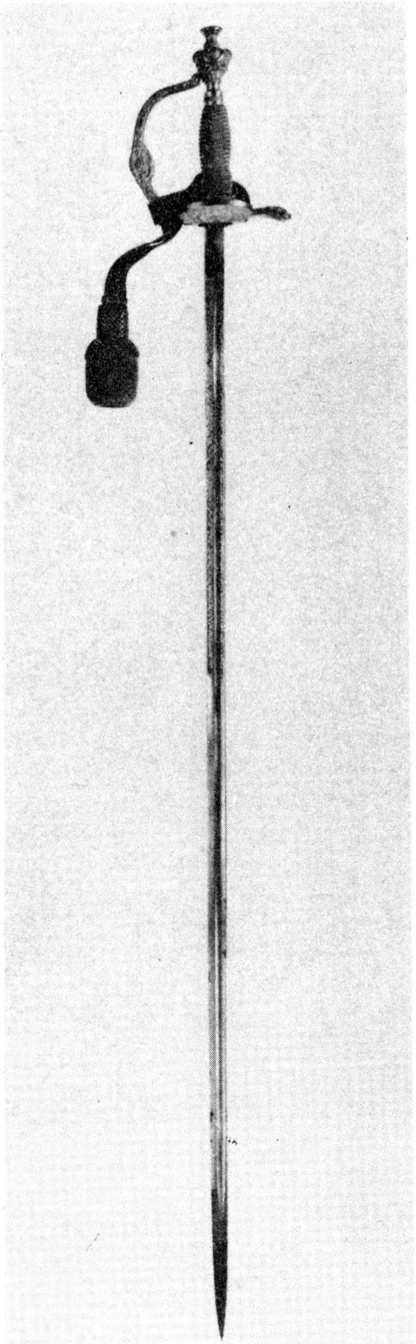

86 *German sword. Cuirassier officers sword (Prussia) patt. 1905–18.*

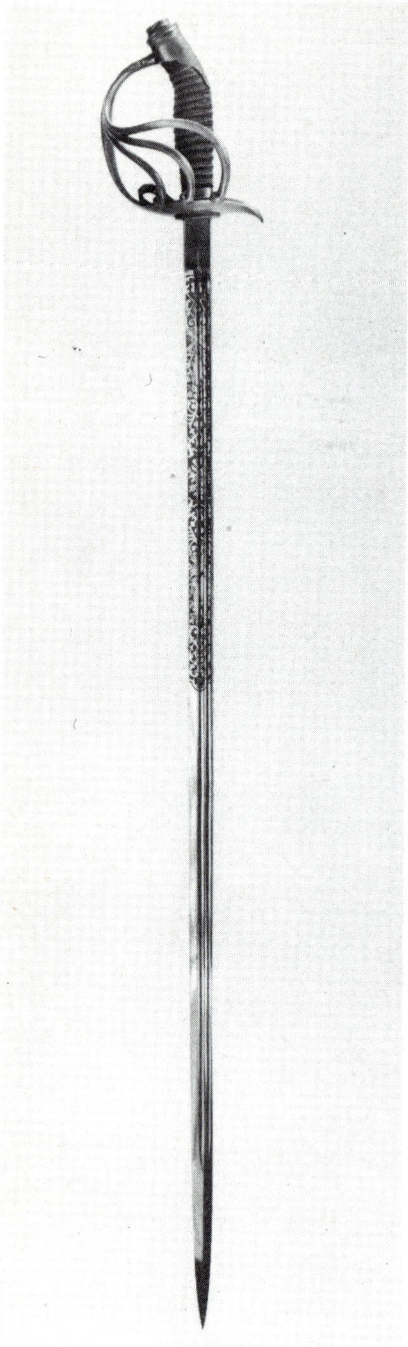

87 *German sword. Infantry officers sword patt. 1911.*

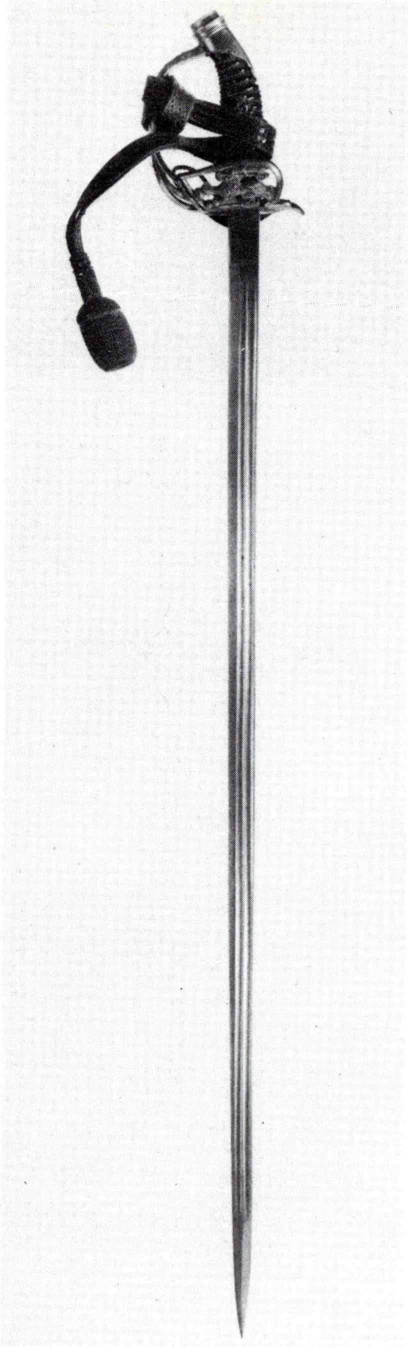

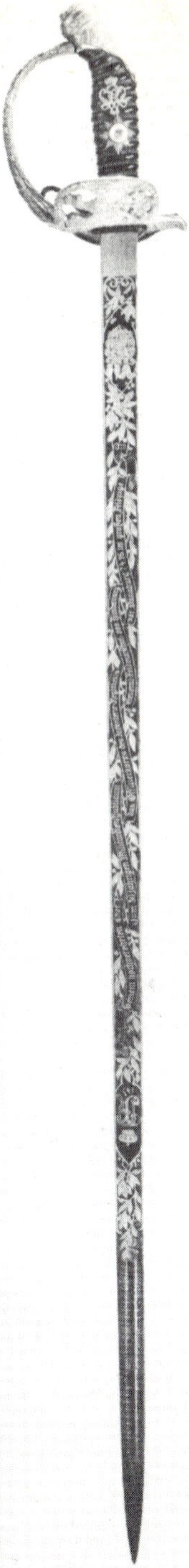

89

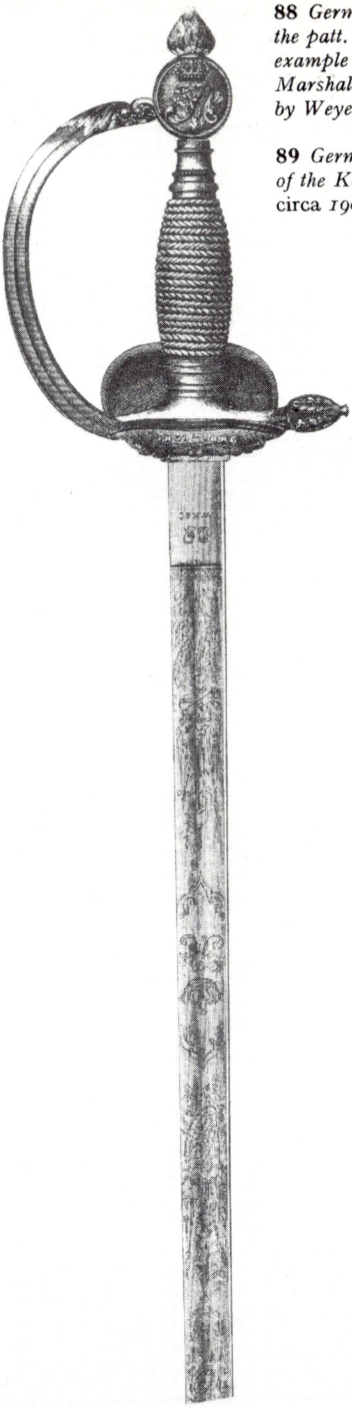

88 *German sword. Presentation sword of the patt. 1911 for Infantry officers. This example presented to General and Field Marshal Von Hindenburg in 1916. Made by Weyersburg Kirschbaum & Co.*

89 *German sword. Infantry Officers sword of the König Augusta Garde-Grenadiers* circa *1908.*

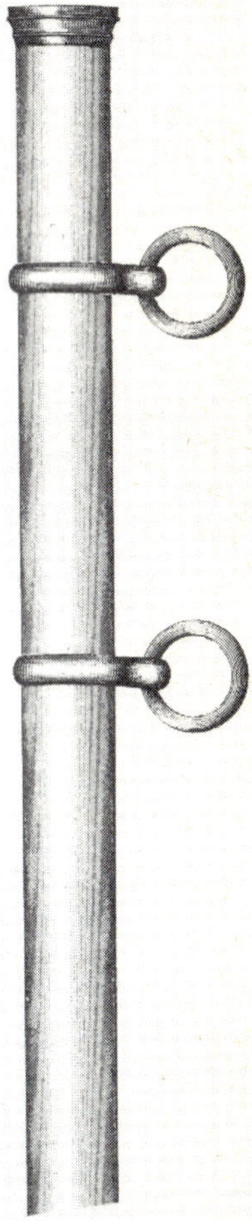

90

91

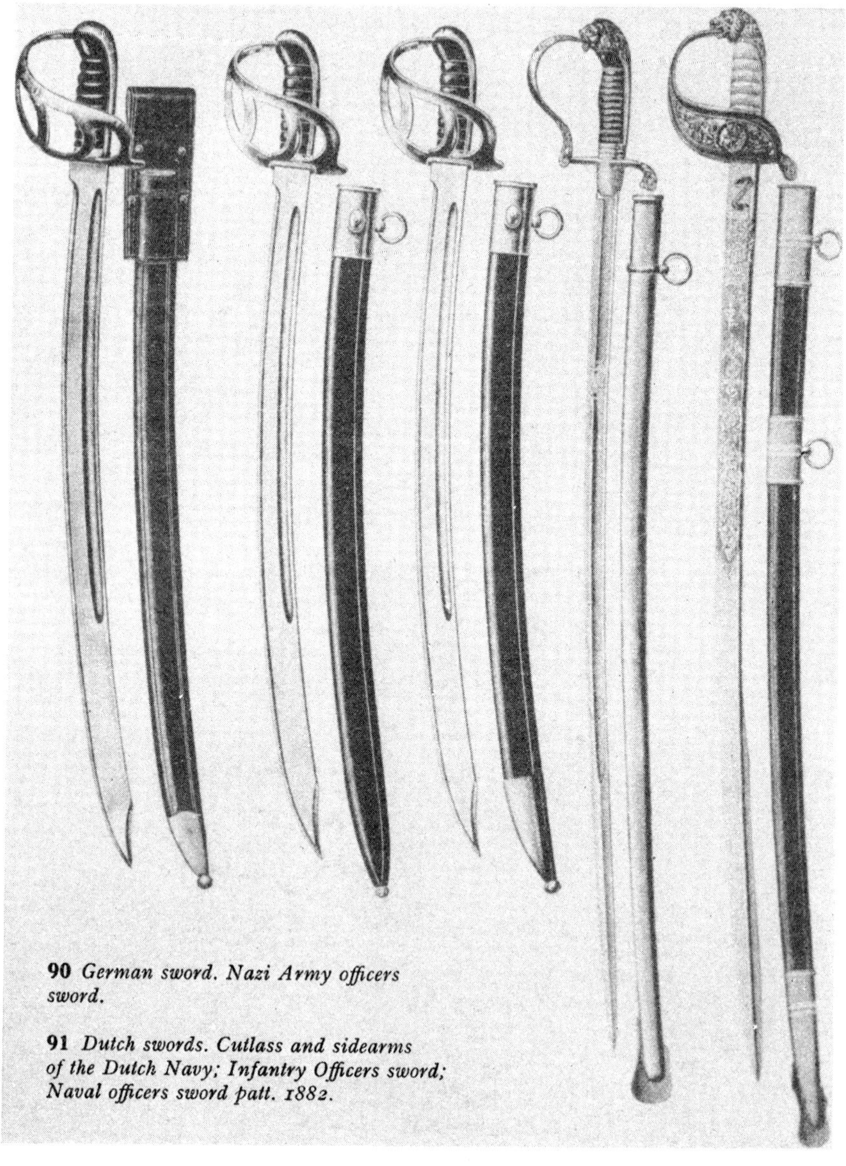

90 *German sword. Nazi Army officers sword.*

91 *Dutch swords. Cutlass and sidearms of the Dutch Navy; Infantry Officers sword; Naval officers sword patt. 1882.*

92 *Danish swords. Artillery NCO's sword patt. 1777; Infantry officers sword patt. 1766; Cavalry officers sword patt. 1798.*

93 *Danish swords. Dragoon sword patt. 1785; cavalry sword patt. 1774; cavalry sword patt. 1799 (a conversion of the patt. 1774).*

94 *Danish swords. Artillery privates hanger patt. 1777; Corporals pattern 1777; Sappers hanger patt. 1808.*

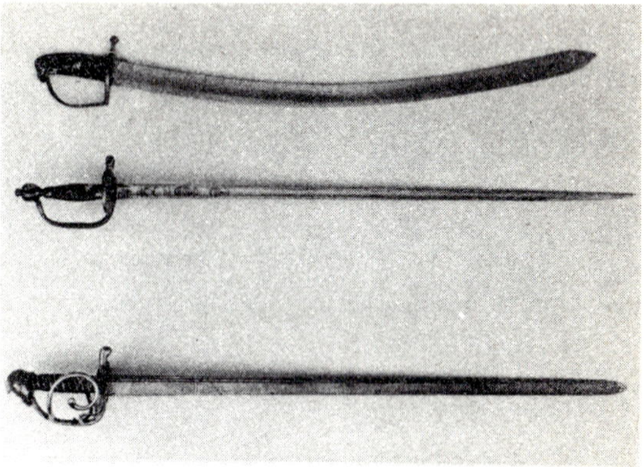

92

93

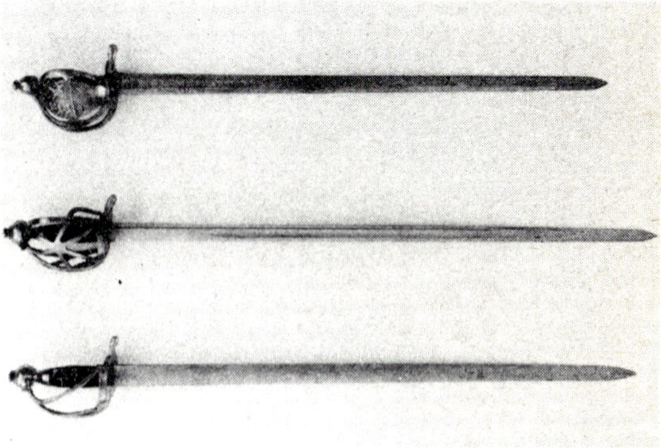

94

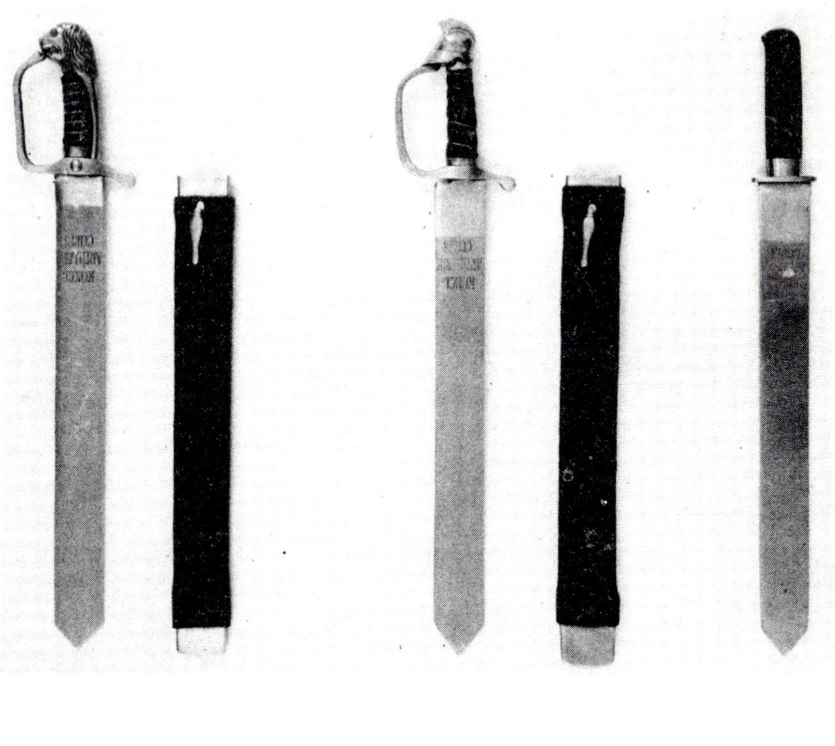

95 *Danish swords. Naval officers dirk* circa *1835; Naval officers sword 1840 (note similarity with British Naval sword patt. 1805); Cadets sword patt. 1761–89.*

96 *Danish swords. Lancers sword patt. 1816 (relegated to Reserve Artillery in 1842); Bosnian pattern sword patt. 1791.*

97 *Danish swords. One of the 323 swords purchased from Belgium in 1848 as an experiment; Light cavalry sword patt. 1839; NCO of the General Staff sword patt. 1820.*

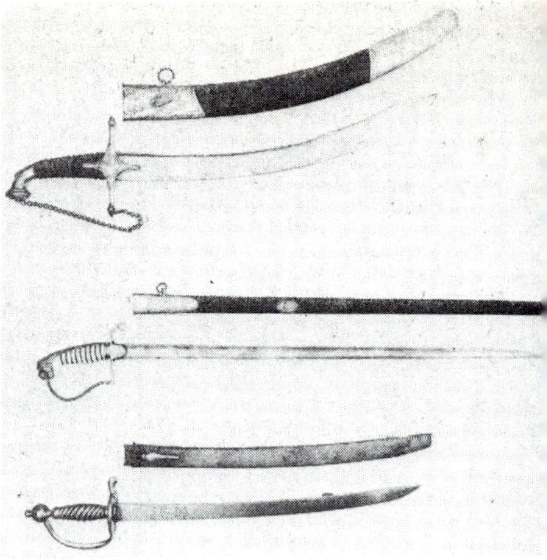

95

96

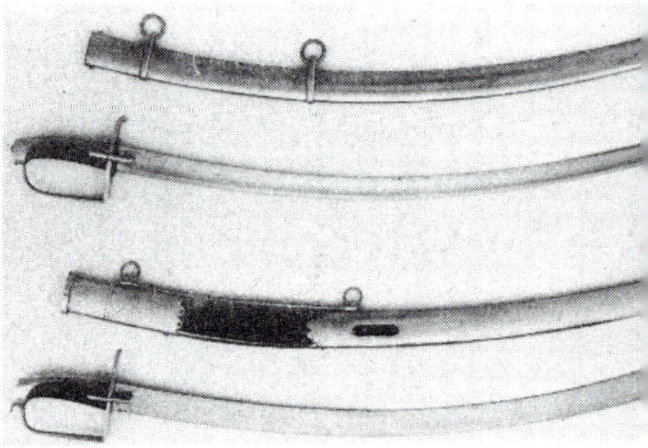

97

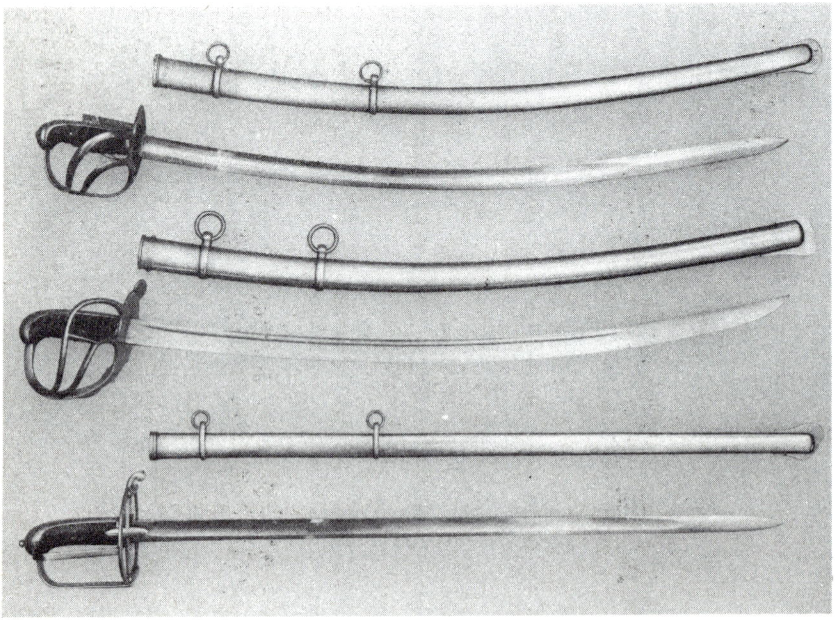

98 *Danish swords. Light cavalry officers sword patt. 1845; cavalry officers sword patt. 1843; officers sword (except Cavalry and Guard) patt. 1837–58.*

99 *Danish swords. Infantry hanger patt. 1854 (later used by Non Combatants); Artisans hanger patt. 1869 (originally a bayonet used by Schlesvig-Holstein on captured Danish rifles in 1848. Spring removed and issued as a sidearm in 1869).*

100 *Danish swords. Officers and NCO's sword patt. 1904; officers sword patt. 1858; Guards Officers sword patt. 1852.*

98

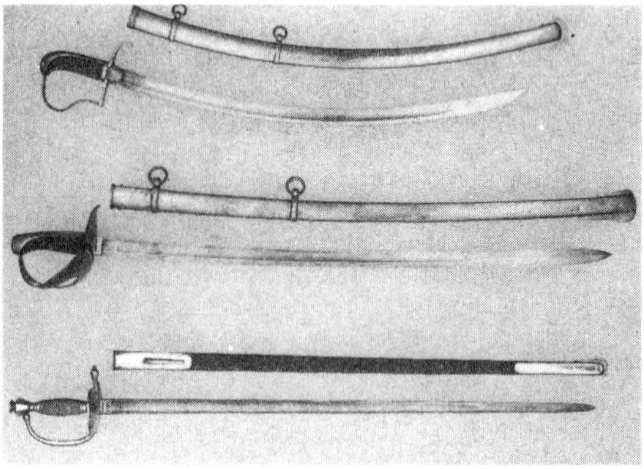

99

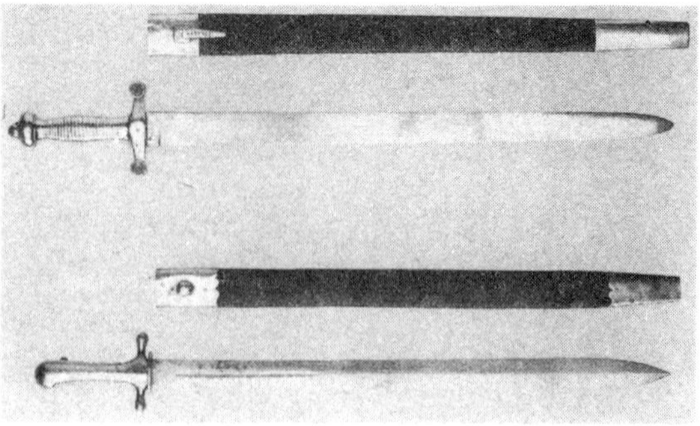

100

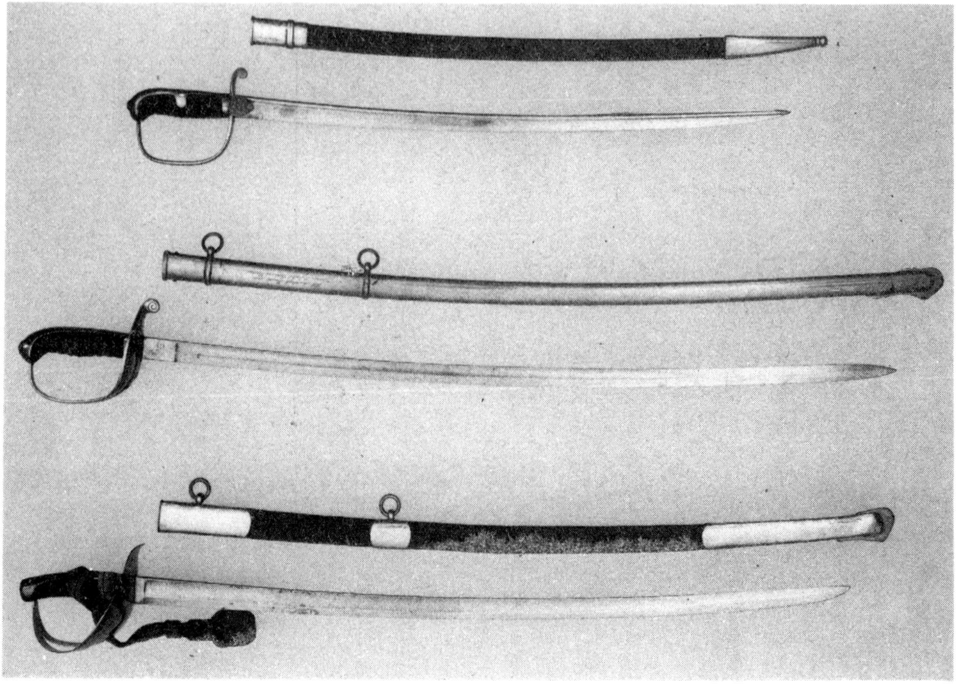

101

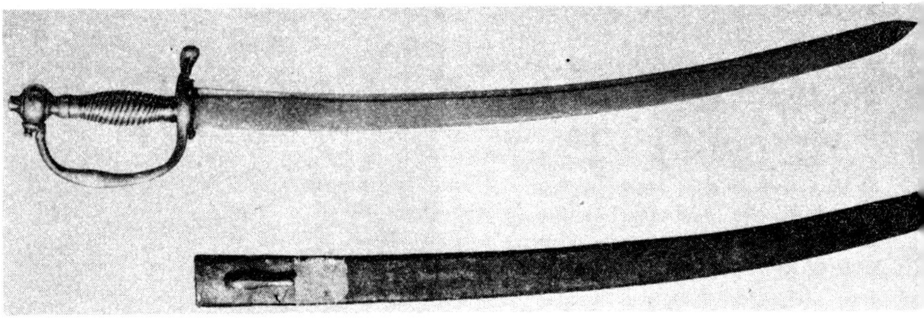

102

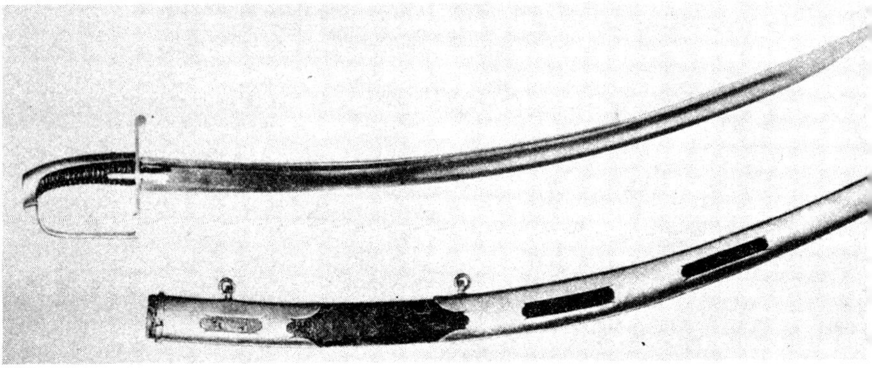

101 *Swedish swords. Infantry hanger patt. 1748.*

102 *Swedish swords. Hussars sword patt. 1759. First sabre adopted in the Swedish Army.*

103 *Swedish swords. Cavalry sword patt. 1777 (used by Smålands and Vastgöta Cavalry regiments).*

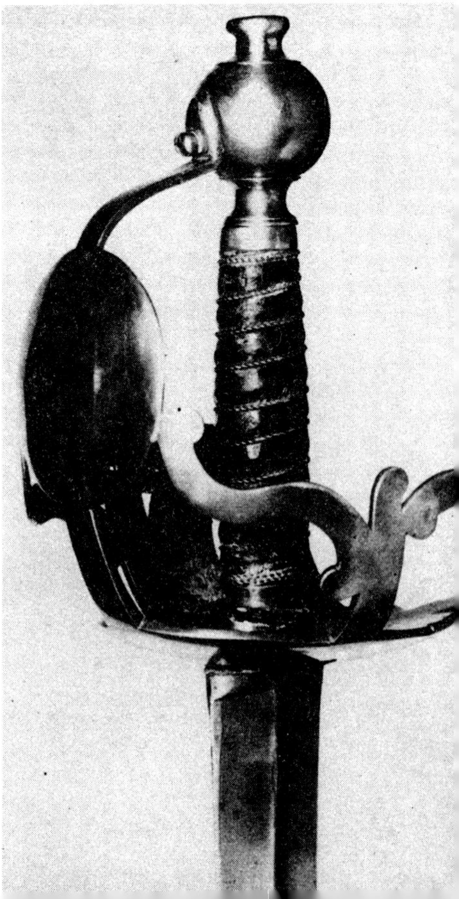

103

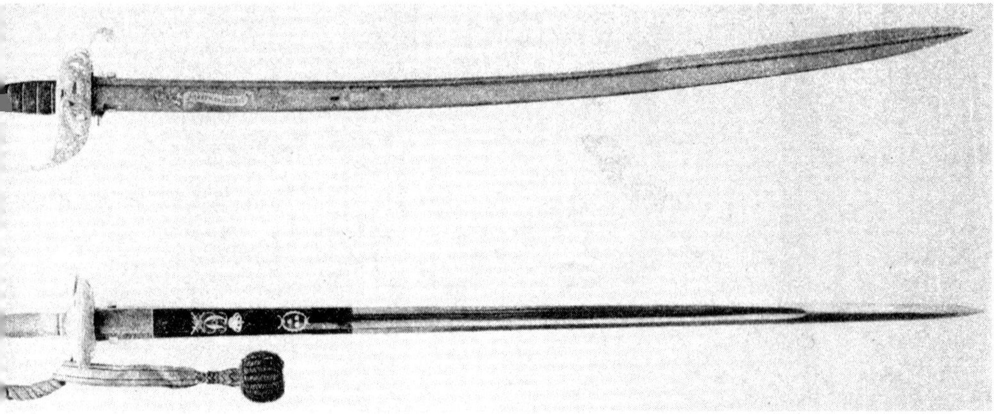

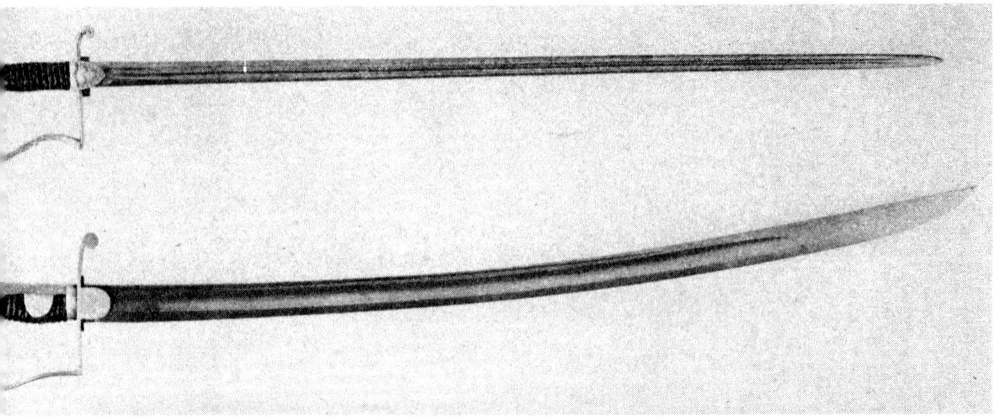

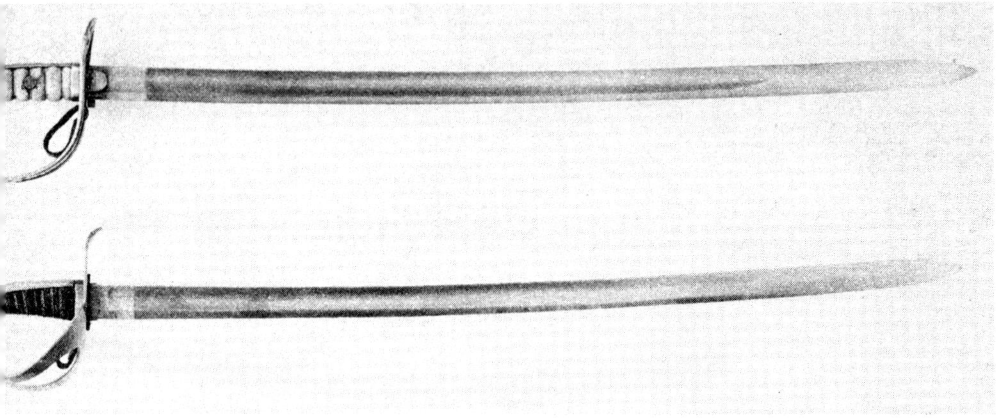

104 *Swedish swords. Infantry officers sword patt. 1859; Infantry officers sword 1820s and 30s.*

105 *Swedish swords. Artillery officers sword patt. 1889; Artillery privates sword patt. 1831.*

106 *Swedish swords. Cavalry troopers swords patt. 1867; cavalry troopers sword patt. 1854.*

104
105
106

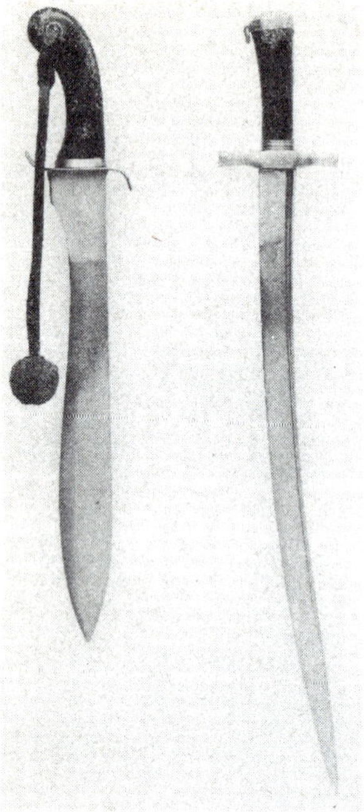

107 *Swedish swords. Infantry facine knife patt. 1848; Infantry hanger patt. 1856.*

108 *Austrian swords. Hussar and Lancers sword patt. 1808; Light Dragoons sword patt. 1798; Heavy cavalry sword patt. 1769.*

109 *Austrian swords. Infantry officers sword patt. 1837; Infantry officers sword patt. 1811; Hussar officers sword patt. 1837.*

110 *Austrian swords. Cavalry sword patt. 1861; Cavalry sword patt. 1845; Infantry officers sword patt. 1862.*

107

108

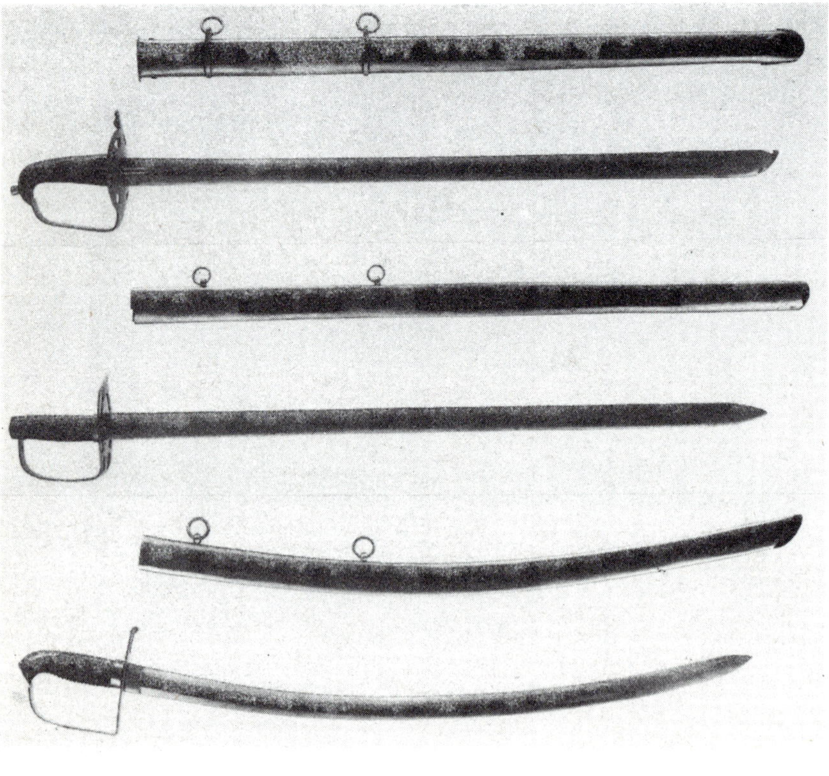

09

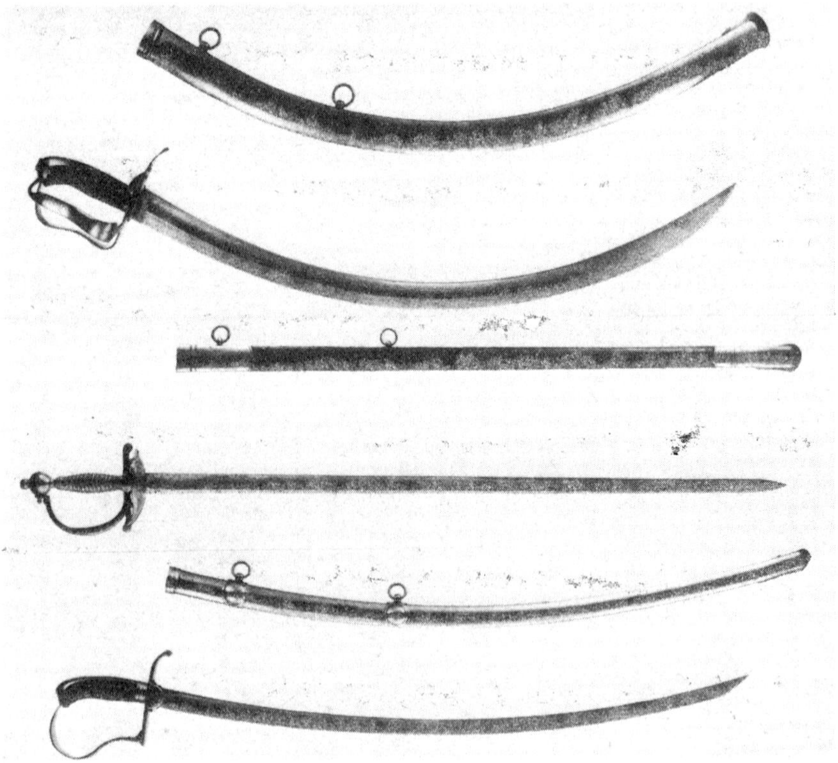

10

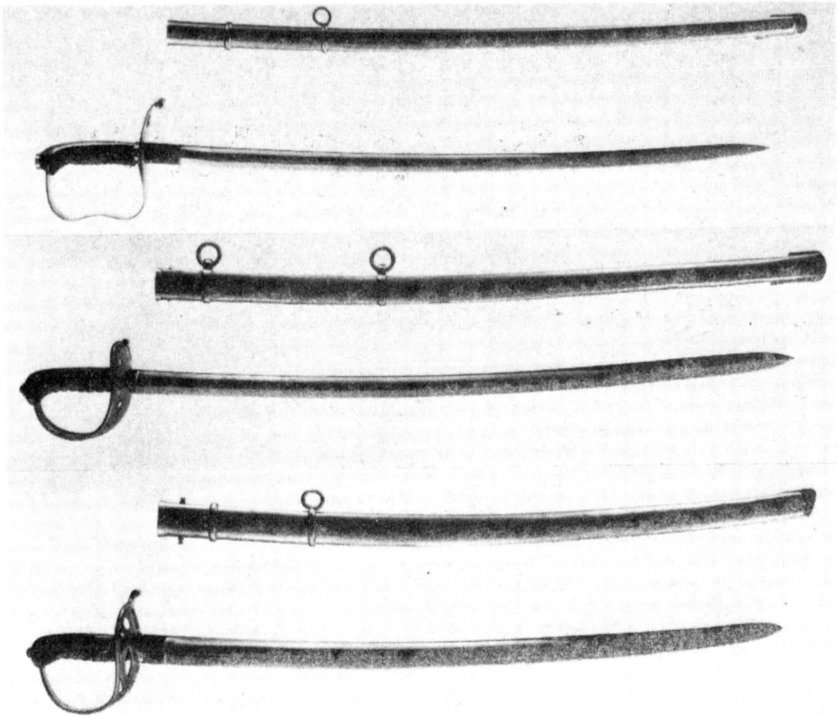

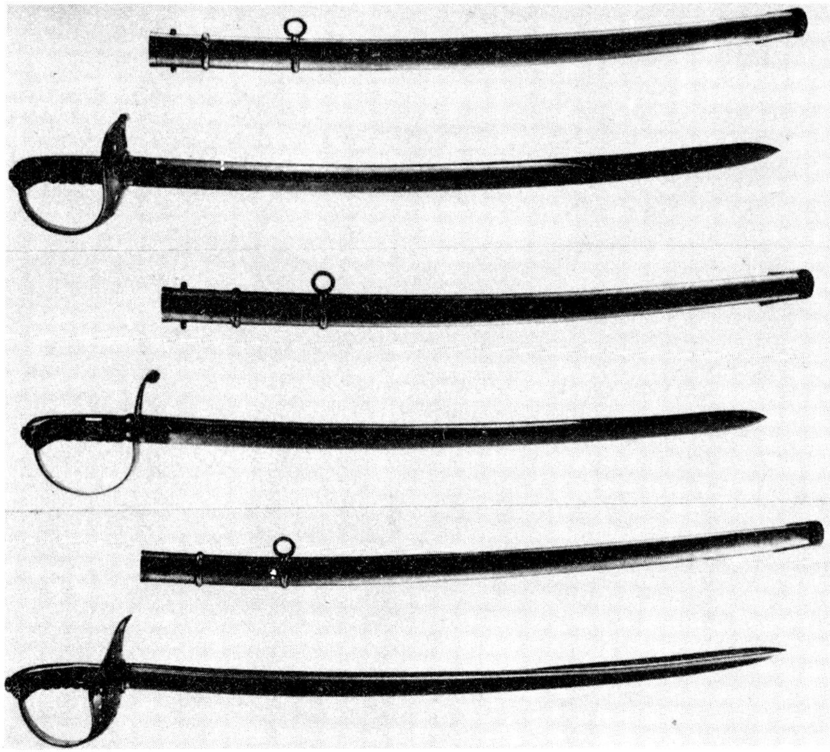

111 *Austrian swords. Cavalry sword patt. 1904; Light Cavalry sword patt. 1877; Cavalry sword patt. 1869.*

112 *Austrian naval cutlass patt. 1862.*

113 *Austrian naval warrant officers hanger patt. 1891.*

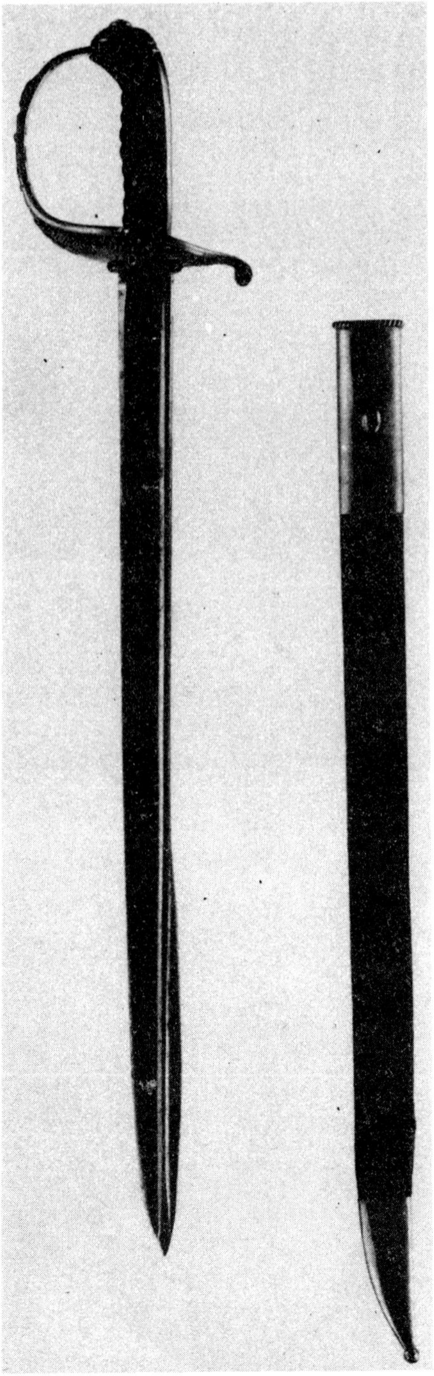

114 *Austrian naval officers sword patt. 1850.*

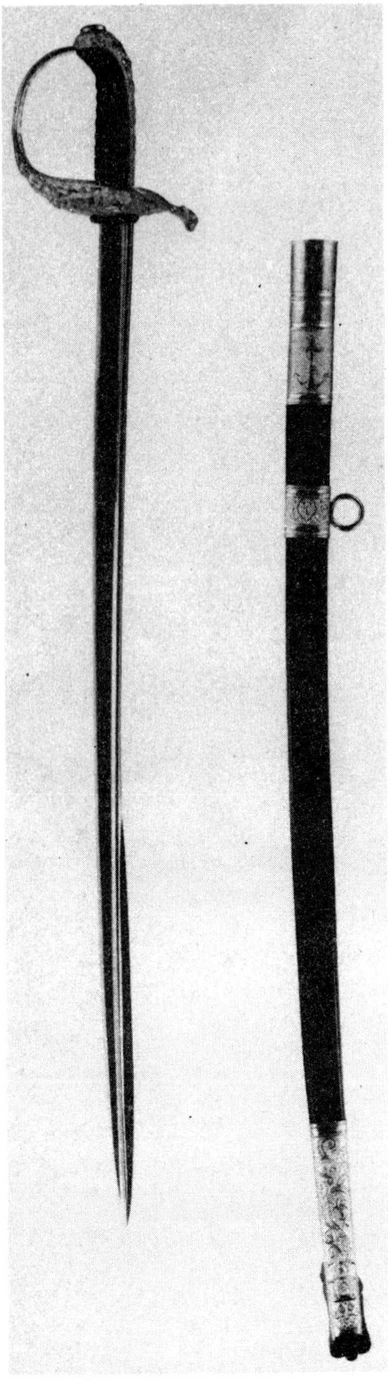

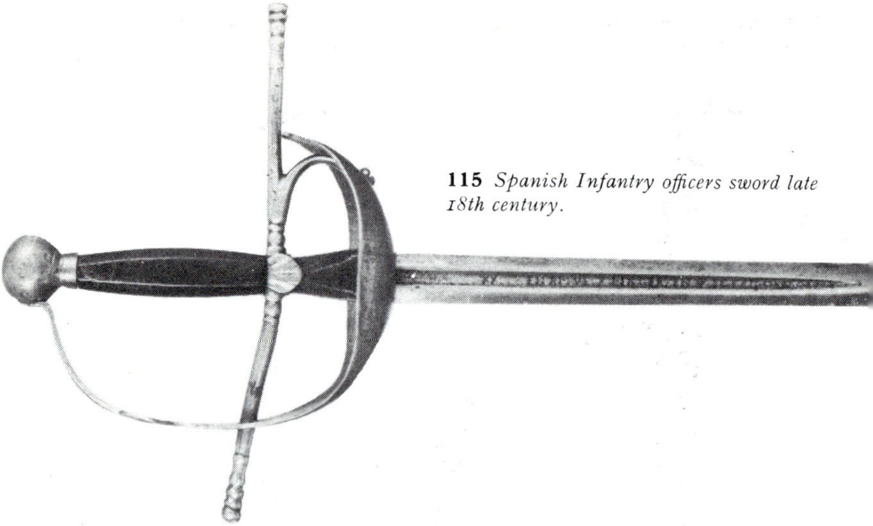

115 *Spanish Infantry officers sword late 18th century.*

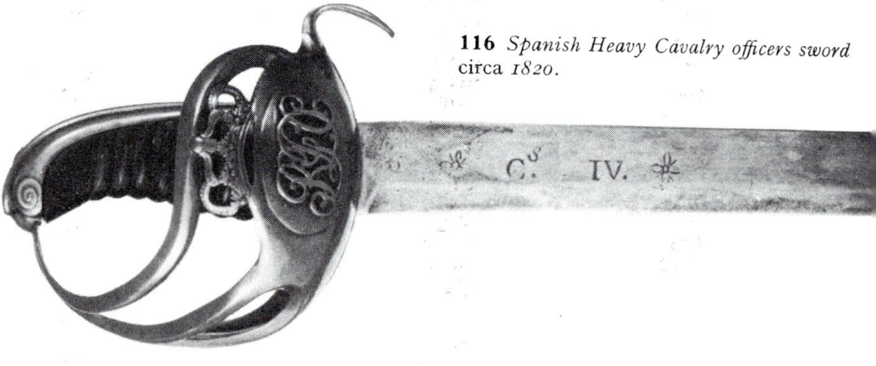

116 *Spanish Heavy Cavalry officers sword* circa *1820.*

117 *Spanish Infantry officers sword patt. 1818.*

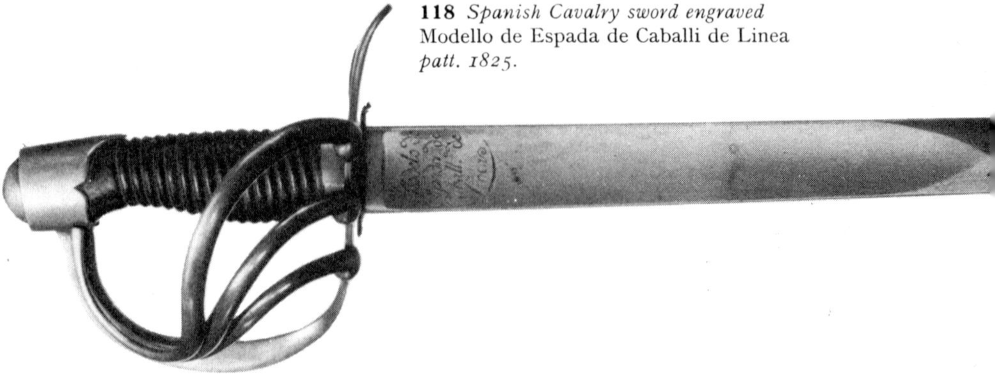

118 *Spanish Cavalry sword engraved* Modello de Espada de Caballi de Linea *patt. 1825.*

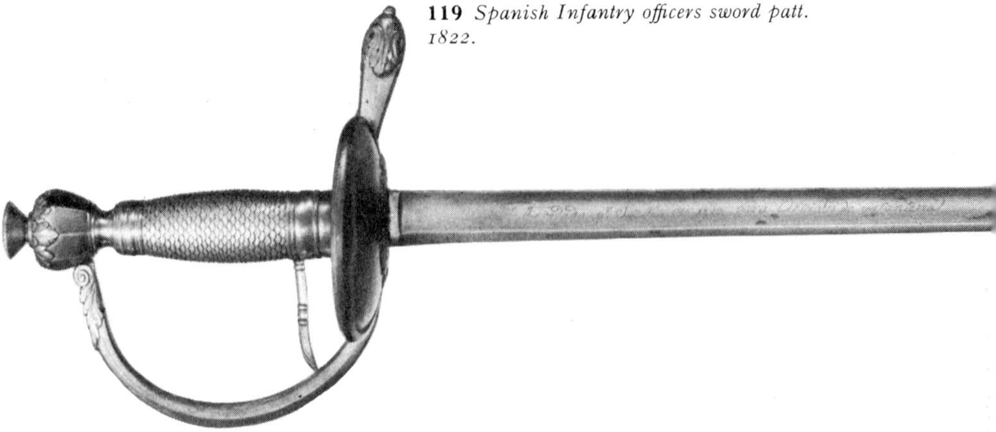

119 *Spanish Infantry officers sword patt. 1822.*

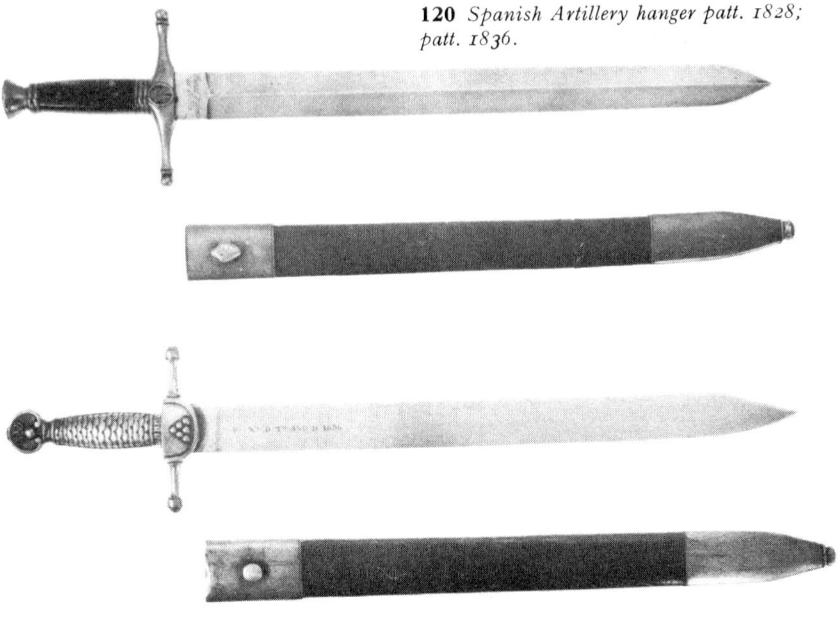

120 *Spanish Artillery hanger patt. 1828; patt. 1836.*

121

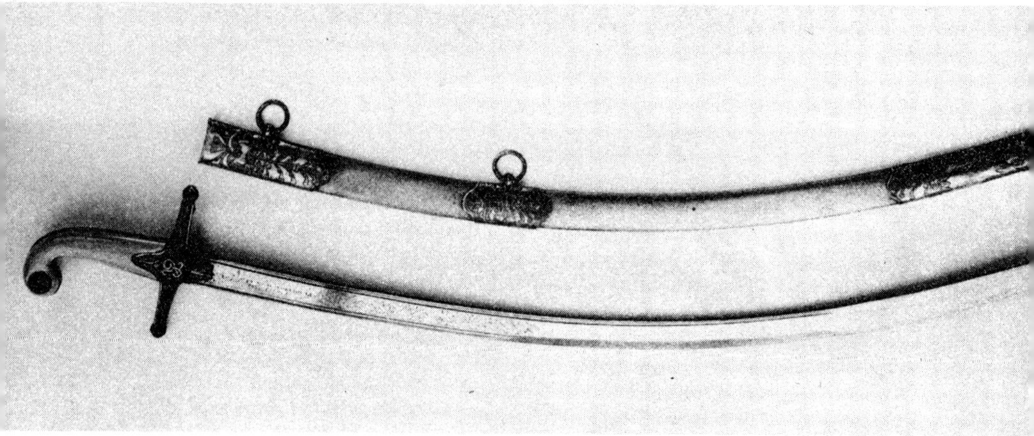

121 *Spanish General officers scimitar marked* FA.N.L.D. Toledo 1842. *Cross guard marked '12' (Queen Isabella II 1833–68).*

122 *Spanish Cavalry sword patt. 1851.*

122

123 *United States. Cavalry sword marked 'American Light Horse'* circa *1785–1800.*

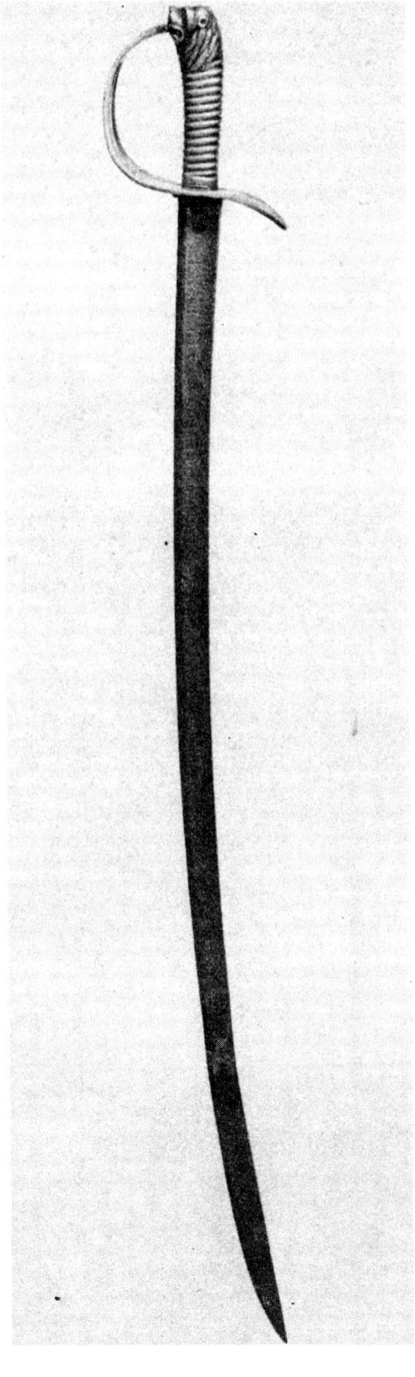

124 *United States. Infantry officers sword* circa *1790–1810.*

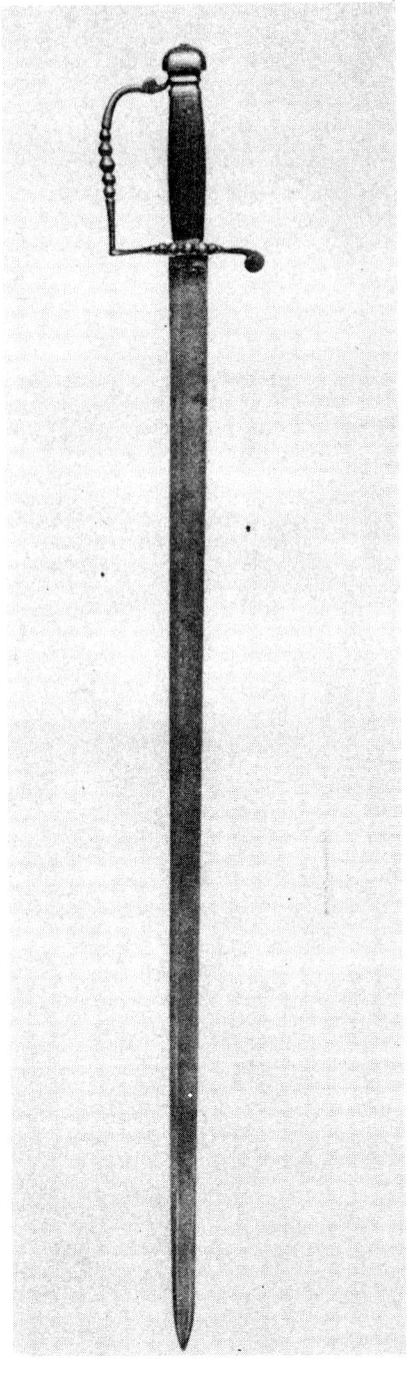

125 *United States. General and Staff officers sword patt. 1832.*

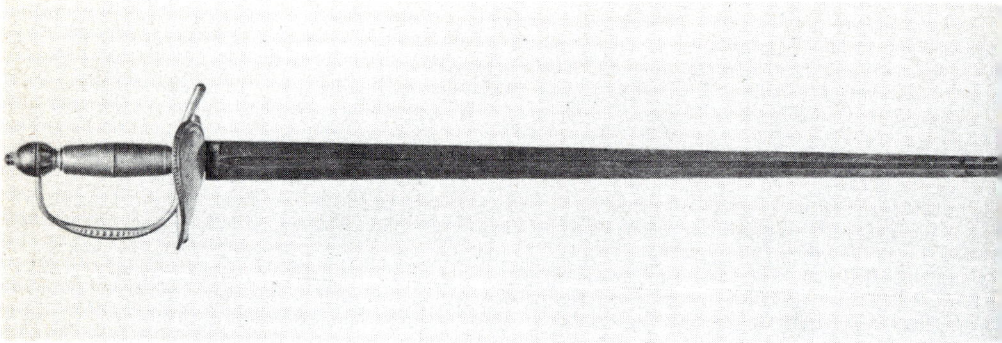

126 *United States. Dragoon troopers sword patt. 1840.*

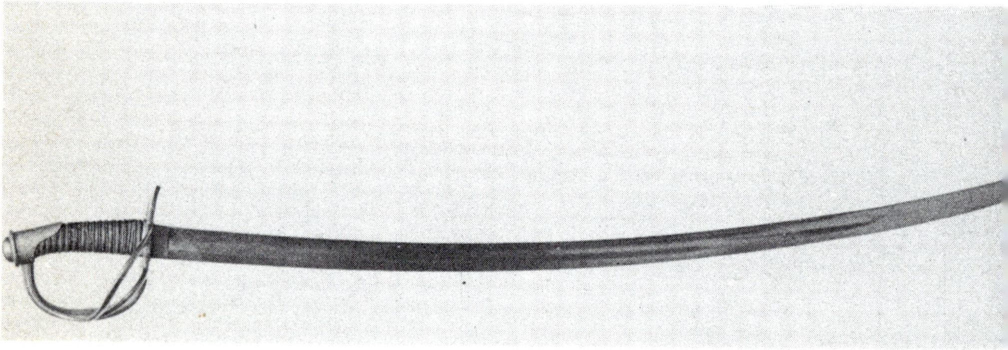

127 *United States. Foot Artillery privates sword patt. 1833.*

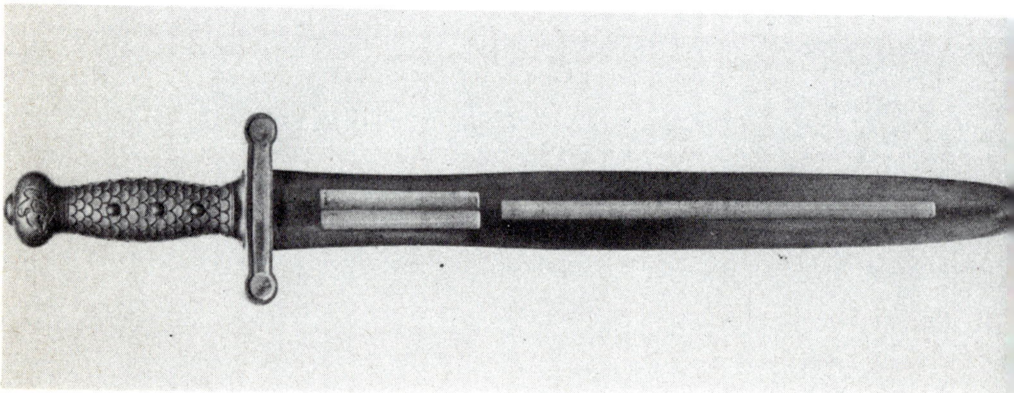

128 *United States. Light Artillery privates sword patt. 1840.*

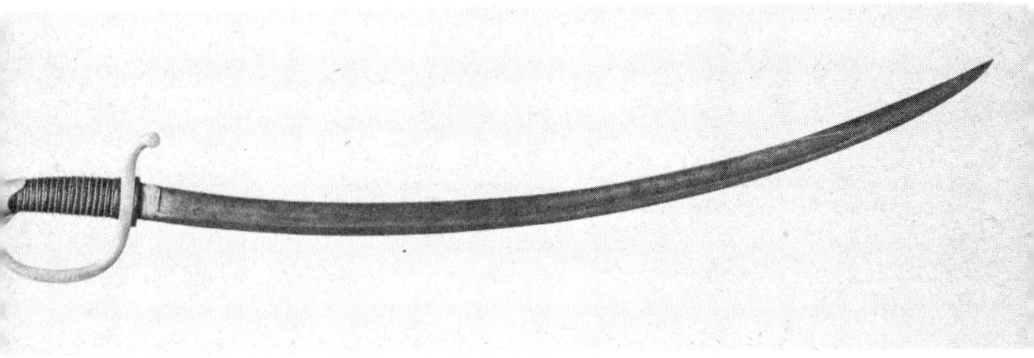

129 *United States. Staff and Field Officers sword patt. 1850.*

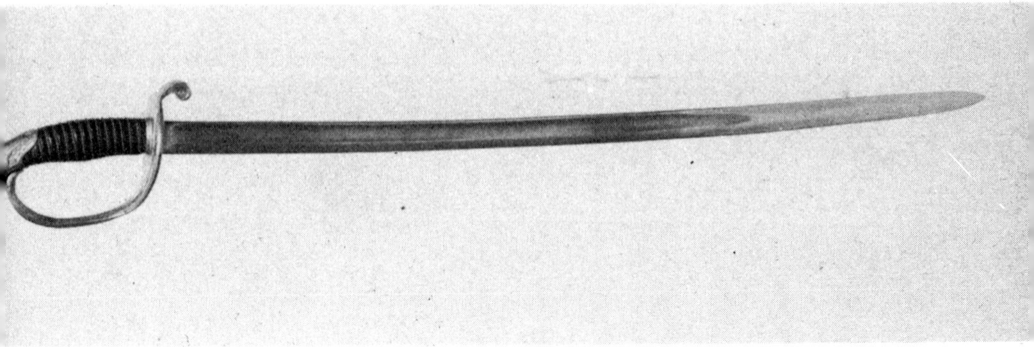

130 *United States. Cavalry officers sword patt. 1872.*

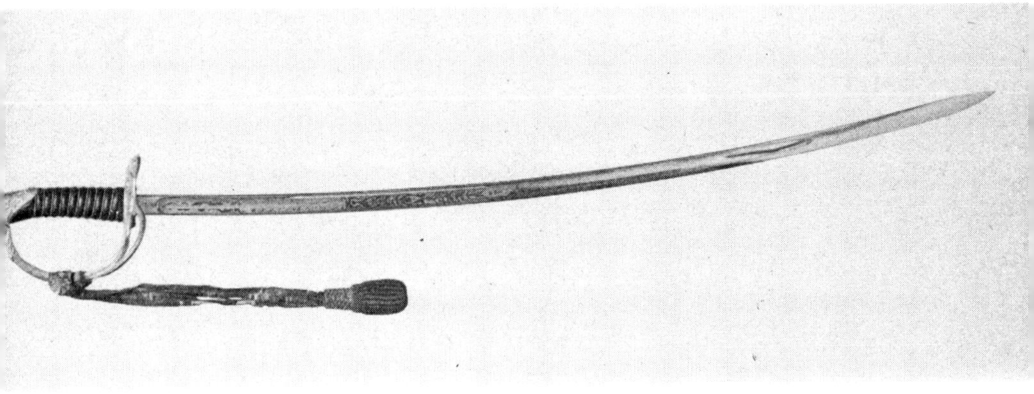

131

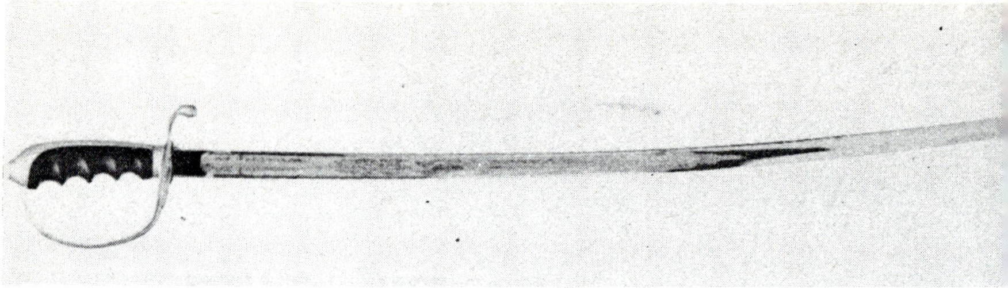

132

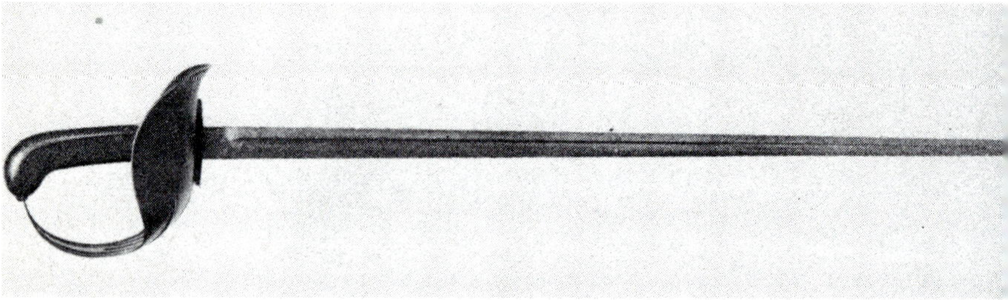

133

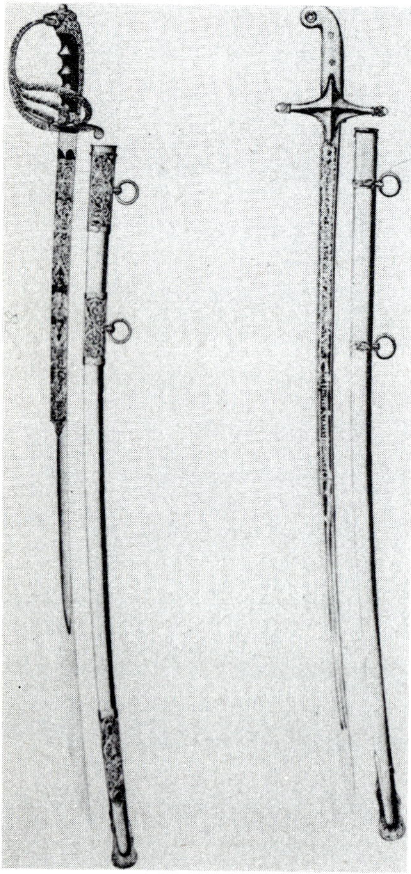

131 *United States. Officers sword patt. 1902.*

132 *United States. Cavalry troopers sword patt. 1913.*

133 *United States. Presentation officers sword of the 1902 patt.; Marine Corps officers sword 1825–1859 and 1875 on.*

134 *United States. US Coast Guard officers sword patt. 1915; Presentation Naval officers sword patt. 1852; Admirals sword patt. 1852; US Navy officers sword patt. 1852; Officers sword patt. 1902.*

135 *Argentine. Cavalry sword; Diplomatic sword; Diplomatic sword; Naval sword.*

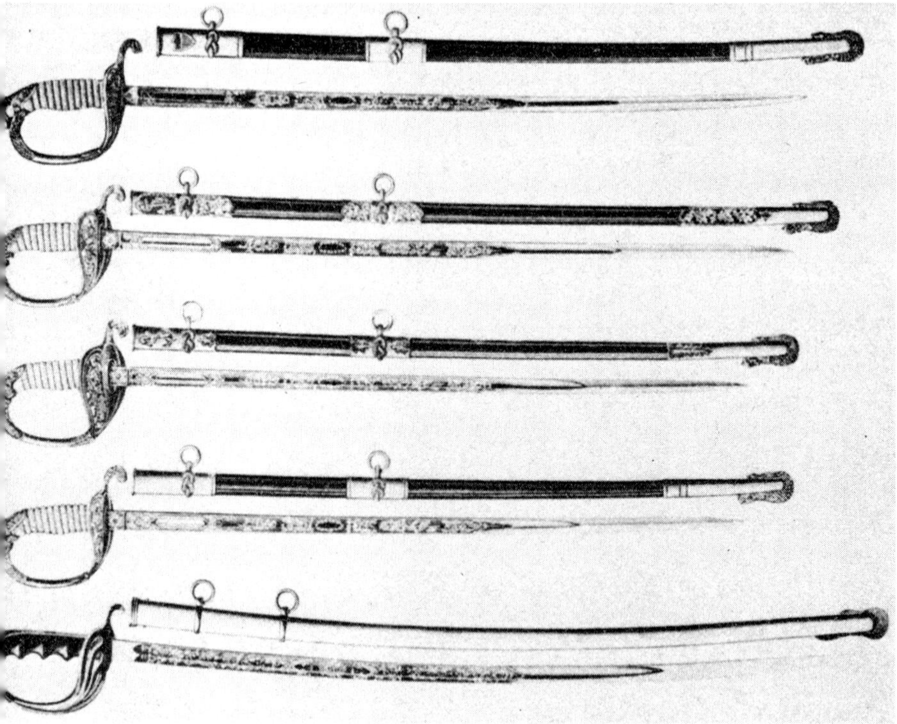

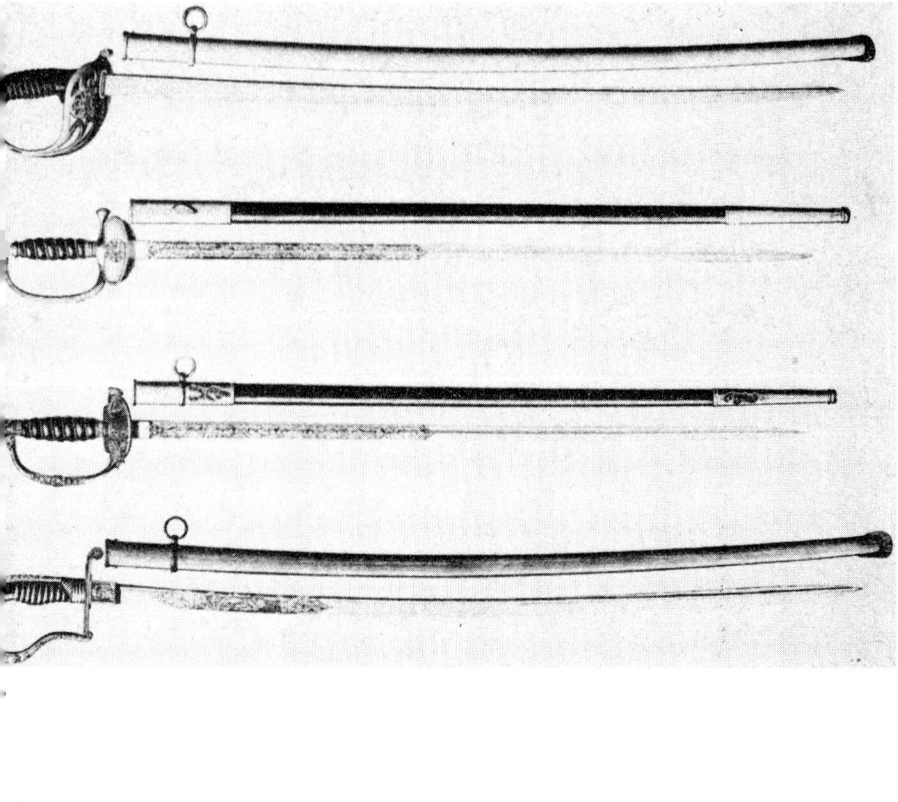

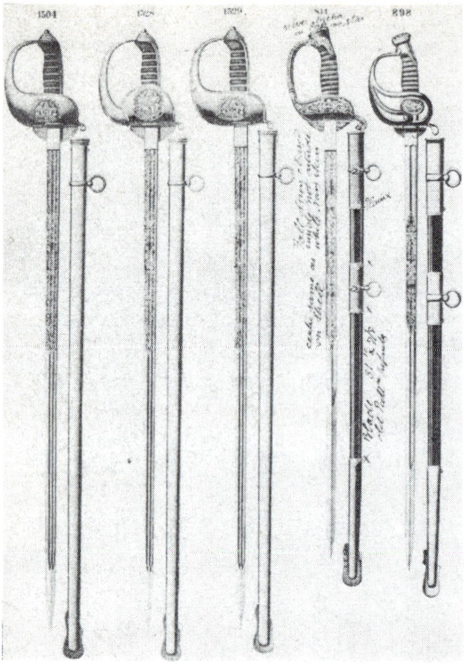

136 *Brazil. Military swords (three variations); Naval officers sword; Naval Warrant officers sword.*

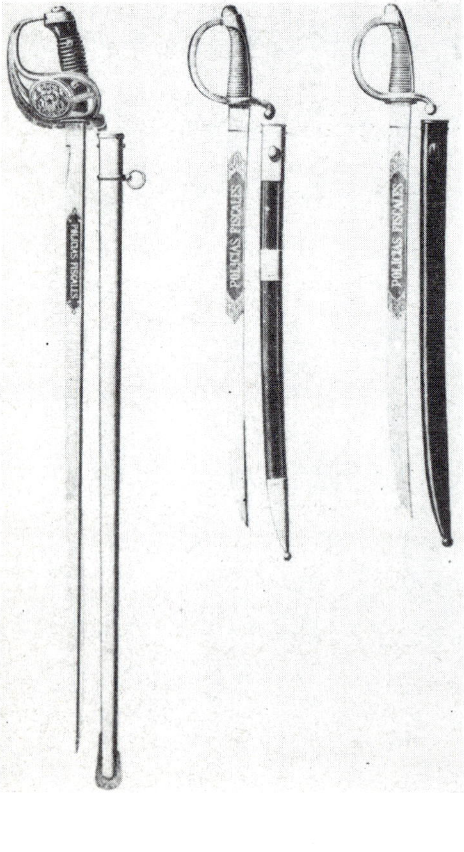

137 *Chile. Police sword; Police hanger; Police hanger.*

138 *Cuba. Navy sword; Cavalry sword; Infantry sword.*

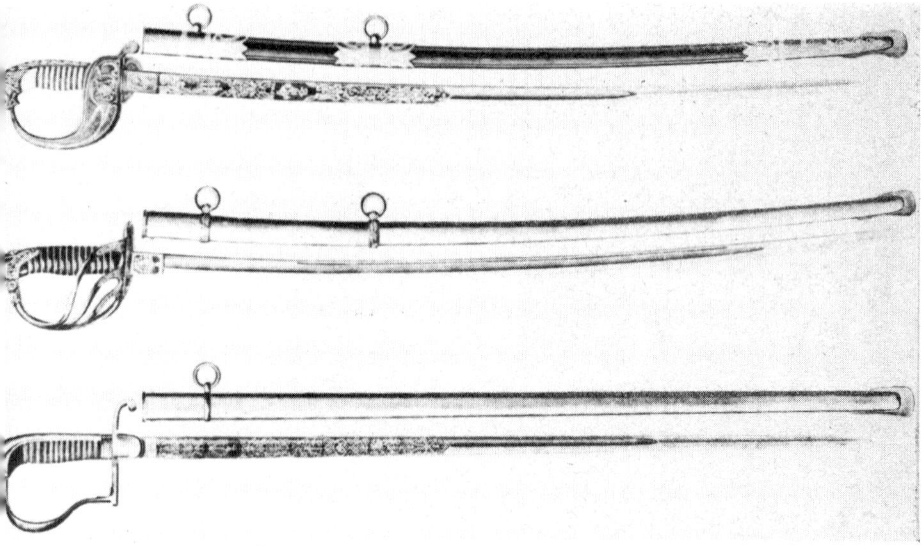

139 *Peru. Military sword. Costa Rica. Cavalry sword. Equador. Infantry sword; Naval sword; Cavalry sword.*

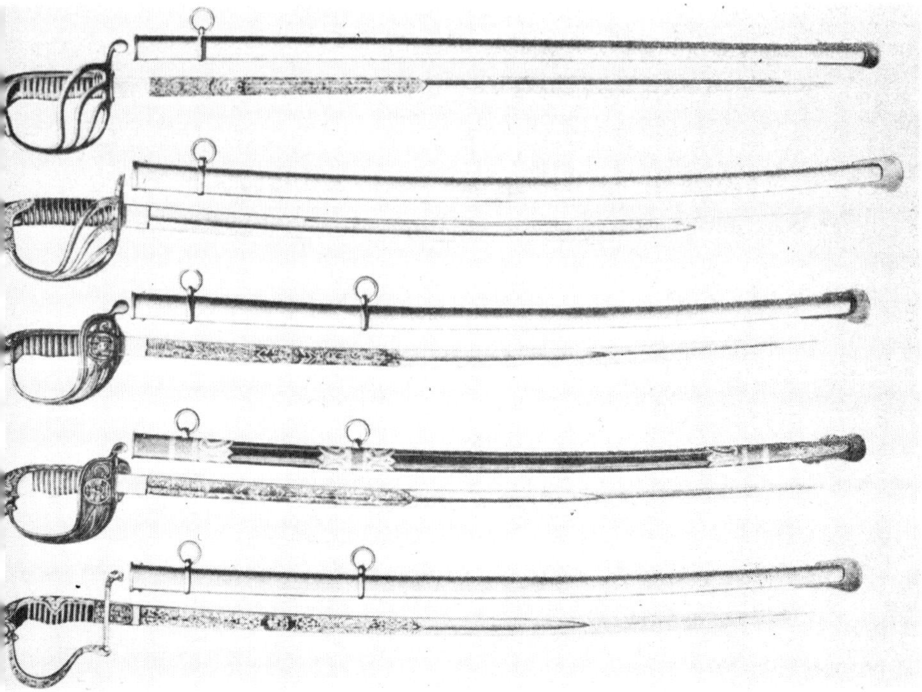

140

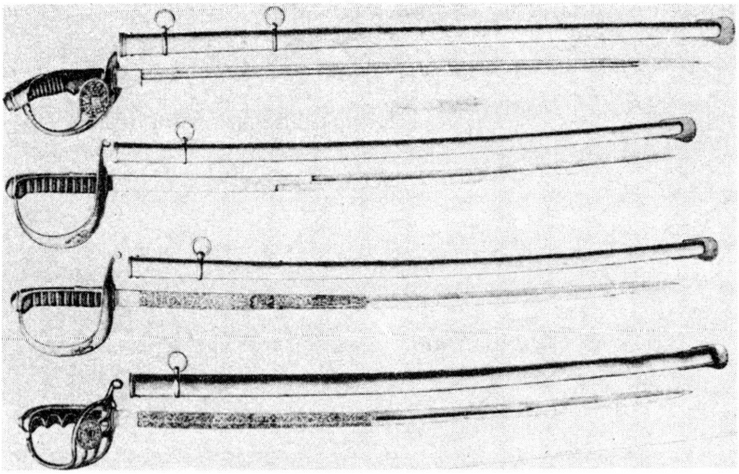

141

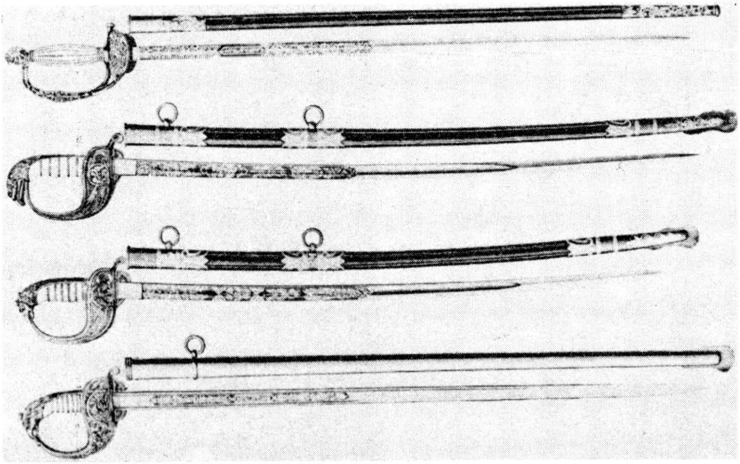

142

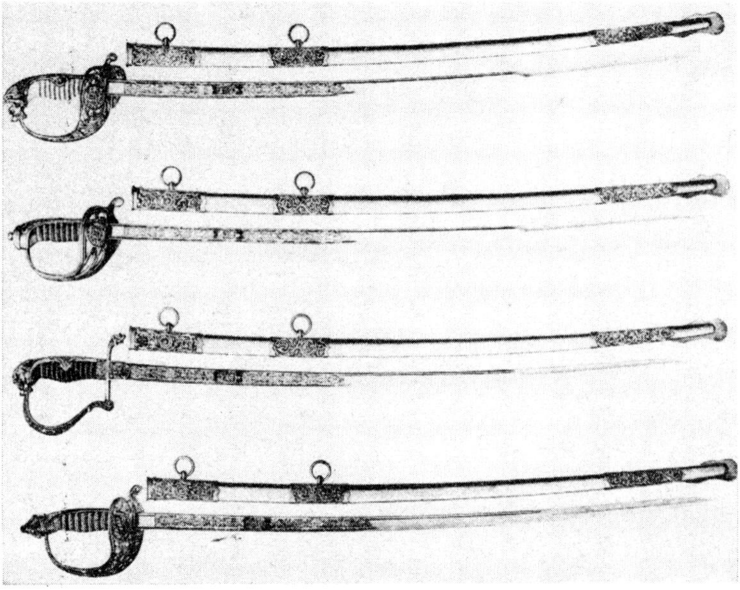

140 *Guatemala. General Officers sword; Infantry sword; Naval sword; Military sword.*

141 *Mexico. Admirals sword; Naval sword; Naval sword; Military sword.*

142 *Venezuela. Naval sword; Infantry sword; Cavalry sword; Naval sword.*

143 *Russia. Imperial Russian officers sword with blade bearing cypher of Nicholas II patt. 1909.*

144 *Russia. Guard Cuirassier sword* circa *1800.*

143

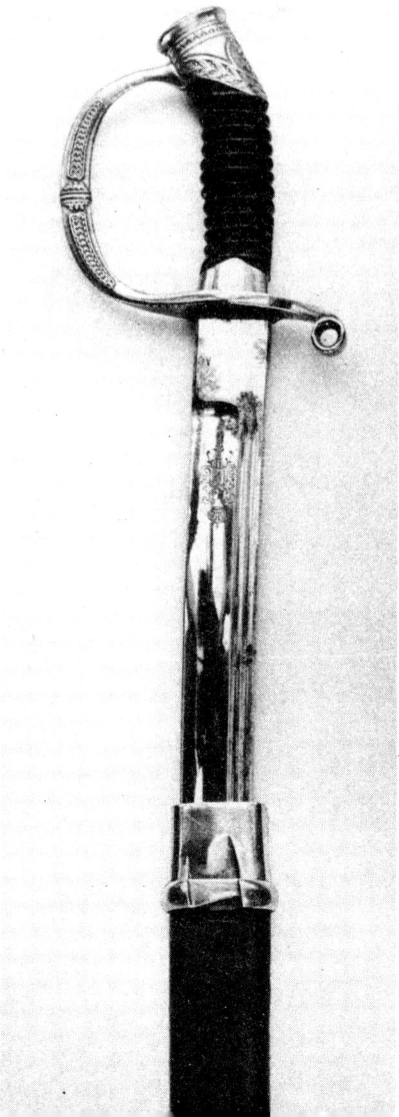

144

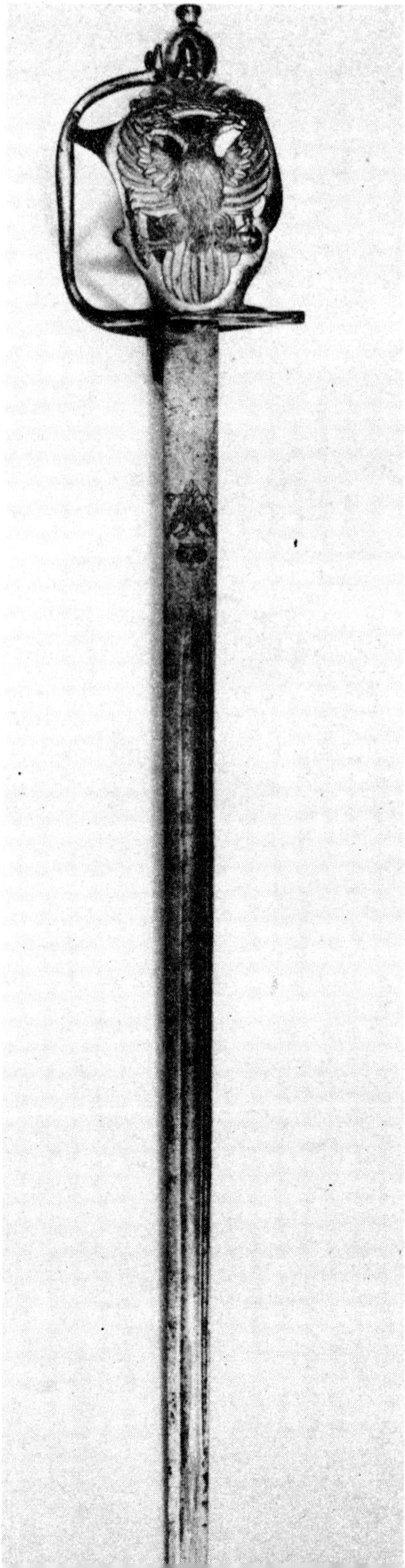

145

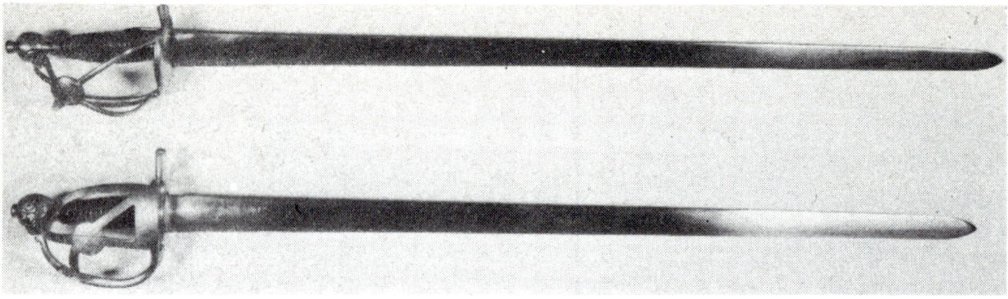

146

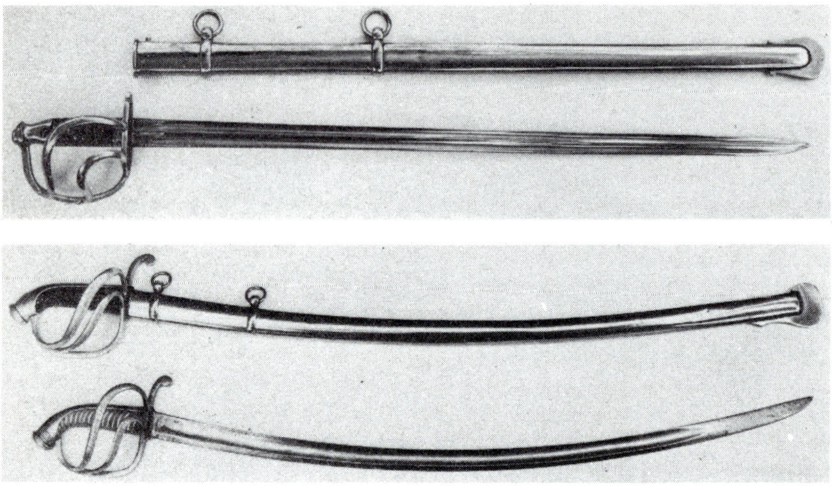

147

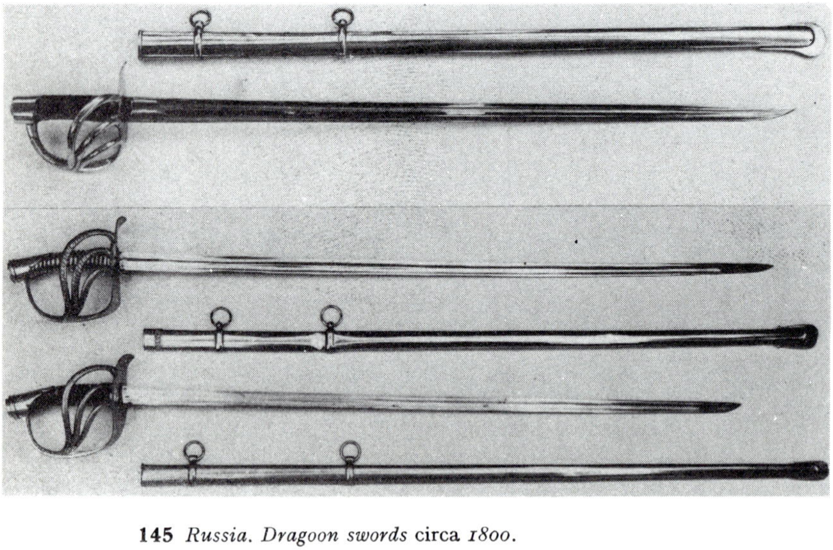

145 *Russia. Dragoon swords* circa *1800.*

146 *Russia. Cuirassiers sword patt. 1809; Cavalry sword patt. 1809 troopers; Cavalry sword patt. 1809 officers.*

147 *Russia. Cuirassier sword patt. 1826: Top: troopers pattern; centre and bottom: officers swords.*

148

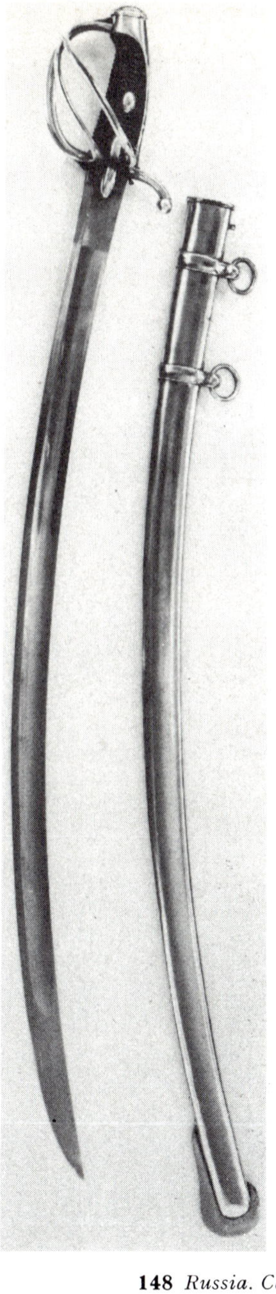

149

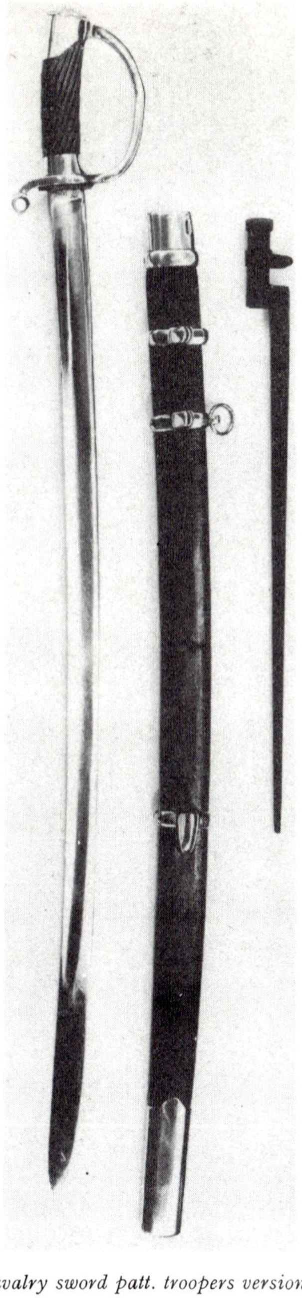

150

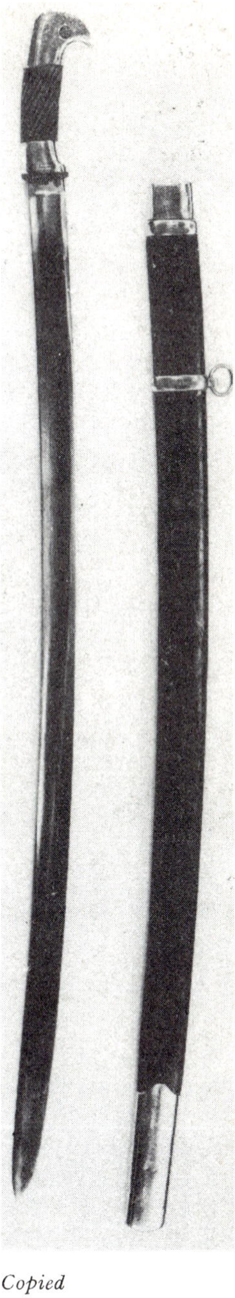

148 *Russia. Cavalry sword patt. troopers version. Copied from the captured French patt. An XI.*

149 *Russia. Dragoon sword patt. 1881, troopers version showing the special scabbard mounts in which the bayonet was carried.*

150 *Russia. Cossack sword patt. 1881, troopers version.*

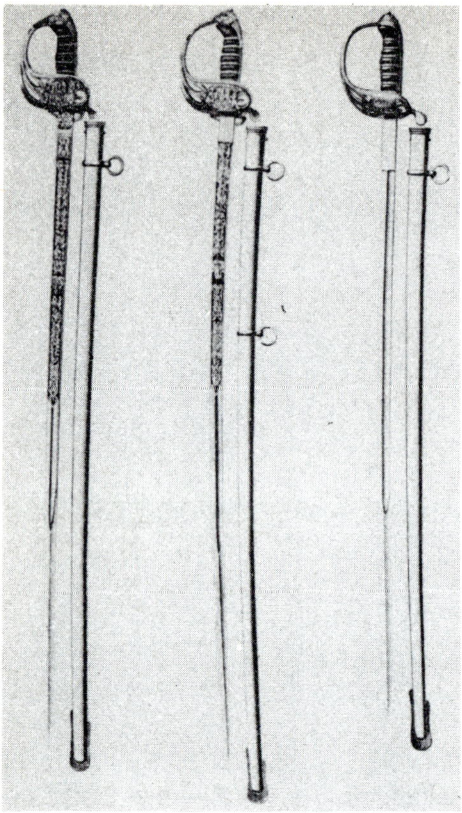

151

1

151 *Siam. Infantry officers sword; Royal Bodyguard officers sword; Infantry NCO's sword.*

152 *Siam. Hilt drawing of a cavalry officers sword.*

153 *Japan. World War II Army officers sword; World War II Naval officers sword.*

153

154 *Indian Army. Cavalry troopers sword Indian State Forces* circa *1910.*

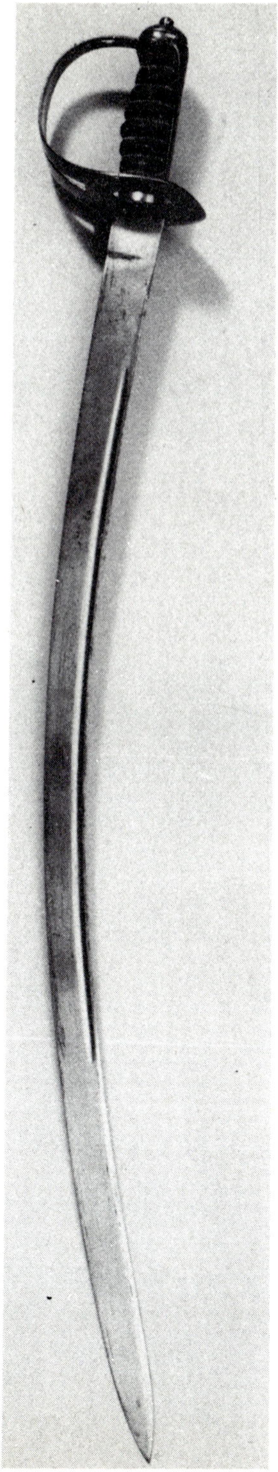

155 *Indian Army. Cavalry troopers sword* circa *1860.*

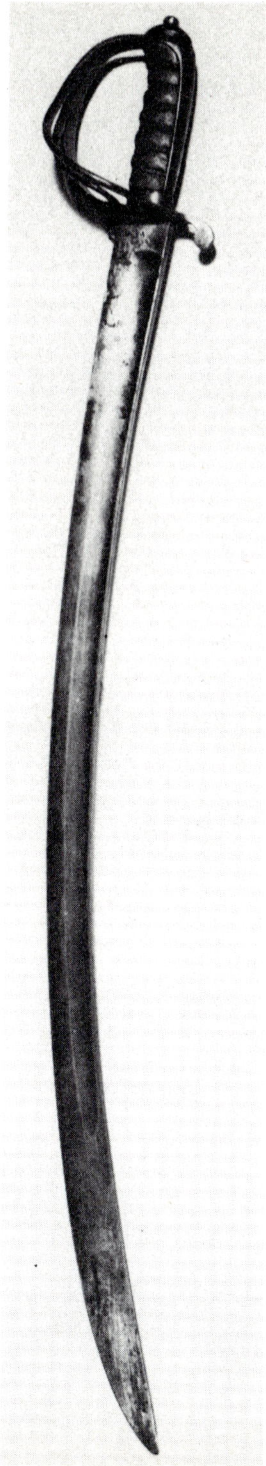

156 *Indian Army. Havildar, Drummers and Mountain Battery sword* circa *1860.*

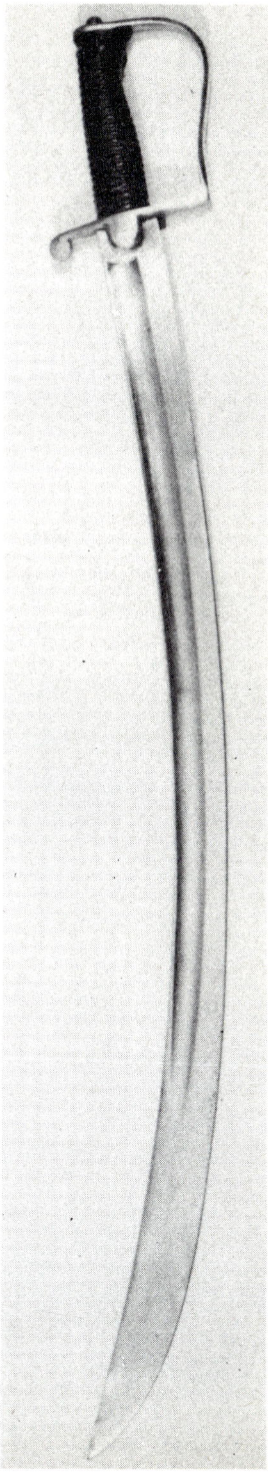

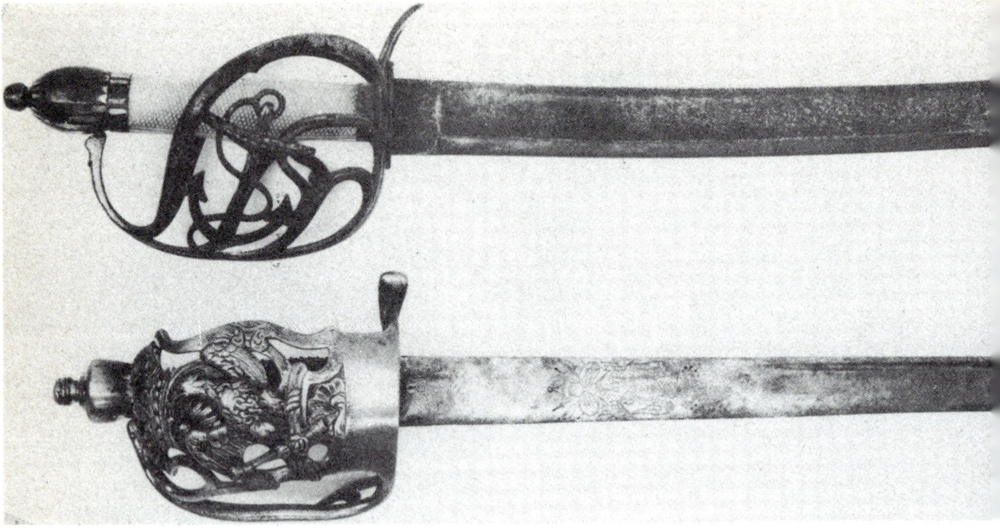

157 *Military swords. British Georgian Naval officers sword* circa *1780; Prussian officers cavalry sword patt. 1732–97.*

158 *Military swords. 19th century small sword; British officers Spadroon* circa *1800; Silver gilt small sword* circa *1750; British Light Cavalry Volunteers sword* circa *1800; Consular sword* circa *1830.*

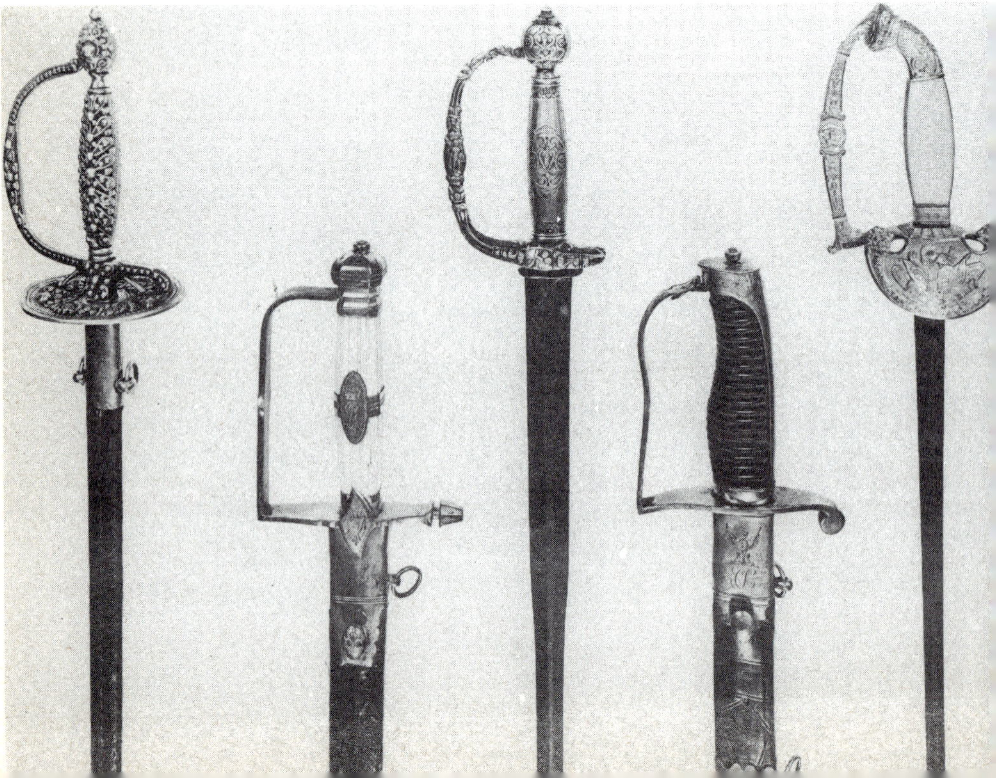

159 *Military swords. British Infantry officers sword patt. 1803; Austrian Infantry officers small sword 19th century; British Yeomanry officers sword* circa *1800; Prussian officers small sword 19th century; British Volunteer officers sword* circa *1800.*

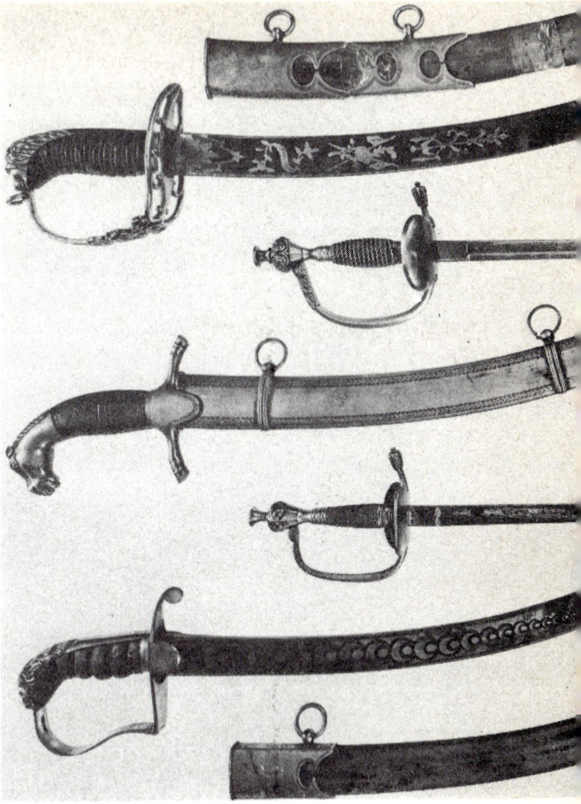

160 *Military swords. British Yeomanry bandsword* (*1st West Yorks Yeo*) circa *1840; French silvermounted hunting sword* circa *1760; French* 'Glaive de Dignitary' circa *1795; 18th century hunting sword; French* 'Sabre de Sappeur' circa *1790.*

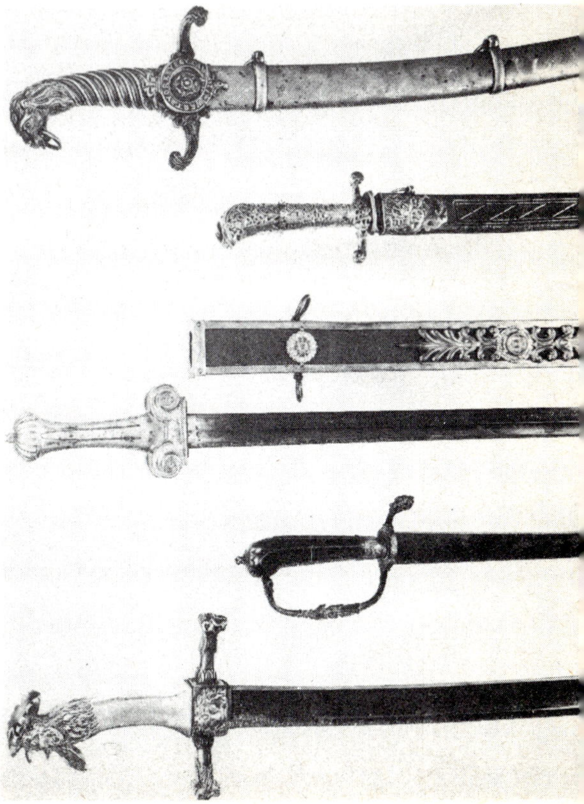

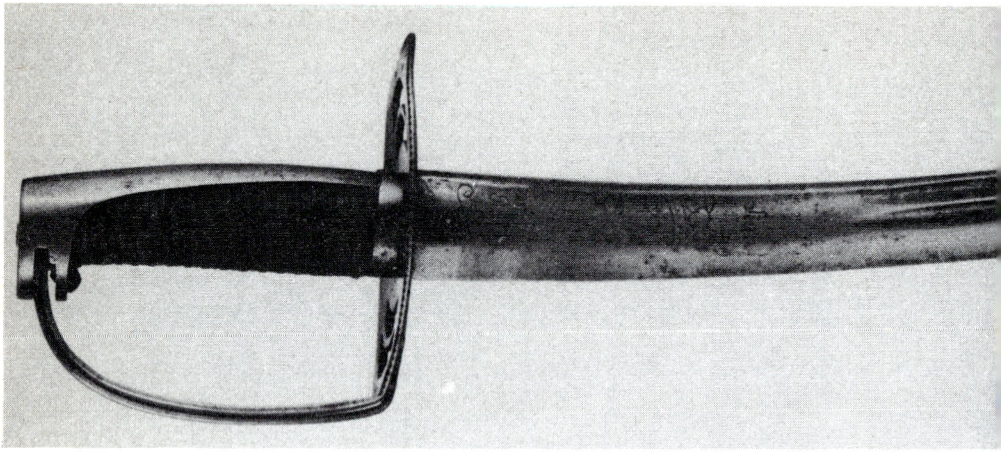

161 *Hungarian sabre with folding guard. 1760.*

162 *Military swords. Russian Dragoon shaska patt. 1881; Nazi German Justice Officials sword; British 1822 patt. Household Cavalry and heavy cavalry officers sword; Imperial German cavalry officers sword; British Naval Warrant officers sword.*

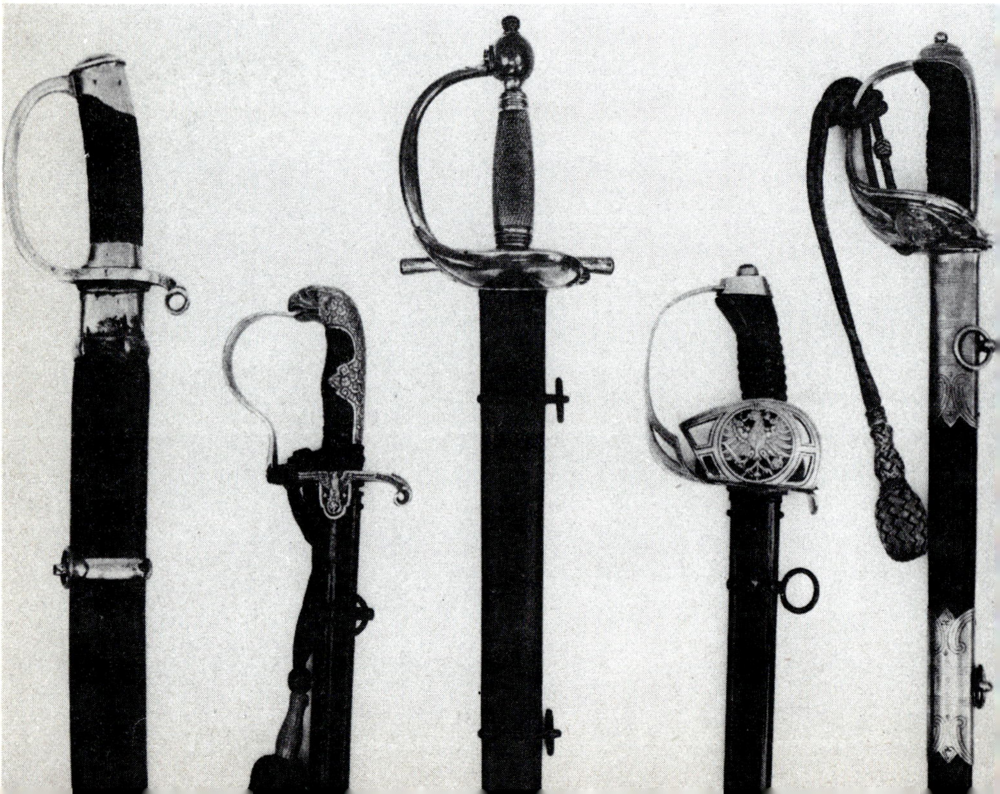

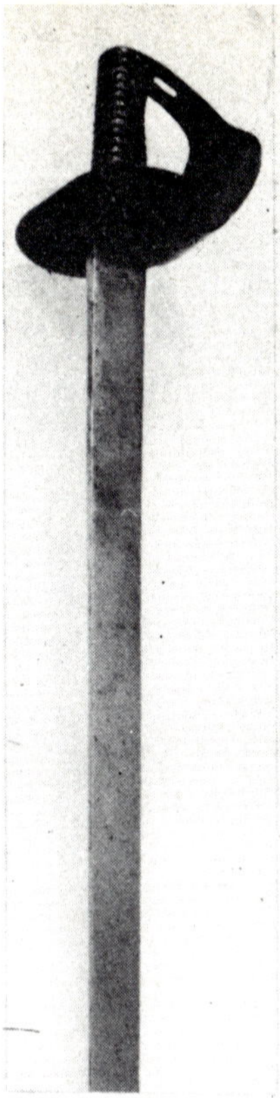

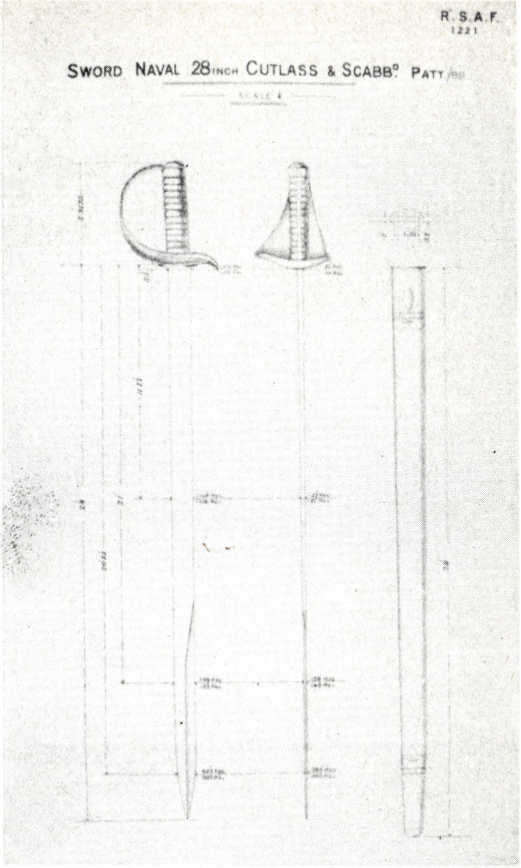

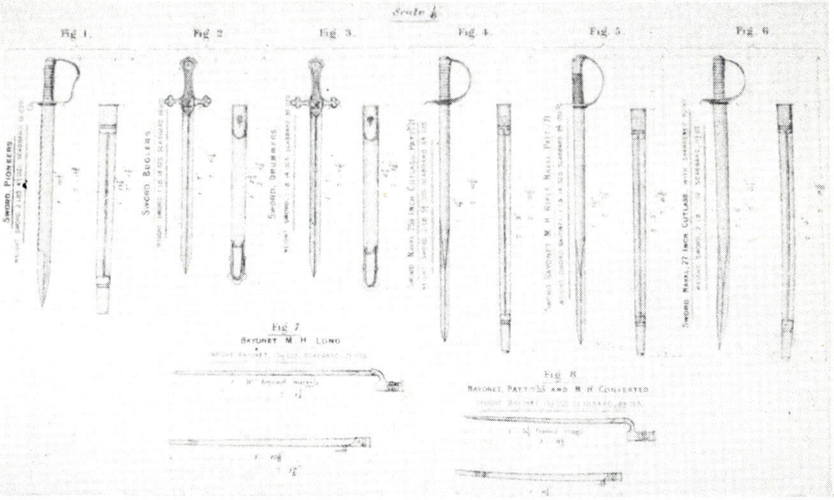

163 *Military swords. British 1803 patt. cutlass; British 1889 patt. cutlass; Plate from 'Table of Small Arms 1892' showing various bayonets and side arms in British service.*

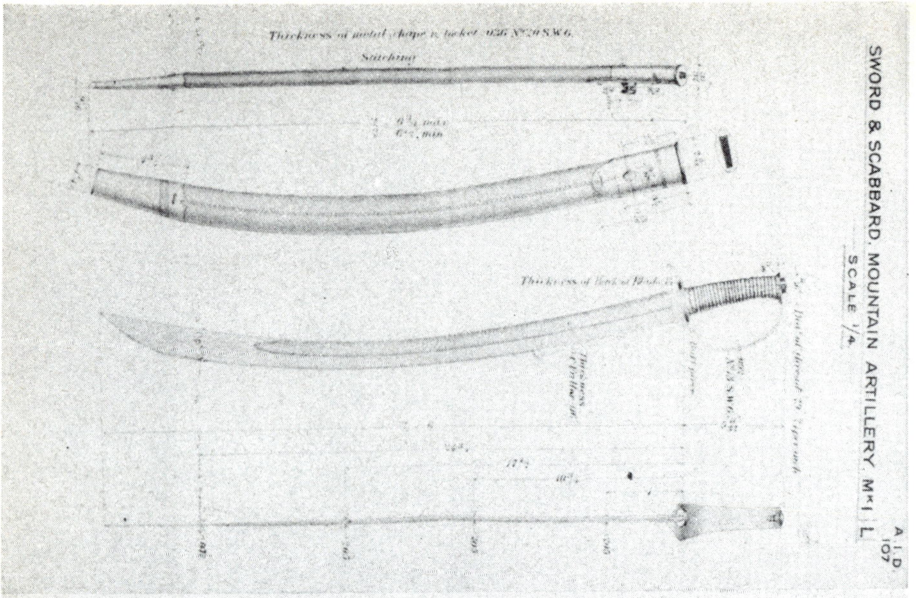

164 *Military swords. British Mountain Artillery gunners sword patt. 1896; Various blades supplied to Abyssinia* circa *1920*.

165

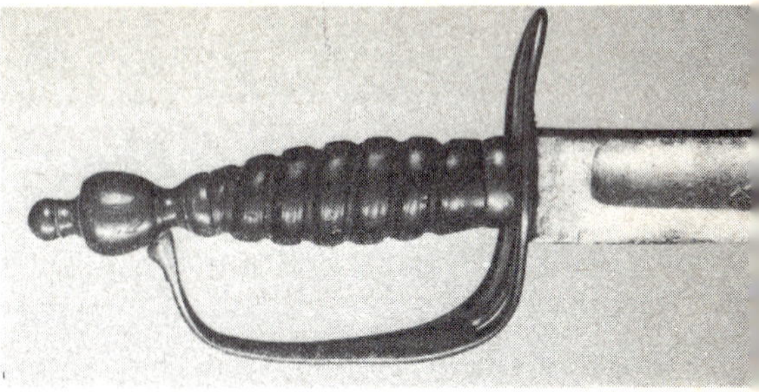

166

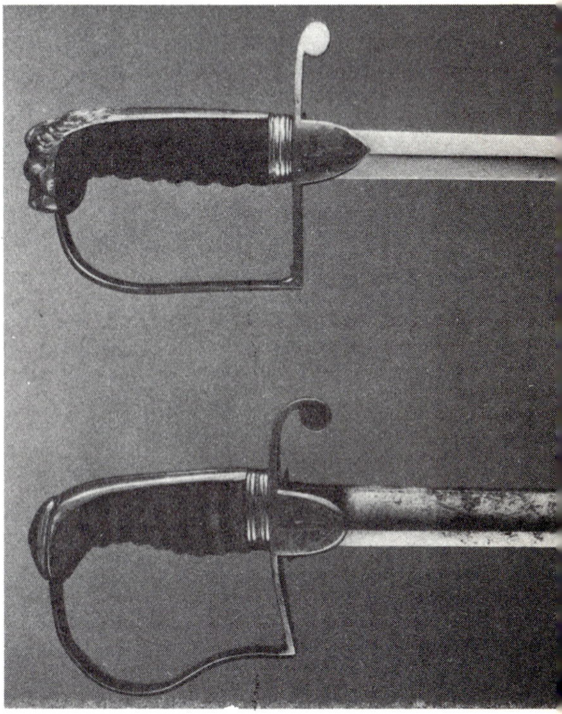

165 *Naval swords. British naval sword with slotted hilt* circa *1770.*

166 *Naval swords. British: Lieutenants 1805; Warrant officer 1805.*

167 *Naval swords. British small swords for Civil branches. 1825–1832. Surgeon; Secretary; Purser.*

167

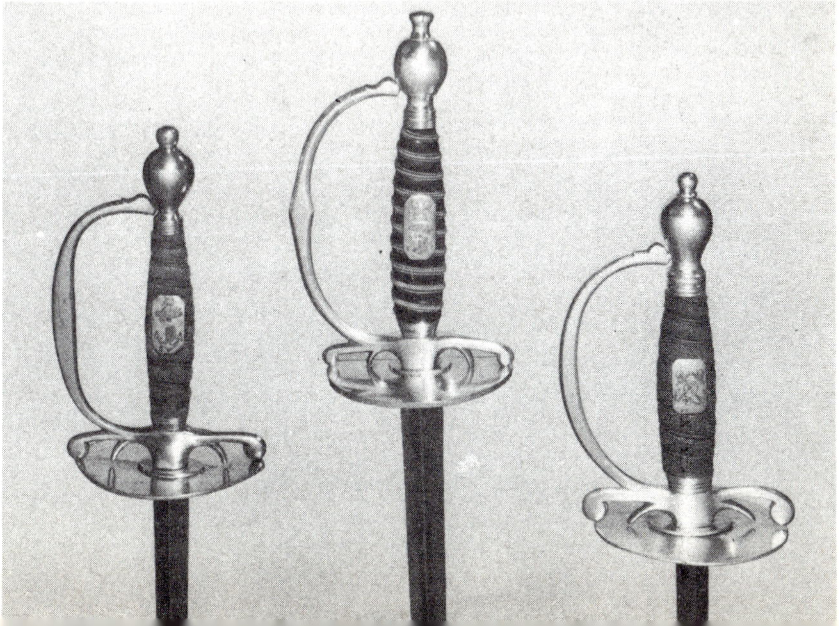

168 *Naval swords. British. Royal Marine Officers sword patt. 1822; Half basket pattern 1827; Bead hilt spadroon* circa *1790.*

169 *Naval swords. Honourable East India Company Marine presentation sword* circa *1840.*

170 *Naval swords. British Naval sword. Patt. with straight blade adopted 1929.*

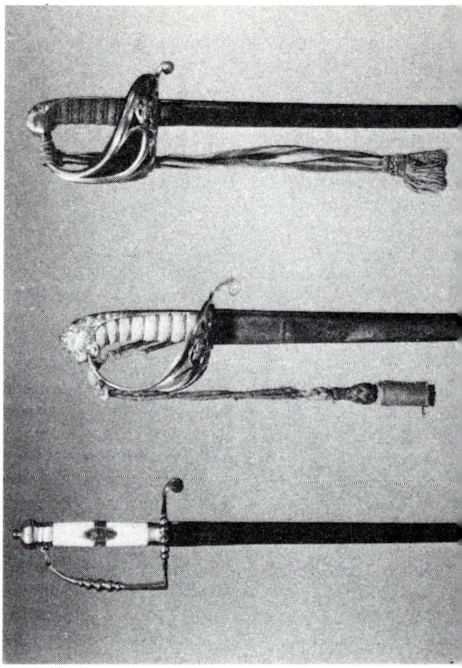

168

169

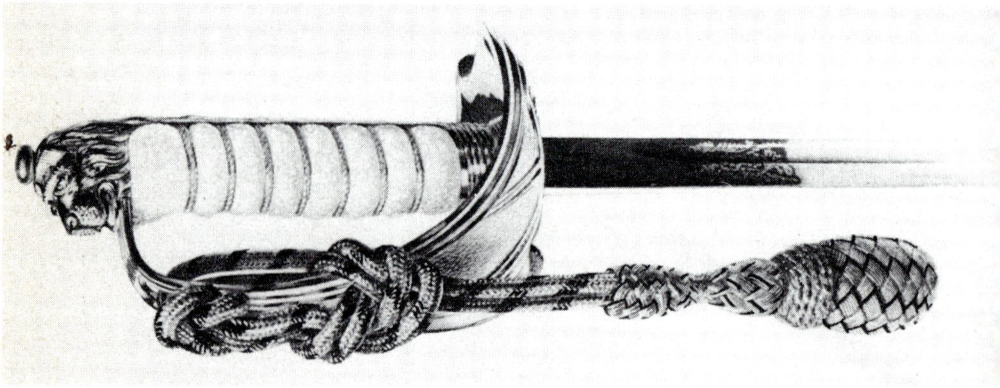

170

171 *Naval swords. Belgian Naval swords and dirk; Patt. 1832; Officers dirk patt. 1893; Patt. 1837.*

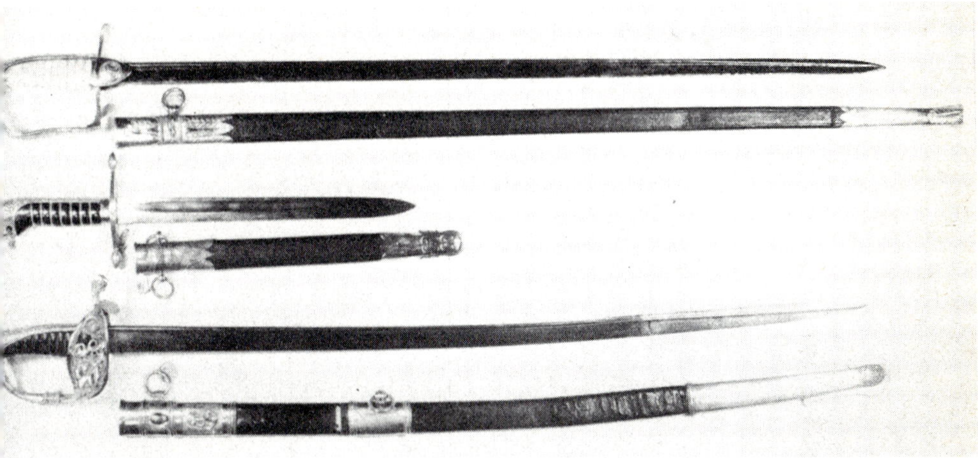

2 *Naval swords. Brazilian Imperial Navy* circa *32.*

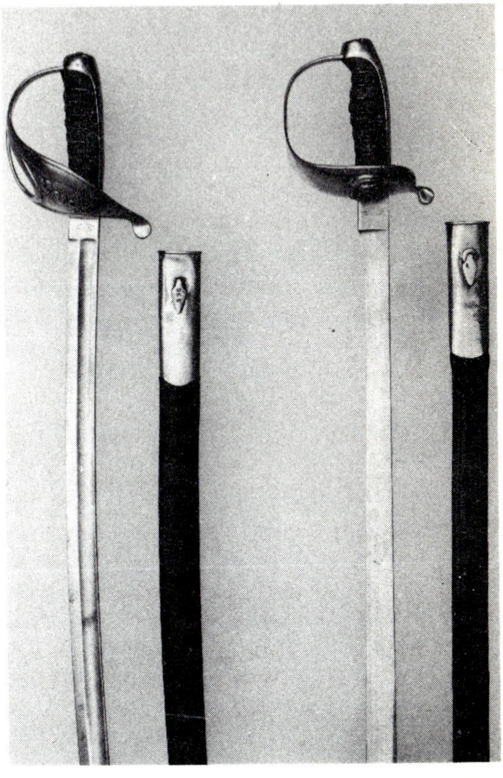

173 *Naval swords. Danish Naval NCO's sword patt. 1871; NCO's patt. 1882.*

174 *Naval swords. French patt. 1805.*

175 *Naval swords. Imperial German Naval officers swords 1871–1918.*

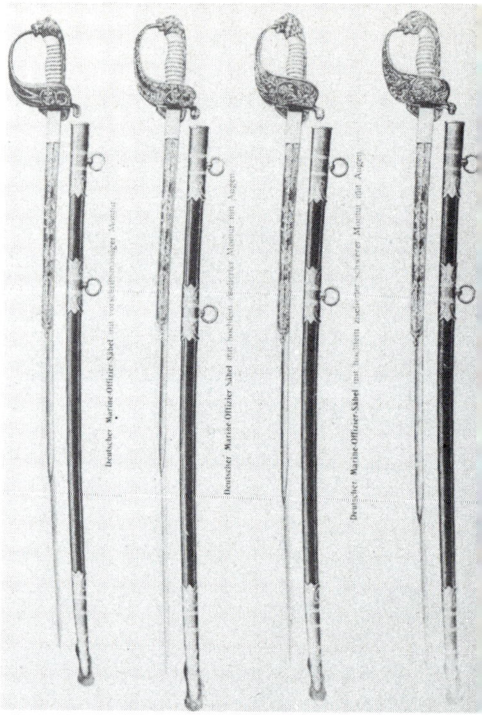

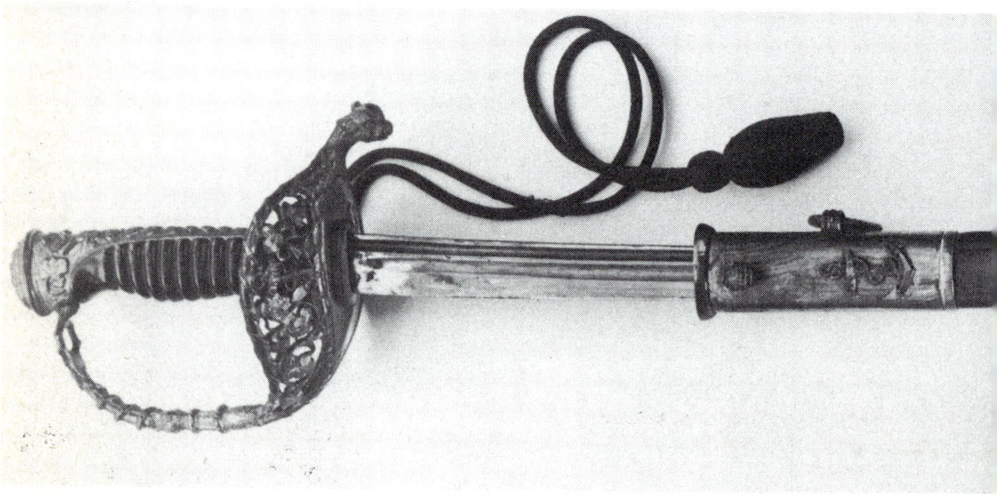

176 *Naval swords. French patt. 1870.*

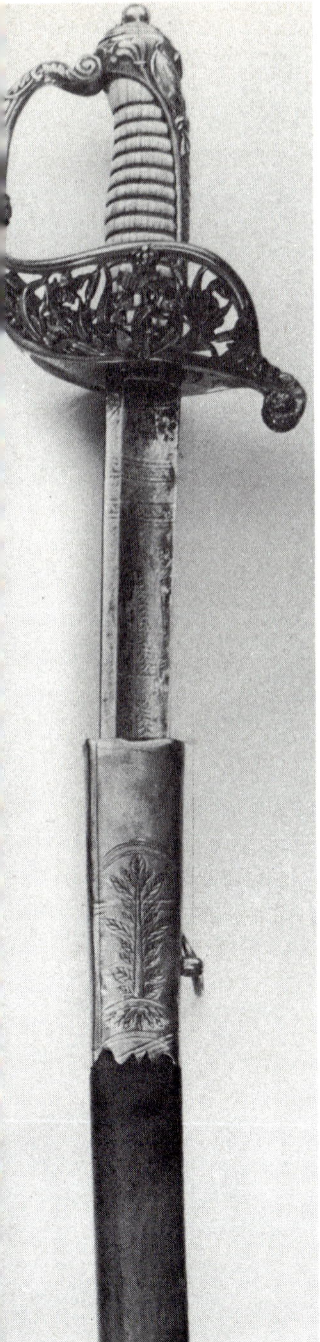

177 *Naval swords. Dutch Naval officers sword patt. 1837.*

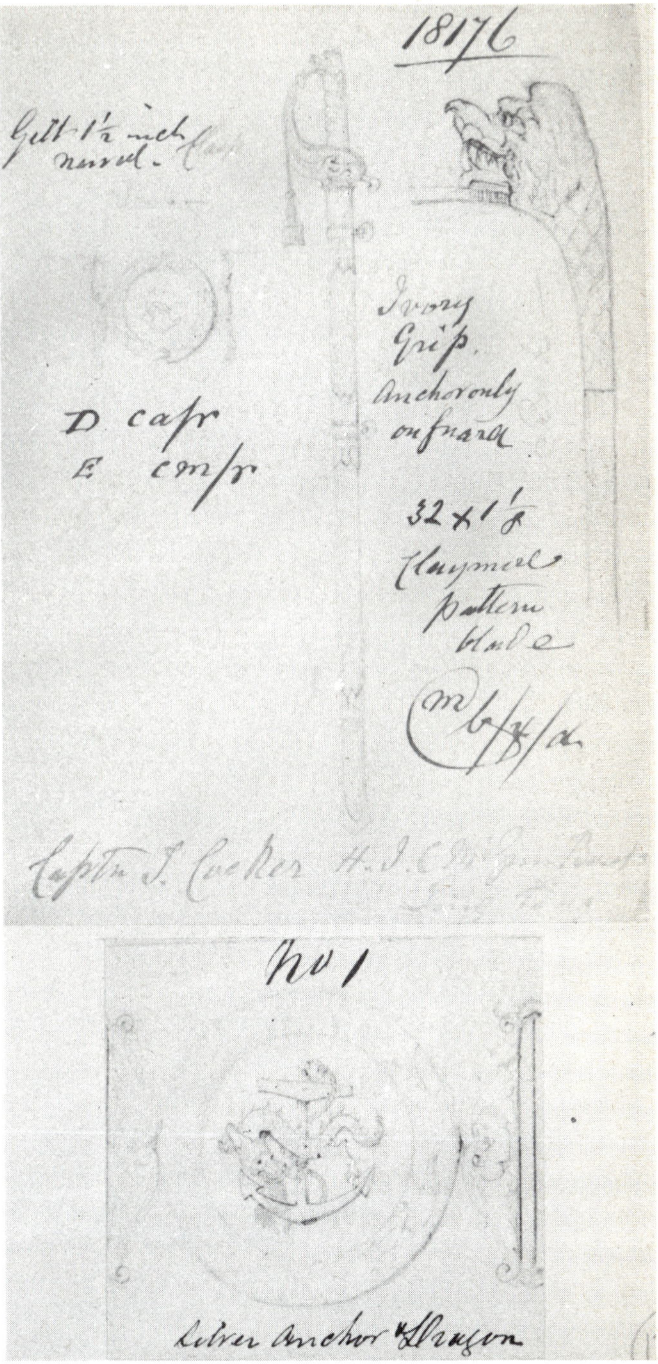

178 *Naval swords. Chinese Maritime Customs. Drawings of sword and belt buckle adopted 1867 and 1872.*

179 *Naval swords. Japan. Drawings of sword and belt buckle adopted January 1872.*

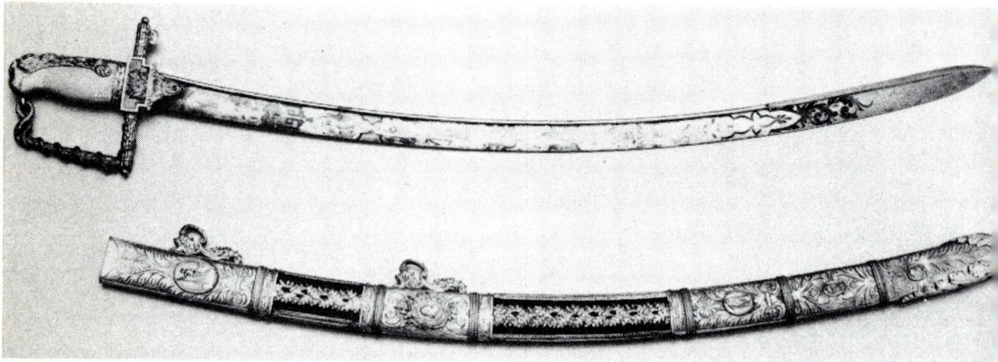

180 *Presentation sword similar in style to that given by the Patriotic Fund at Lloyds.* Circa *1840.*

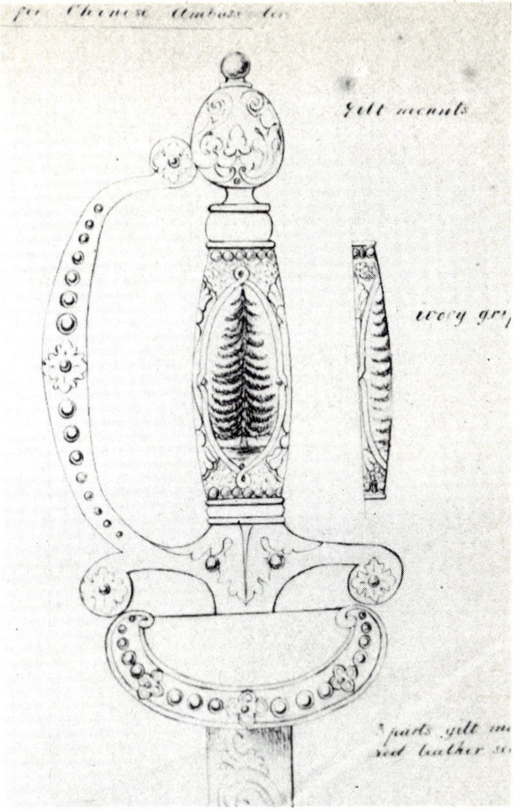

181 *Diplomatic small sword for Chinese ambassador* circa *1870.*

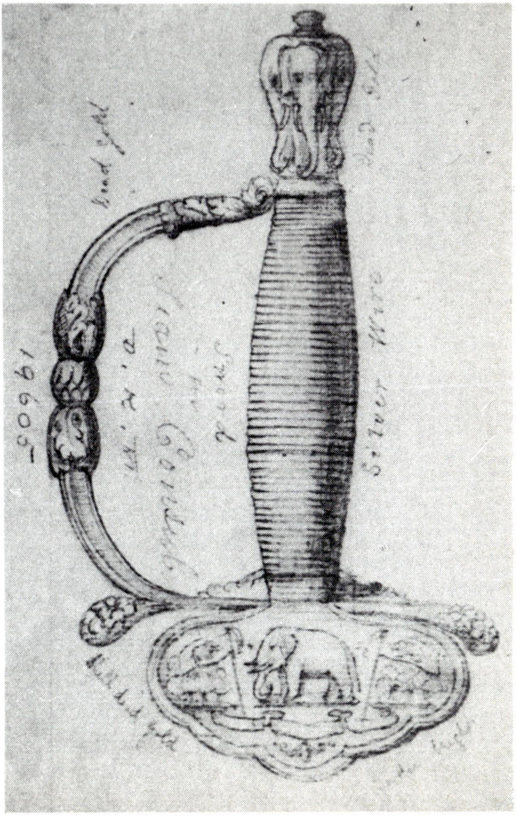

182 *Diplomatic small sword for Siamese Consul* circa *1875.*

183 *British court sword of a military officers at court* circa *1875.*

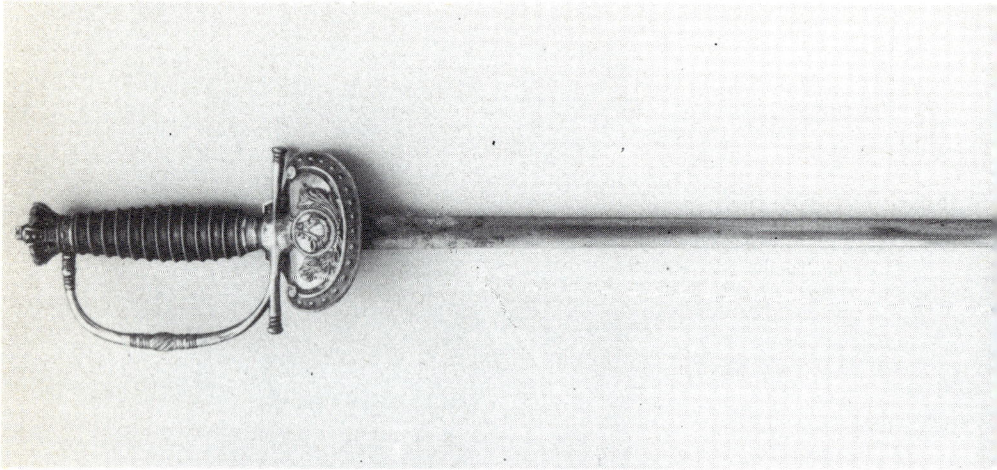

184 *British Diplomats sword* circa *1910.*

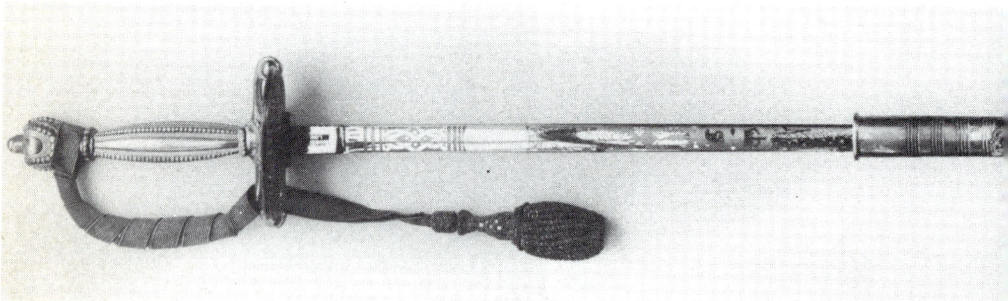

185 *British. Military bandsword 1845.*

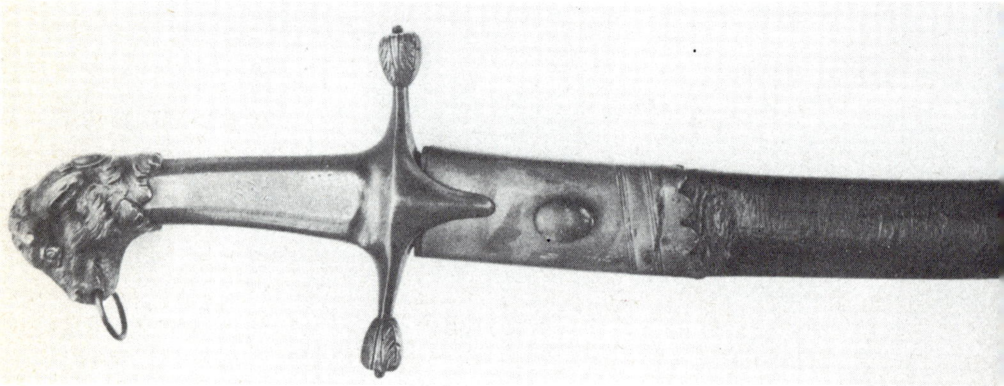

186 *British Police and Prison warders hanger* circa *1830*.

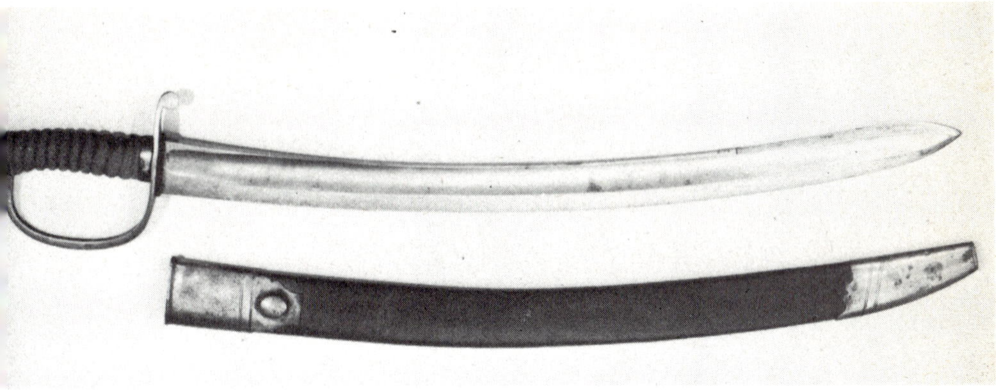

187 *Indian Pulouar 19th century*.

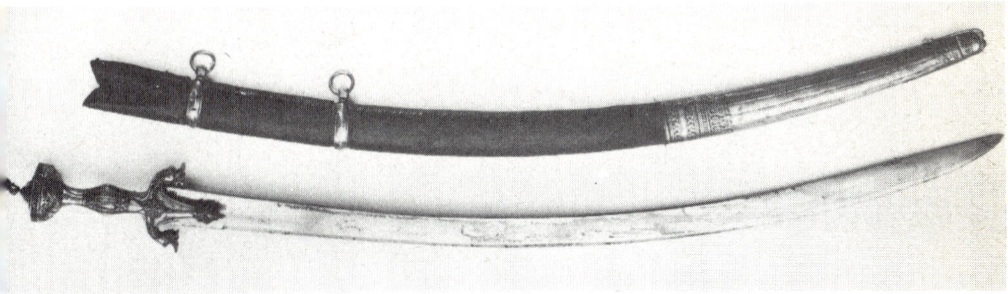

188 *Persian shamshir 19th century*.

189 *Indian Tular 19th century.*

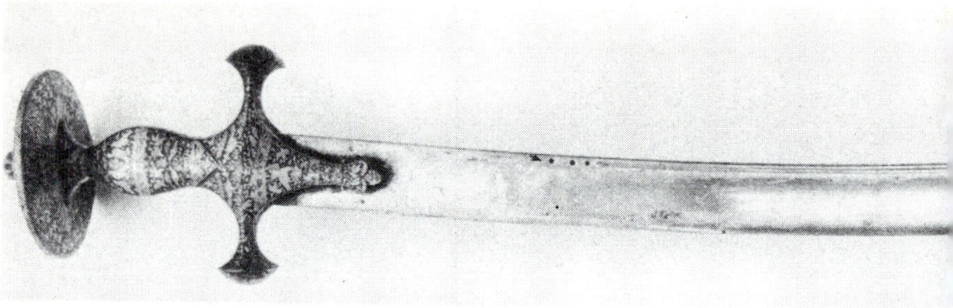

190 *Indian Firangi or spiked hilted tulwar 19th century.*

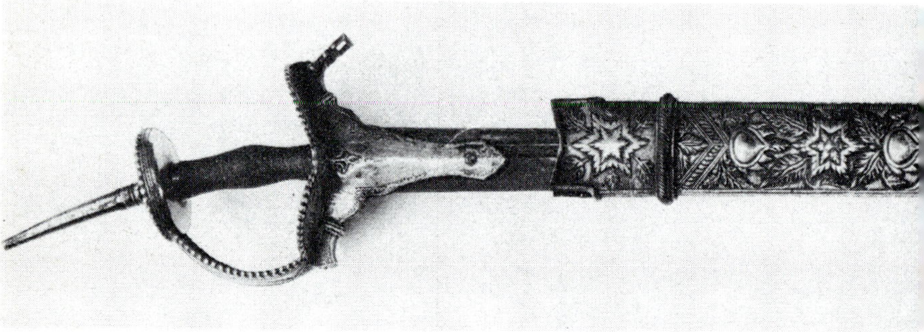

191 *Persian shamshir; Persian scimitar; 19th century.*

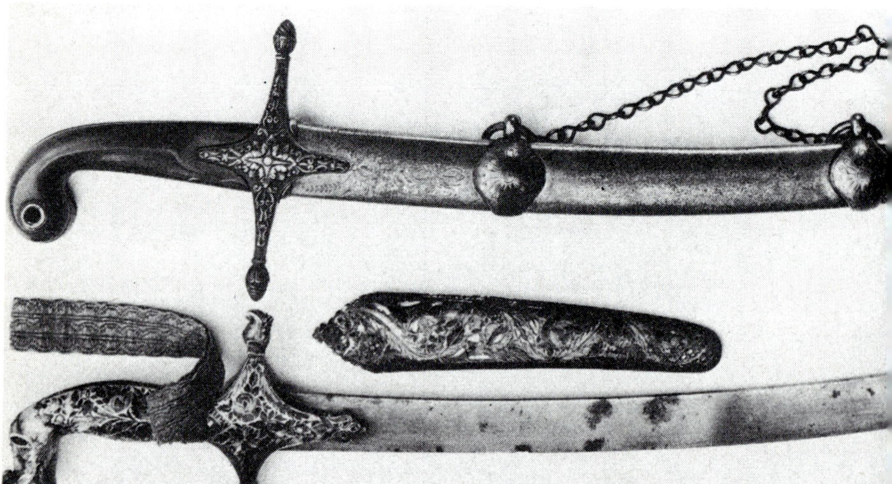

192

192 *Caucasian shashka; Turkish yataghan; Arab sabre; Burmese dha; Russian shashka.*

193 *Russian shashka. 19th century.*

194 *Large ceremonial kukri; Burmese dha; Japanese katana dismounted showing component parts of the sword.*

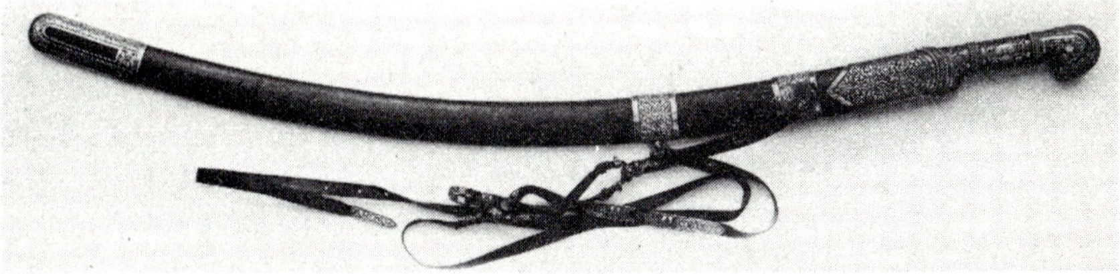

193

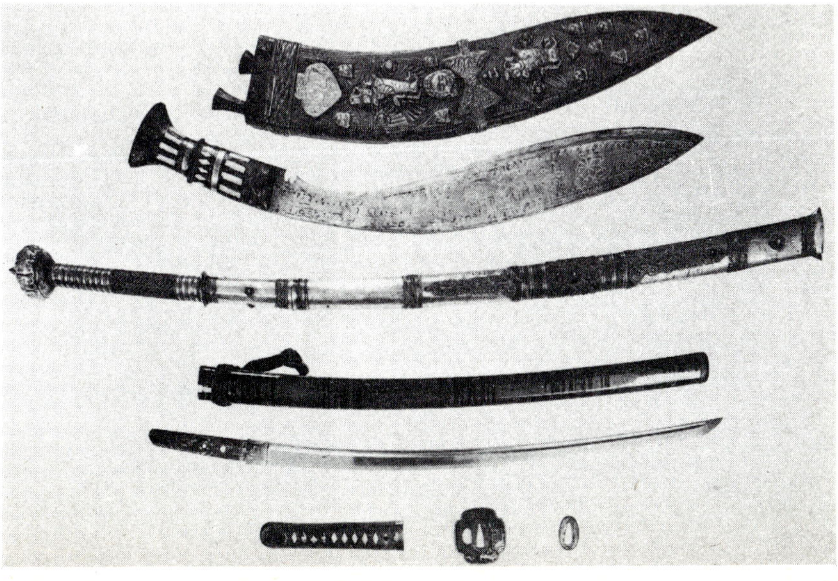

194

195 *Indian two handed Firangi or spiked hilt tulwar, 18th century; Japanese Naval officers sword* circa *1900; Victorian copy of a 16th century Claymore.*

196 *Indian broad bladed tulwar; French made bowie knife; Indian jambiya; India bi-furcated dagger; Moroccan jambiya.*

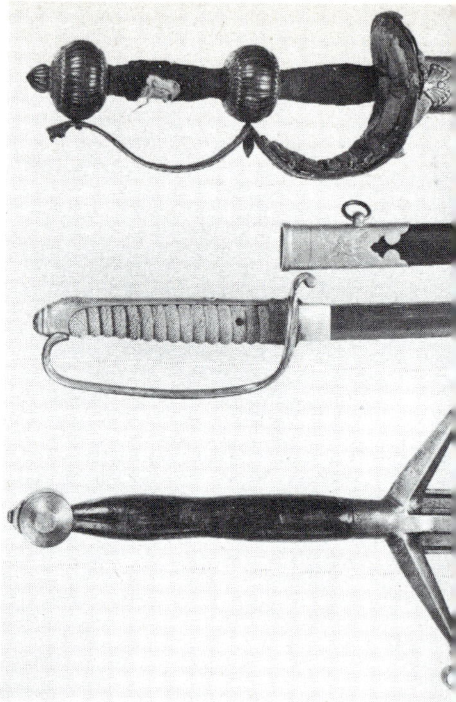

195

196

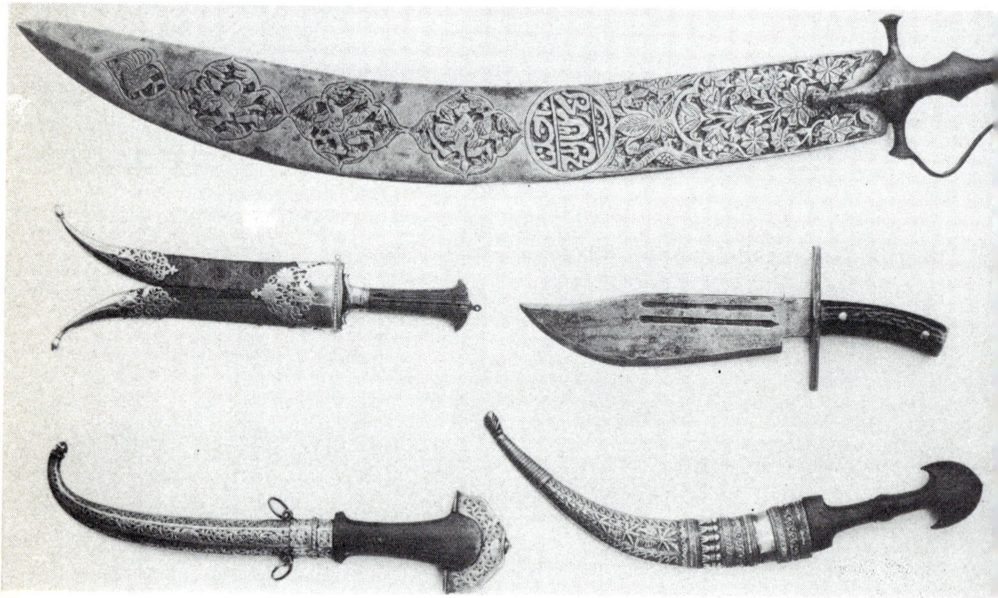

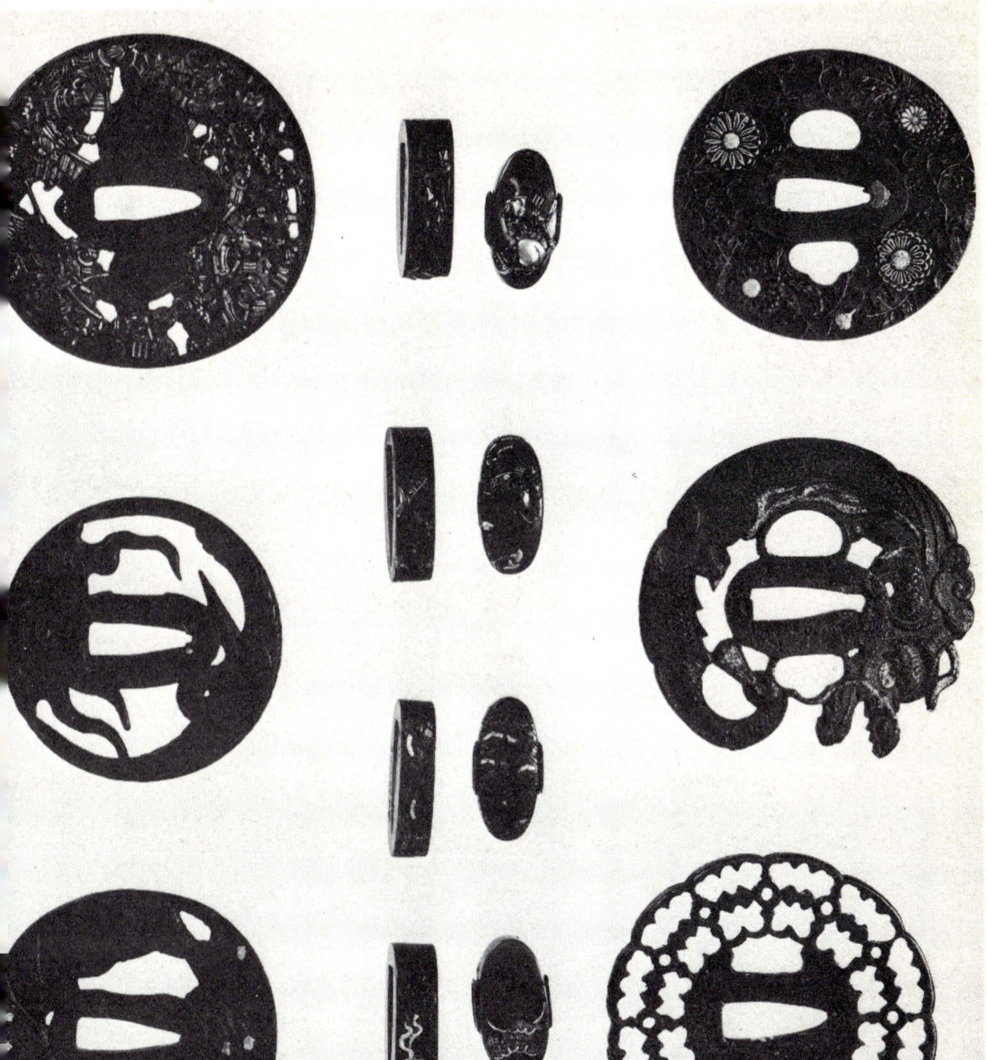

197 *Japanese sword hilt furniture. Tsubas; Kashira; Fuchis.*

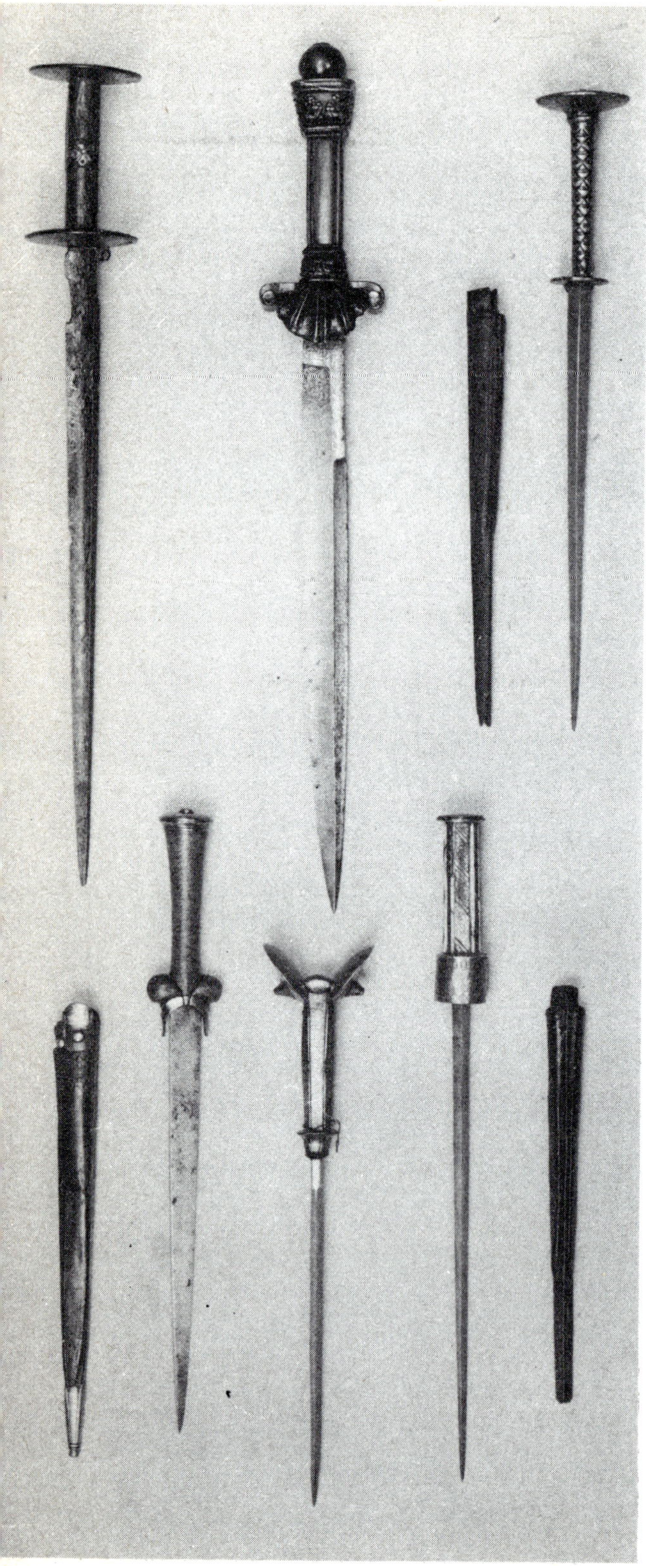

198 *Daggers. Rondel dagger French* circa *1440–50; French dagger* circa *1500; German dagger* circa *1530; Flemish kidney dagger or ballock dagger 1450–60; Italian ear dagger 16th century; German rondel dagger* circa *1450.*

199 *Swiss dagger with cast scabbard depicting Holbein's 'Dance of Death' 1592. Nazi German daggers were probably copied from this style. A cross hilted dagger with similar pattern scabbard.*

200 *Italian. Dividers in the form of a dagger 1630–40; Italian sword breaker and dagger* circa *1600.*

199

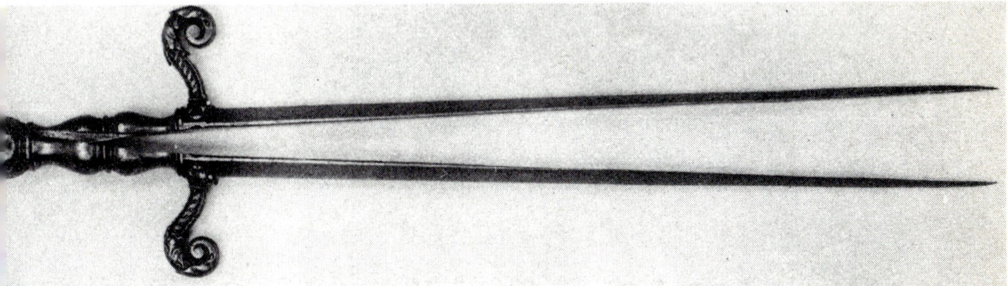

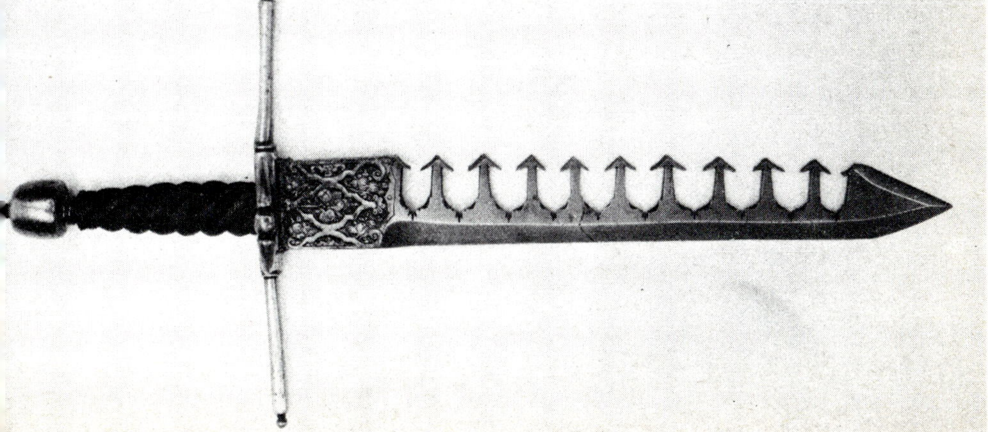

201 *Italian left hand dagger* circa *1610; Italian left hand dagger* circa *1620; German stiletto* circa *1610; German left hand dagger 1620.*

202 *Spanish or Italian dagger 19th century; Italian stiletto mid-17th century; Italian left hand dagger 17th century; Italian quillon dagger* circa *1600; British naval dirk* circa *1800.*

203 *Flintlock pistol hunting sword* circa *1760; German hunting cutlass; French double barrelled percussion pistol knife* circa *1850.*

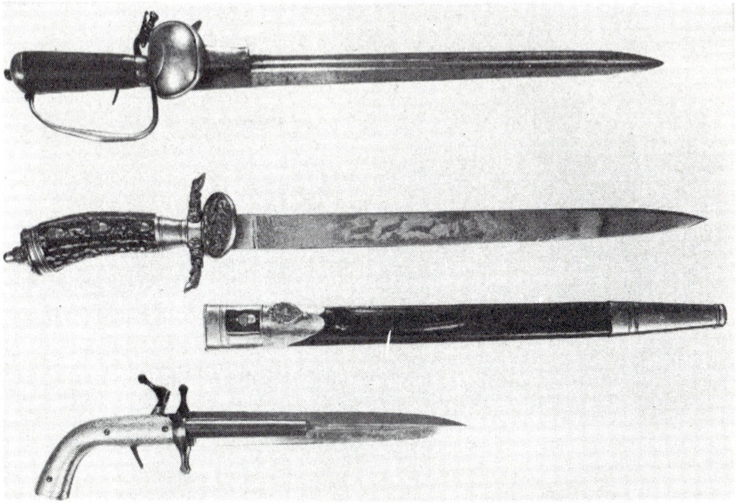

204 *Set of eviscerating instruments.* Trousée de Chasse, *large knife and six others German* circa *1732.*

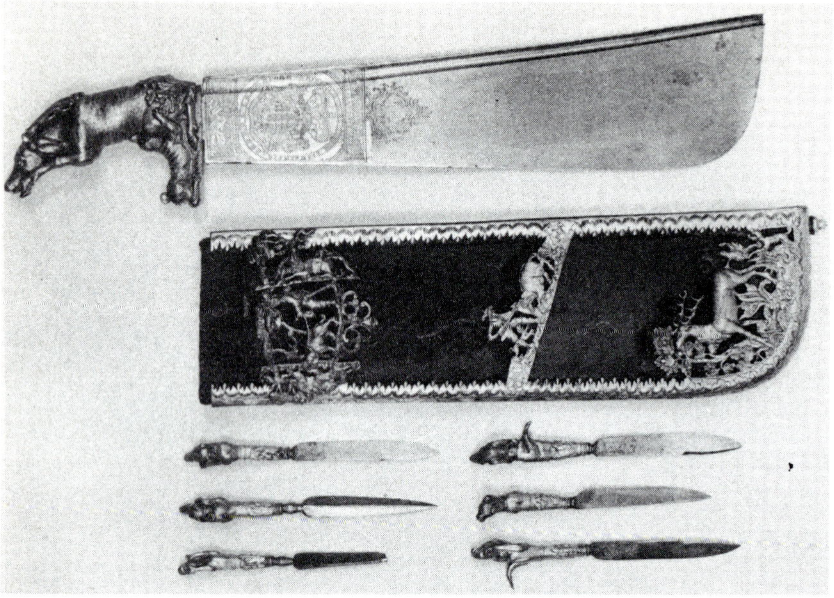

205 *Left hand daggers. German in imitation of the Spanish style 1645–50; Spanish (?) 1650; Spanish 1660; Spanish 1640–50; Italian* circa *1660.*

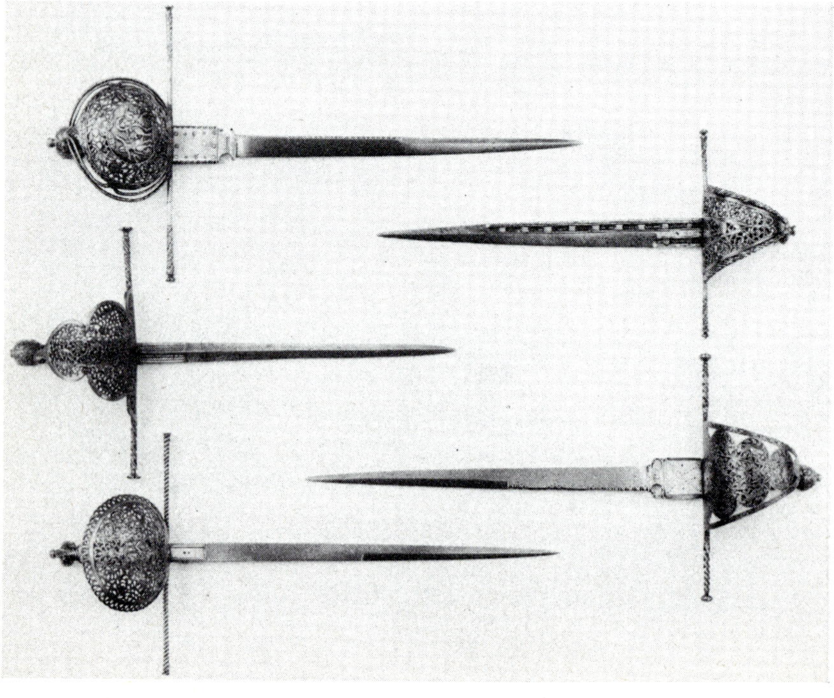

206 *Scottish dirks. 18th century clan dirks.*

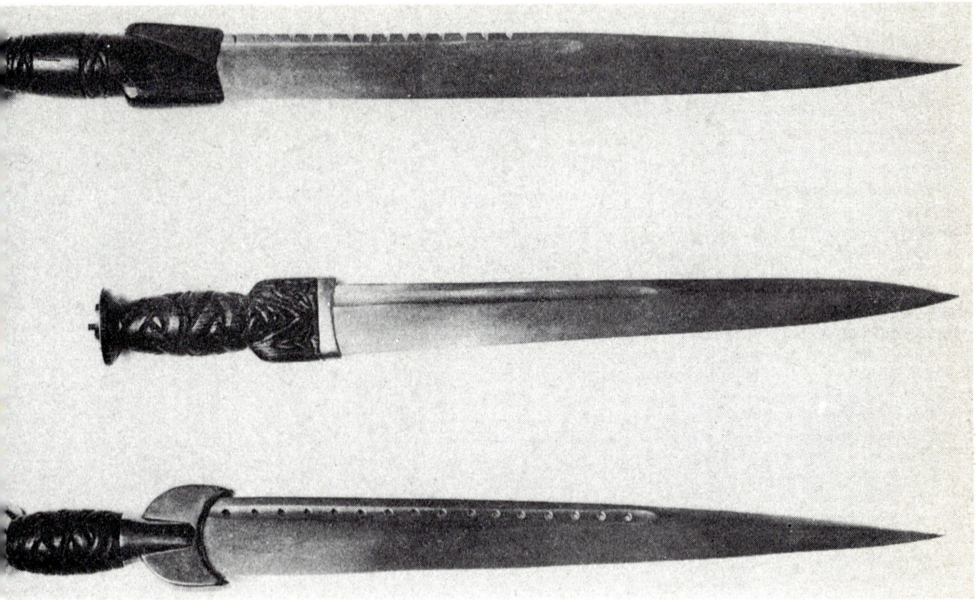

207 *Scottish dirks. 18th century clan dirks.*

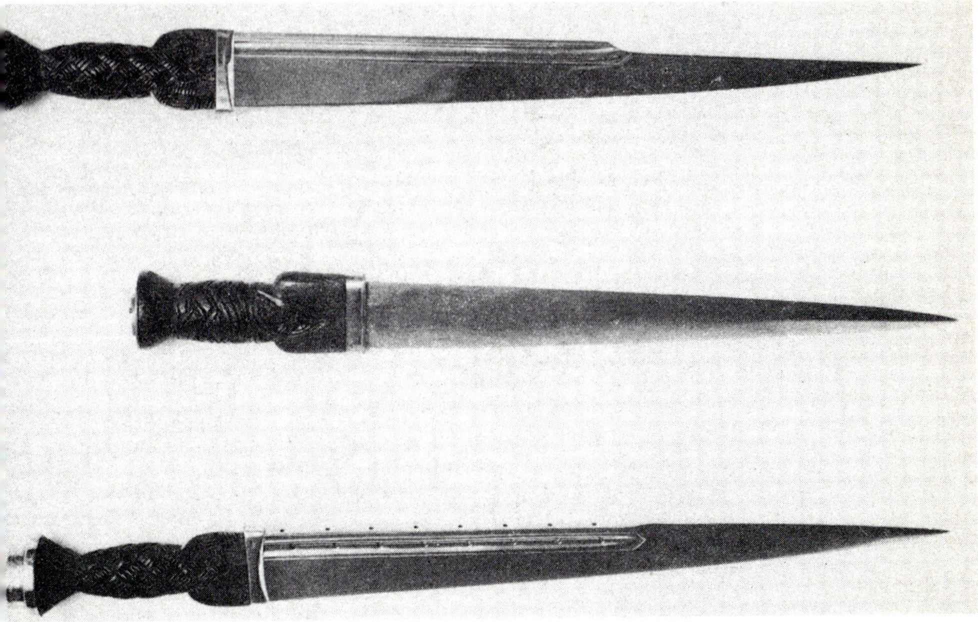

208 *Scottish dirks. Lord Lieutenant of Aberdeen 1862; Civilian* circa *1830; Kennedy clan* circa *1890.*

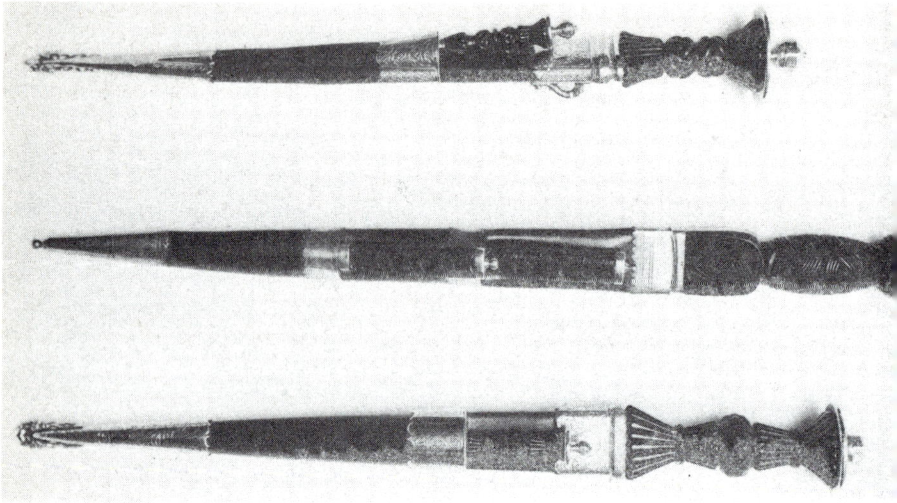

209 *Scottish dirks. 71st Highland Light Infantry* circa *1850; London Scottish Volunteers* circa *1880; Princess Charlotte of Wales Loyal Macleod Fencibles 1800.*

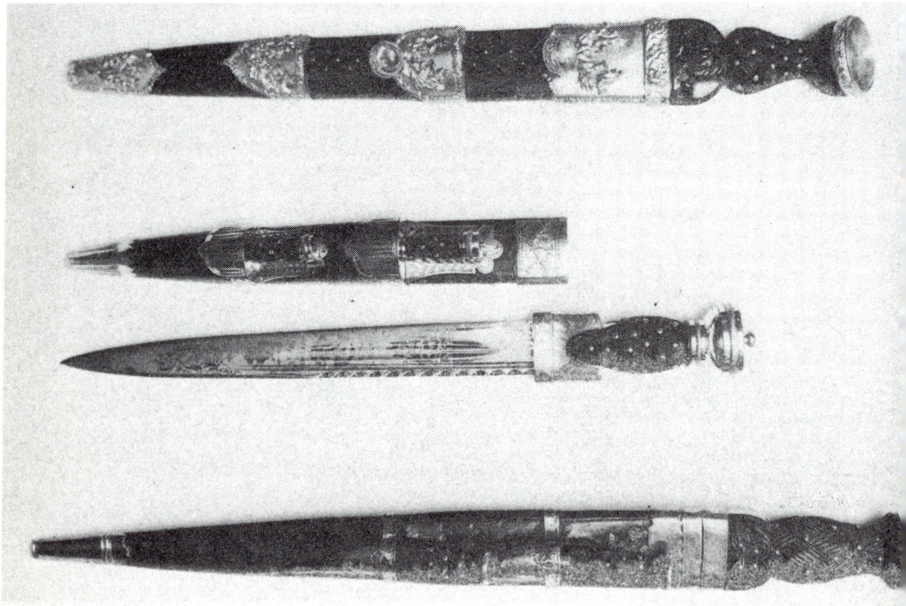

210 *Scottish dirks. Civilian dirks.* Circa *1870; 1920; 1883.*

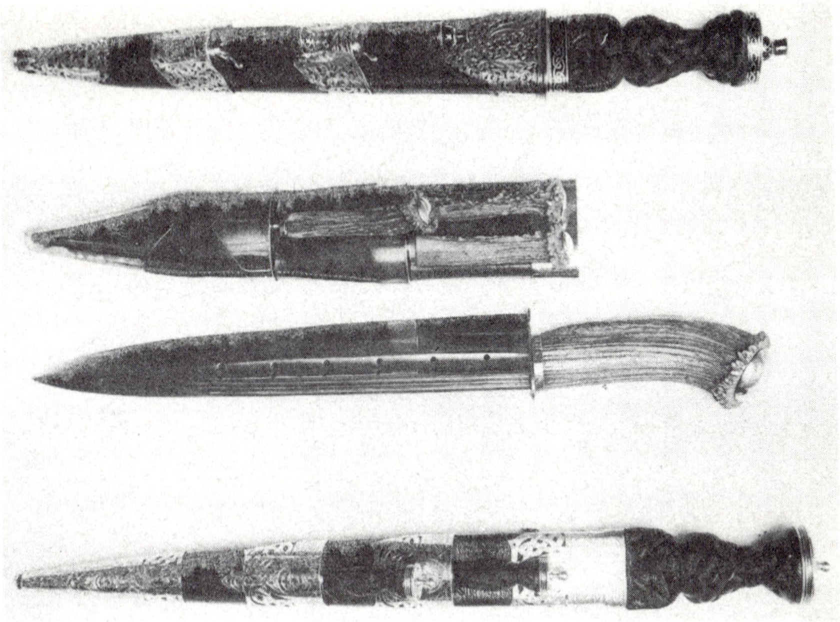

211 *Scottish dirks. Highland Light Infantry Militia* circa *1861; Seaforth Highlanders 1830; Clan dirk 1700* (*reproduction*).

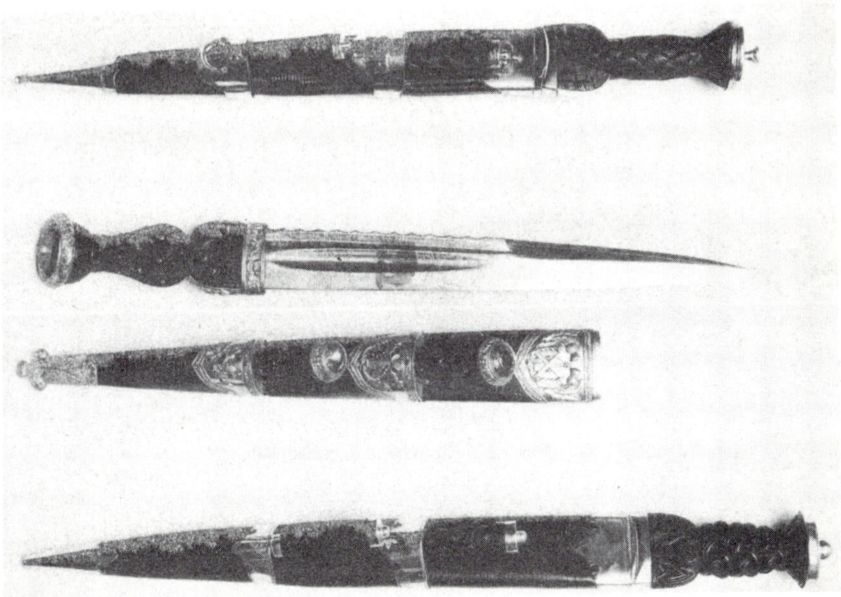

212 *Scottish dirks. 79th Cameron Highlanders* circa *1850; Seaforth Highlanders* circa *1890; Cameron Highlanders* circa *1890.*

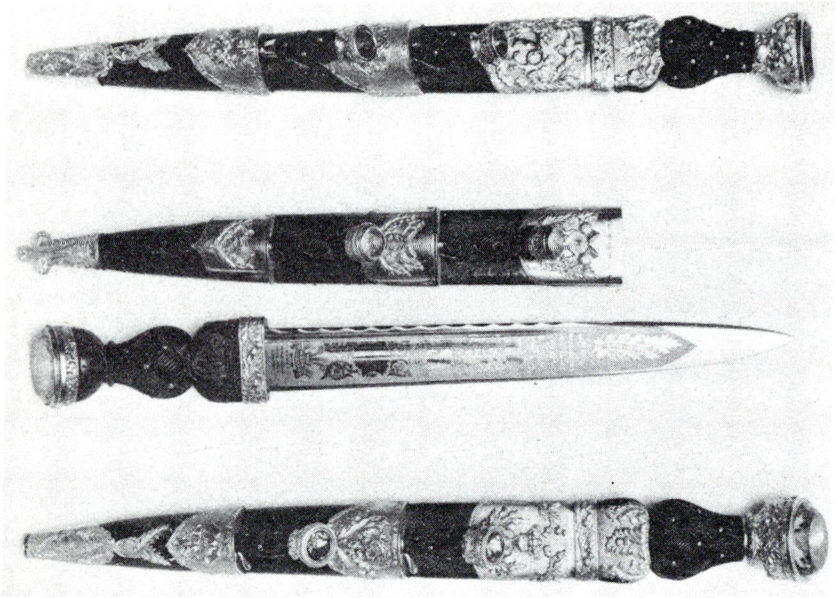

213 *Scottish dirks. Argyll and Sutherland Highlanders* circa *1881; Argyllshire Highlanders* circa *1870; Aberdeenshire Highland Militia* circa *1850–60.*

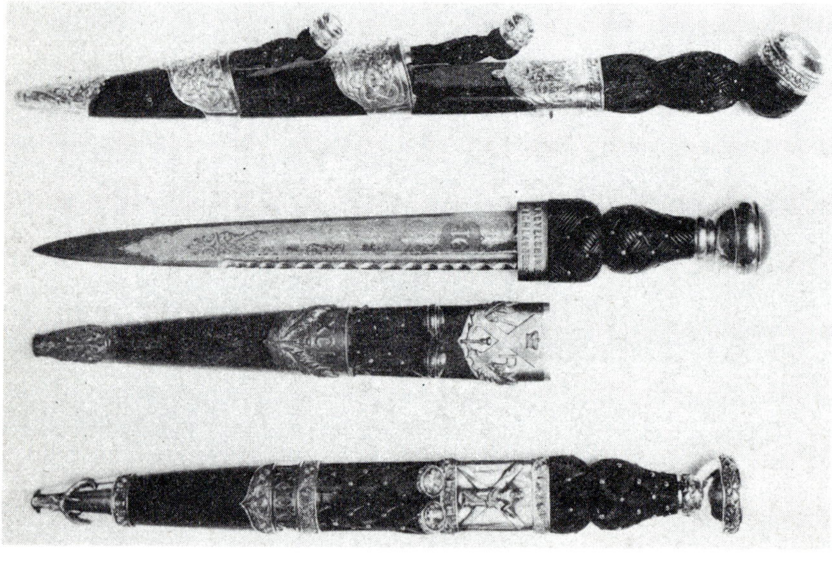

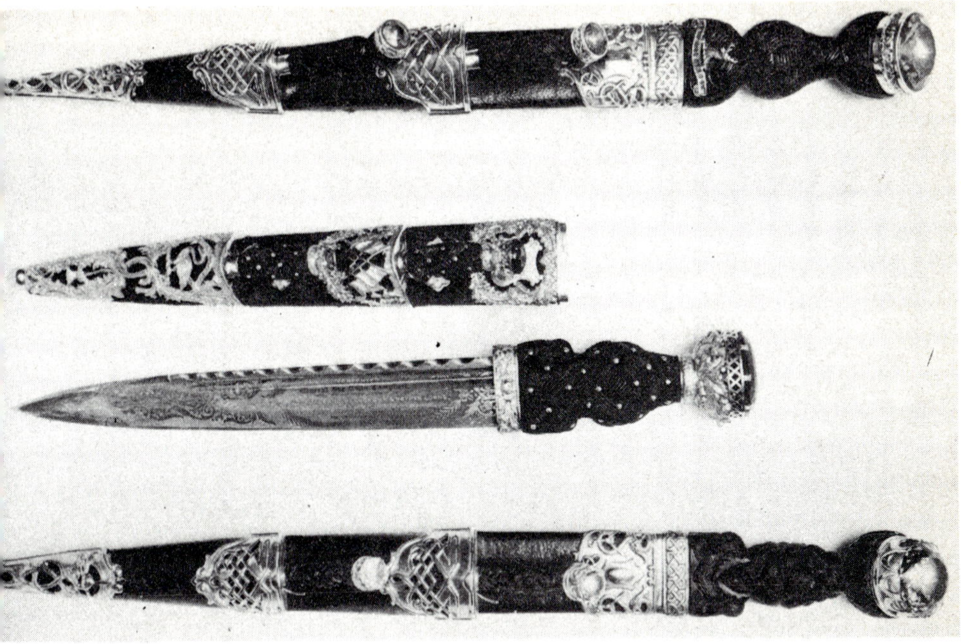

214 *Scottish dirks. Presentation dirks to Mackenzie Frazer 1902; General Colin Campbell 1856; 1873.*

215 *Scottish Skean dhus. Black Watch; Gordon Highlanders; Highland Light Infantry; Seaforth Highlanders; Cameron Highlanders. All* circa *1910.*

215

216

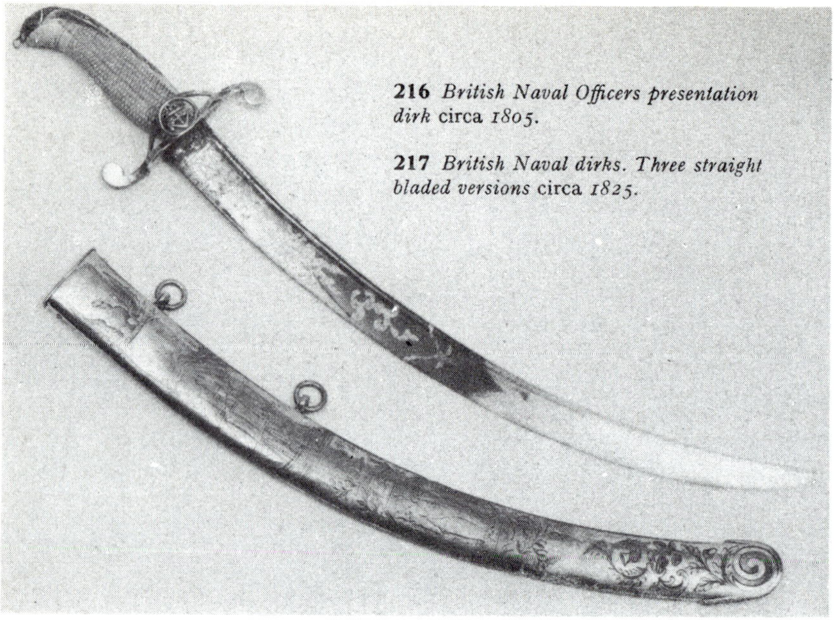

216 *British Naval Officers presentation dirk* circa *1805*.

217 *British Naval dirks. Three straight bladed versions* circa *1825*.

217

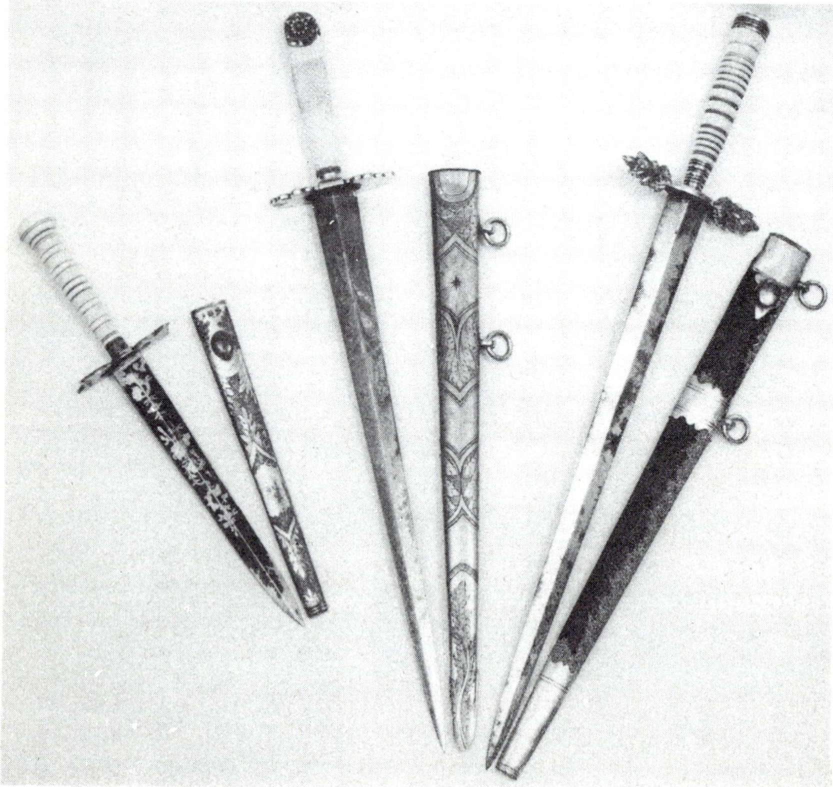

218 *British Naval dirks. Patt. 1856; Patt. 1879; Patt. 1879 (after 1891). Further version of Patt. 1856.*

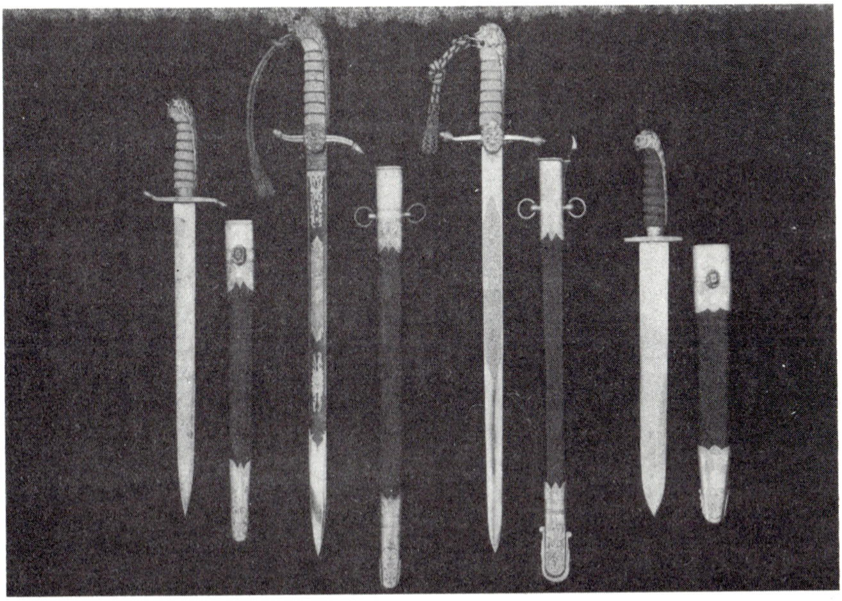

219 *German Naval dirks. Imperial Navy 1871–1918; Navy dirk 1929–38.*

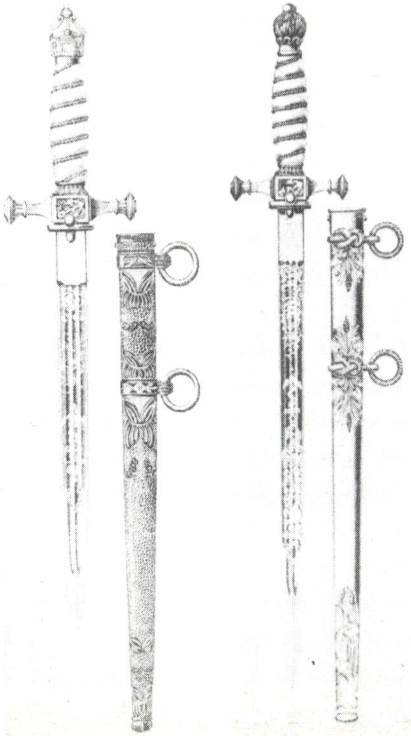

220 *German Naval dirks. Two versions of the side arm used by Midshipmen 1872–90 and by Engineer Cadets 1890–1918.*

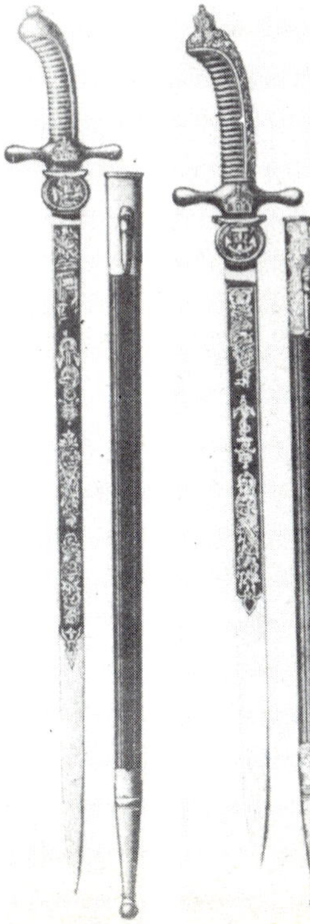

221 *Mexican dirks. Military cadets dirk* circa *1910; Naval cadets dirk* circa *1910.*

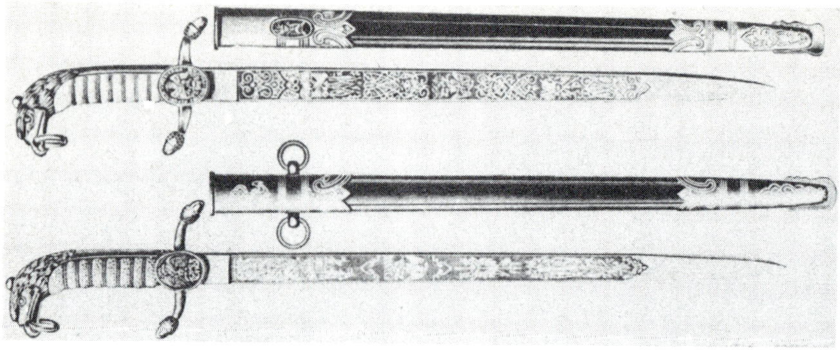

222 *Dirks supplied by Eickhorn of Solingen, Germany to South American countries; Naval dirk; Musicians dirk.*

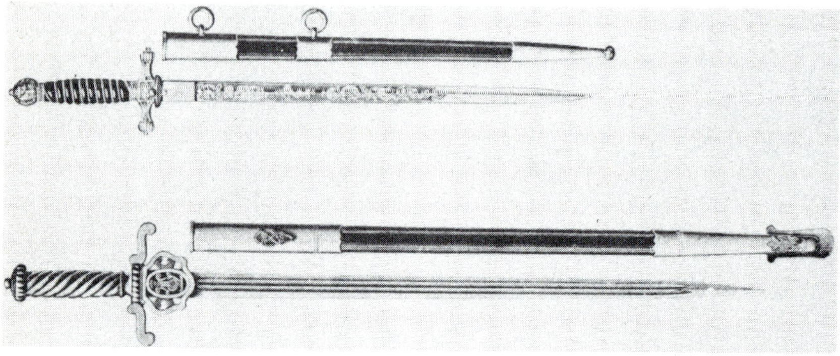

223 *Saw backed bladed bowie knife 1965; Prototype Royal Air Force survival knife by Wilkinson 1958; German hunting knife by Puma 1970; Folding bowie knife; Swedish barrel knife; Wilkinson RJH jungle knife.*

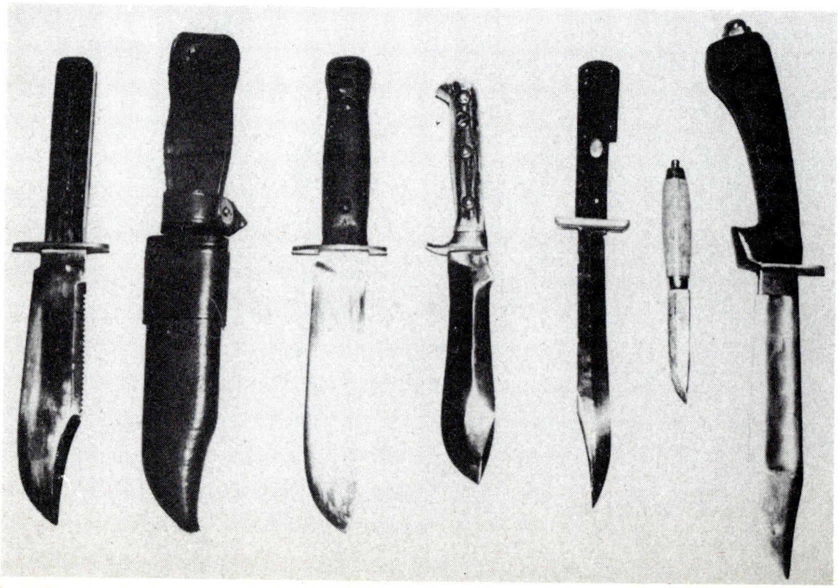

224 *Indian all steel* katar *or punch dagger; English plug bayonet* circa *1680; Japanese gold mounted* aikuchi; *Imperial German dress dagger; Sheffield bowie knife mid-19th century; German silver mounted bowie knife mid-19th century.*

225 *British bowie knife* circa *1865; British bowie knife cum skinning knife* circa *1860; Large British bowie knife by G. Wostenholm marked 'IXL'* (*I Excel*)*; Sheffield made bowie knife* circa *1870; Bowie knife with gazelle horn grip.*

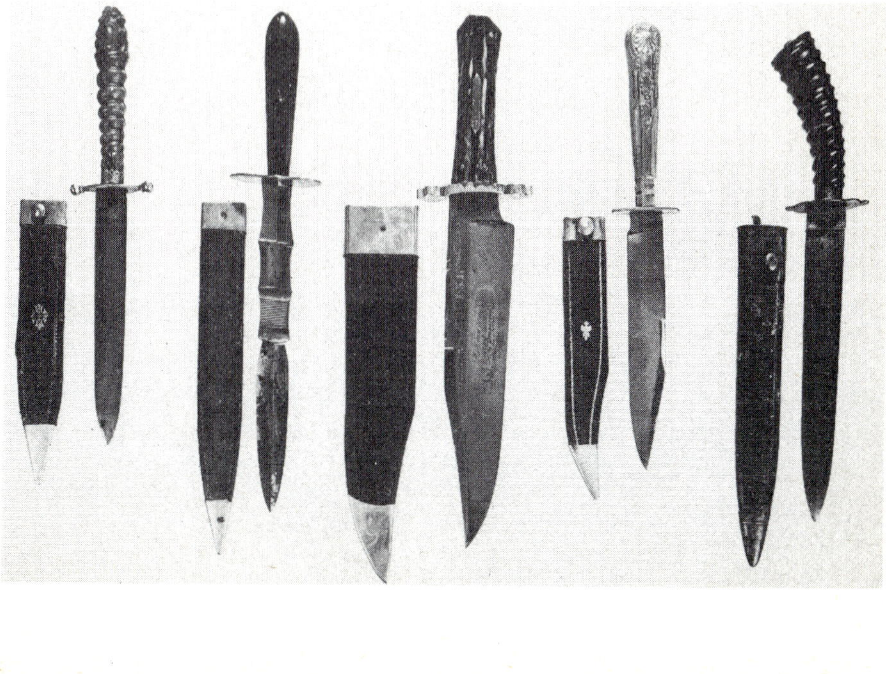

226 *British Commando knife (Commemorative version made by Wilkinson Sword Ltd in 1946); Russian Commando knife* circa *1942* and **227** *Shakespeare knife by Wilkinson* circa *1880 designed by Col. Shakespeare of the Indian Army.*

226

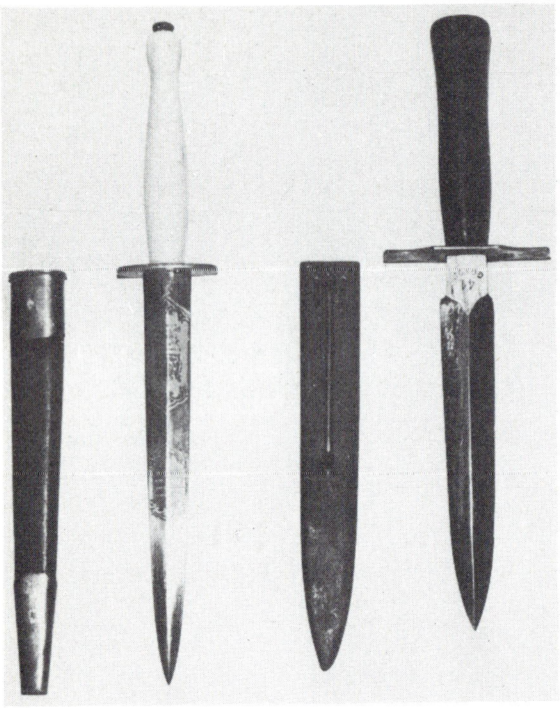

227

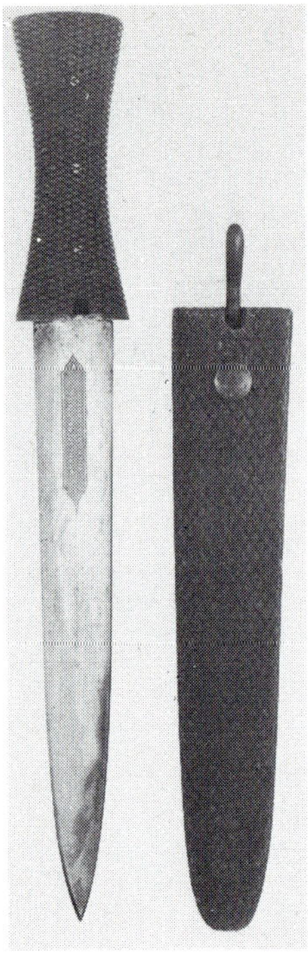

228 *Japanese* Hachiwara *or parrying weapon; Japanese silver mounted* aikuchi; *Japanese* tanto.

228

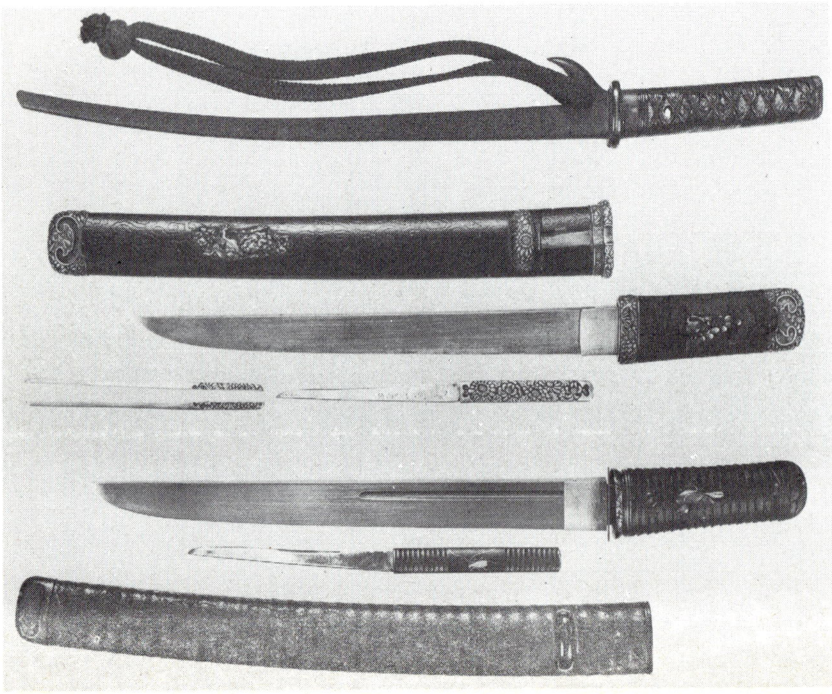

229 *Kukri with 10½ins blade and silver engraved and pierced mounts to the sheath*, and **230** *Indian 19th century* katar; *Indian 19th century betel nut knife; Arab 19th century jambiya; Indian* khanjar.

29

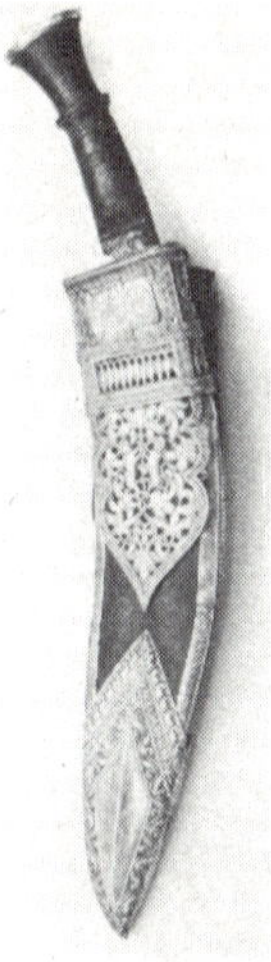

230

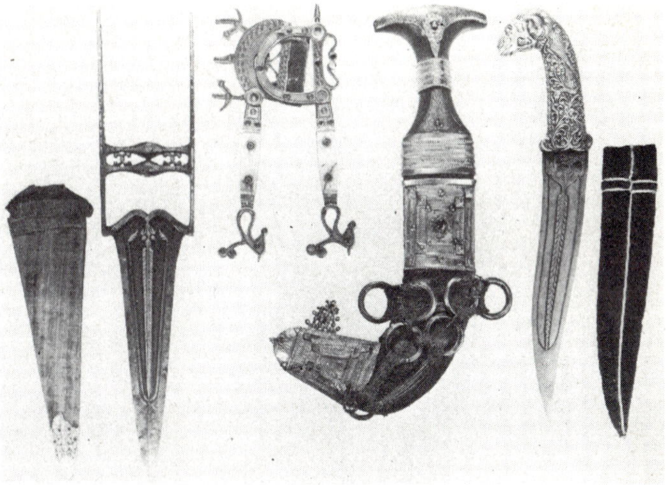

231 *Japanese* hamidachi *dagger; Cossack* kindjal; *Indian* khanjar; *Persian* kard; *Persian* kard.

31

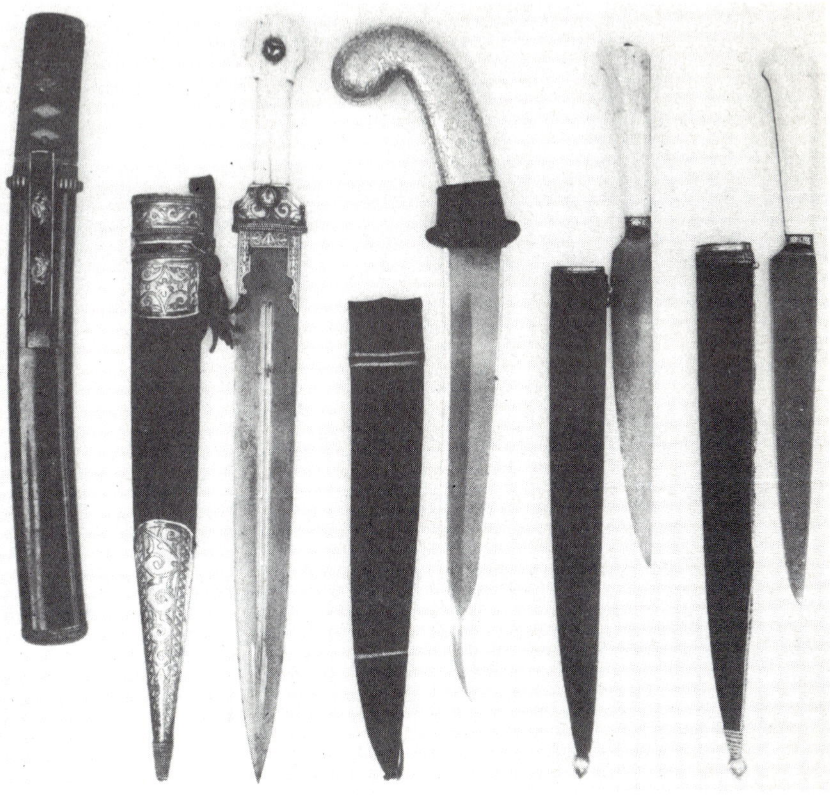

232 *German naval dirk early 19th century; British naval dirk* circa *1800; Plug bayonet late 17th century; Split socket bayonet early 18th century; Japanese* aikuchi; *Tibetan brass exorcising dagger; Tibetan exorcising dagger; Indian jambiya.*

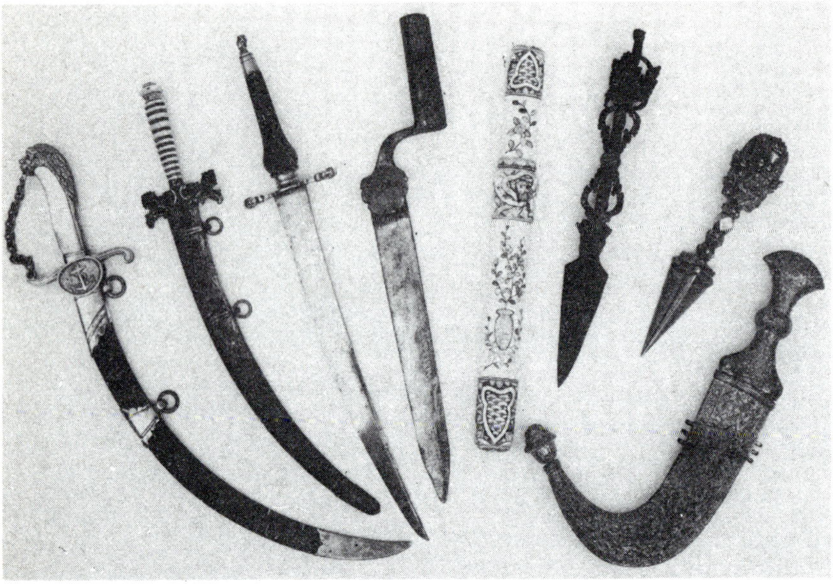

233 *Japanese* kwarken; *Javanese* kris; *Arab jambiya; Caucasian* kindjal; *Japanese* aikuchi.

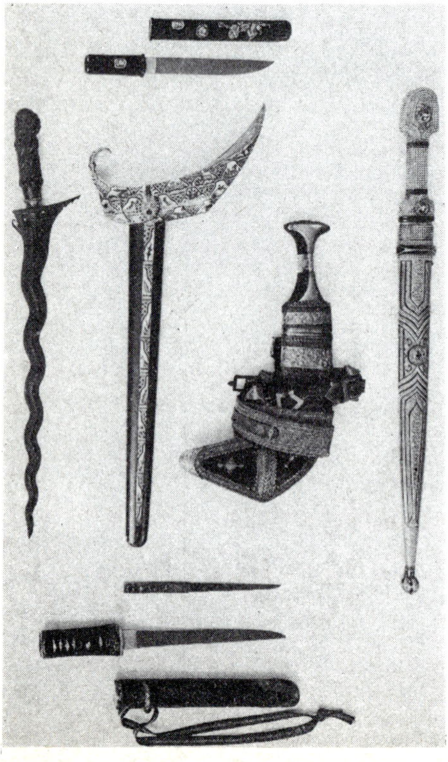

234 *Cossack* kindjal.

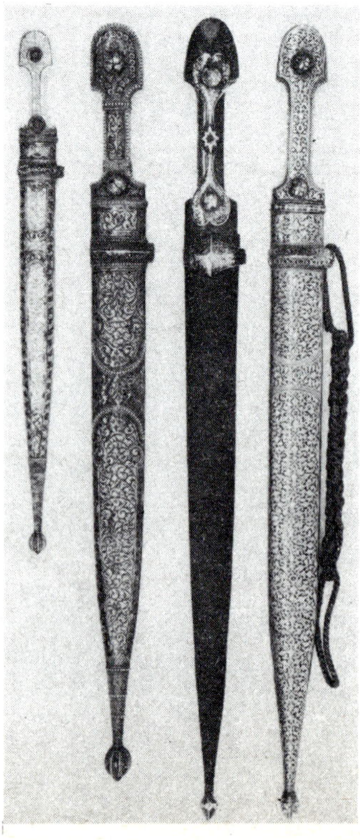

Indian kindjals. *Far right: Indian* anum.

Arab jambiya; Indian 18th century gold and elled dagger.

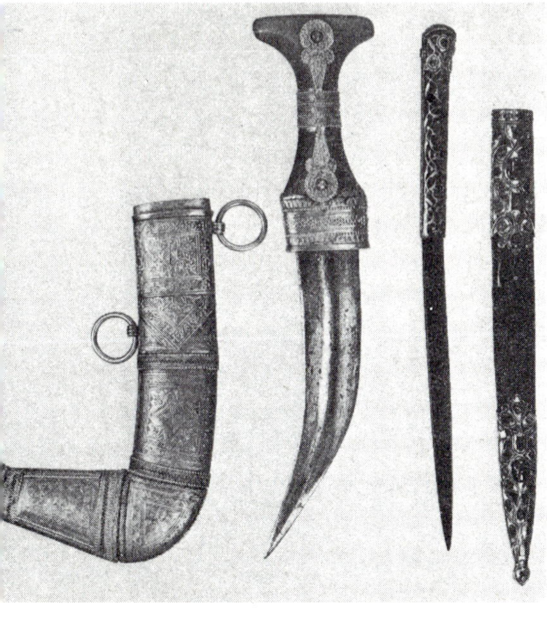

237 *Sumatra* kris; *Malay* kris.

238 *Indian* pata *or gauntlet sword 19th century; Gold hilted* kris; *Indian* pata *or gauntlet sword.*

239 *Indian jambiya; Indian Pesh Kabz; United States Krag model 1898 bowie blades bayonet; British 1858 pattern bayonet for Irish constabulary carbine.*

240 *Beaver tailed bowie knife, American* circa *1860; Ivory hilted stiletto* circa *1860; British naval dirk* circa *1810; American bowie knife* circa *1850.*

238

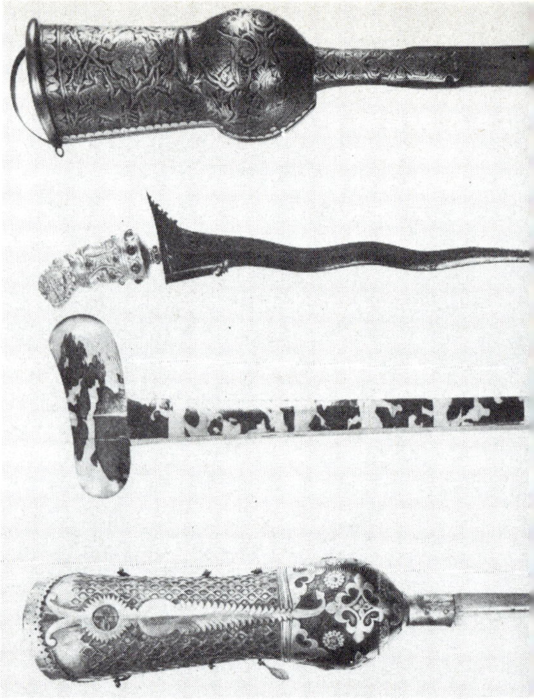

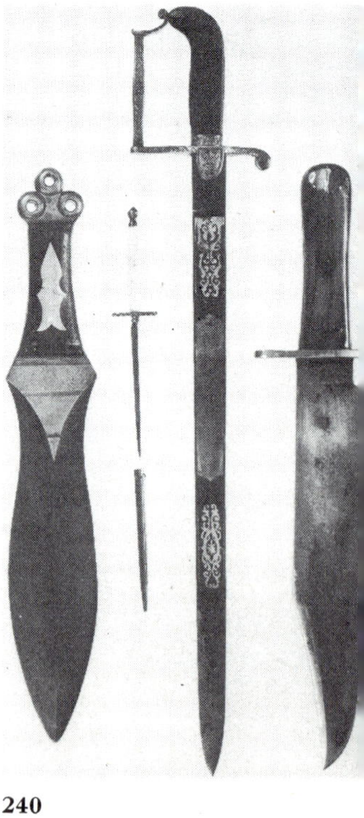

239 **240**

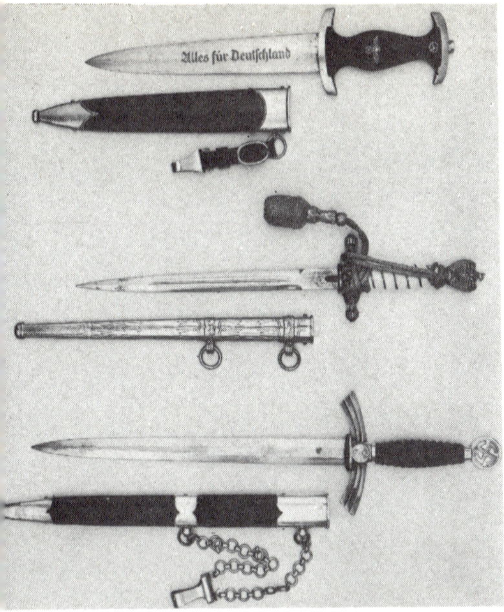

242

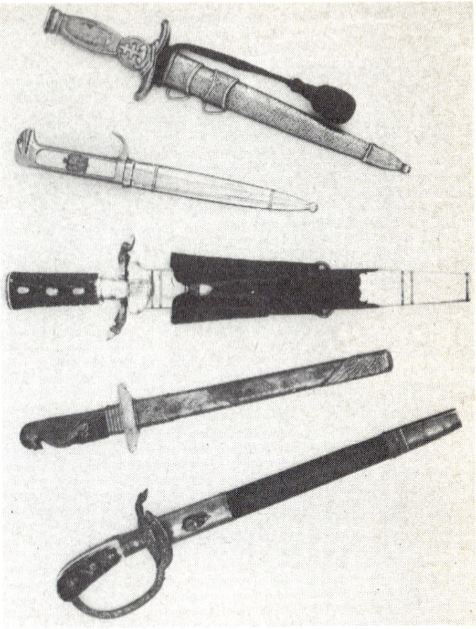

241 *Nazi German. SA dagger 1933;* Kriegsmarine (*Navy*) *dagger 1938;* Luftwaffe (*Air Force*) *flyers dagger 1935.*

242 *Nazi Slovak Air Force dagger; Italian Fascist dagger* circa *1940; Imperial German hunting dagger; Japanese Air Force dagger; Nazi German Forestry officials dagger.*

243 *Imperial Austrian naval officers dirk 19th century; Nazi RLB Officers dagger; Roumanian Air Force officers dagger 1940.*

243

244 *England. Plug bayonets, 17th century* and **245** *Swedish. Plug bayonet* circa *1680.*

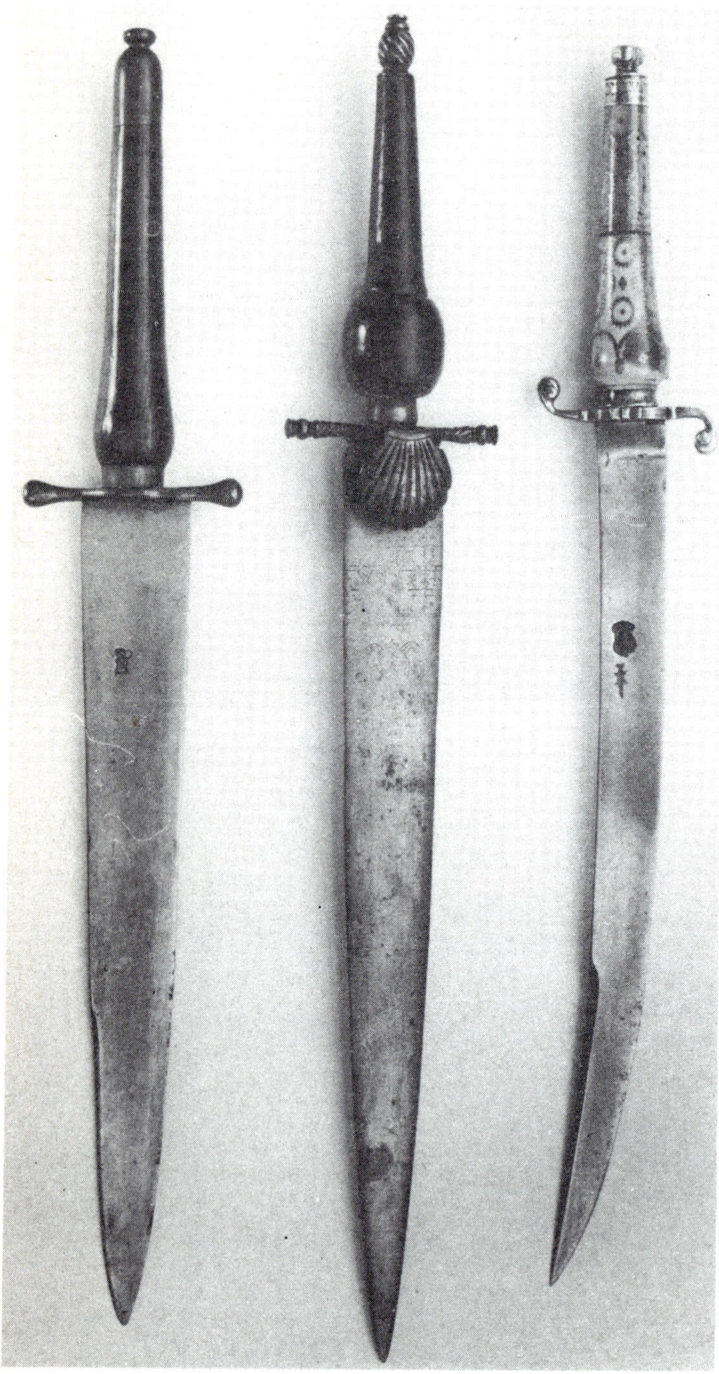

244

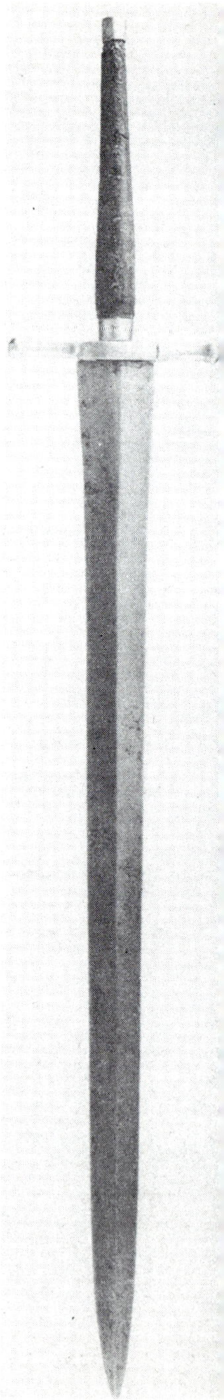

245

246 *Sweden. Hilt of plug bayonet showing spring for correct fit, patt. 1692.*

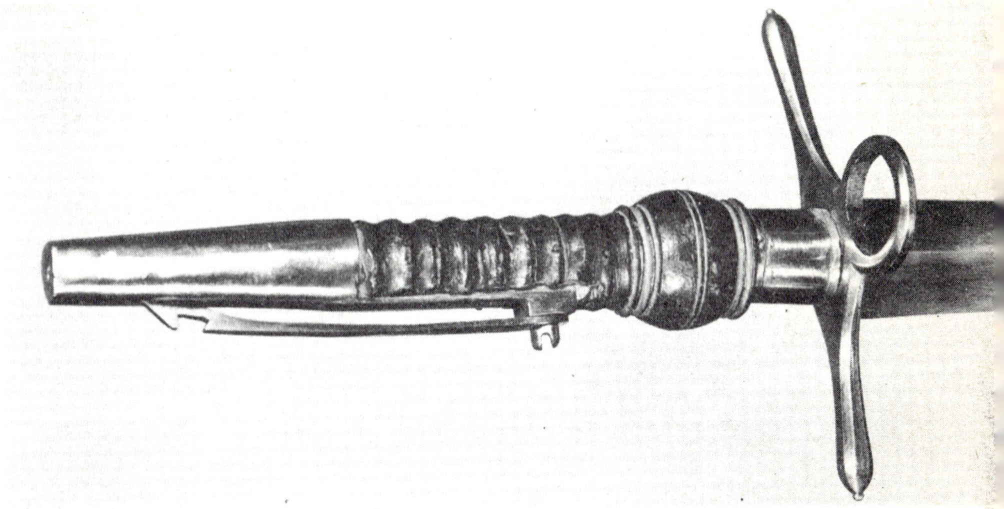

247 *Sweden. Socket bayonets with locking screws, patt. 1699; patt. 1701.*

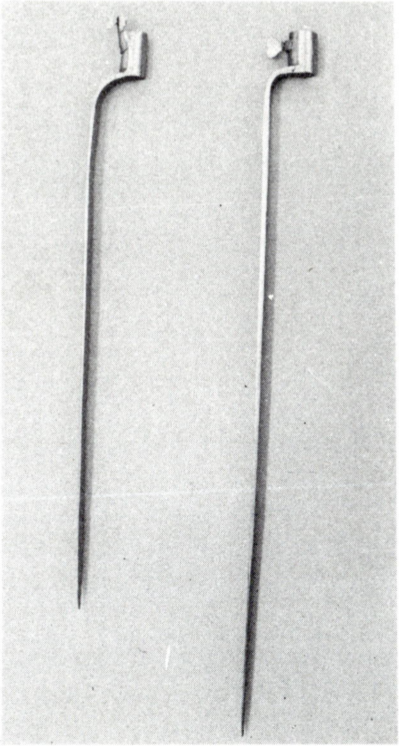

248 *Sweden. Socket bayonets with locking screws, patt. 1699; patt. 1738.*

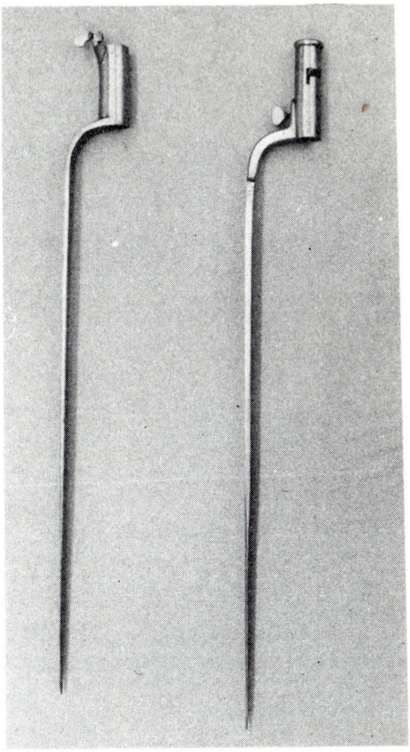

249 *Sweden. Socket bayonets with locking screws and rings, patt. 1700–1701; patt. 1716; patt. 1716.*

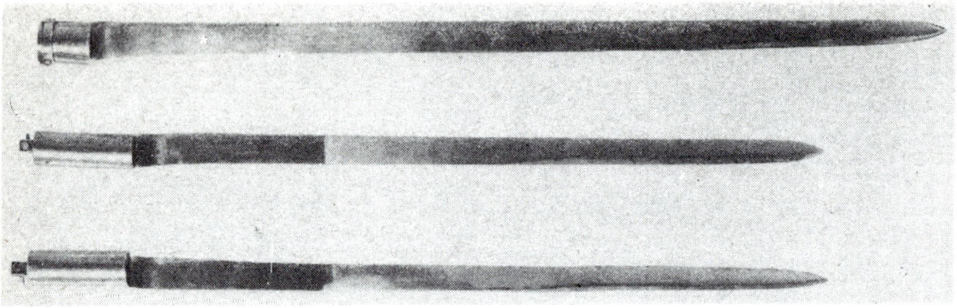

250 *British. Socket bayonet Irish Constabulary 1840; Split socket bayonet* circa *1705.*

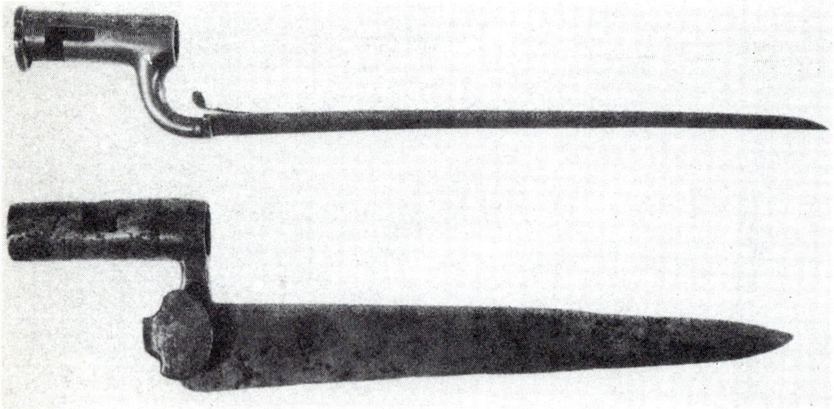

251 *British. Plug sword bayonet* circa *1690; Vivian Carbine bayonet patt. 1841.*

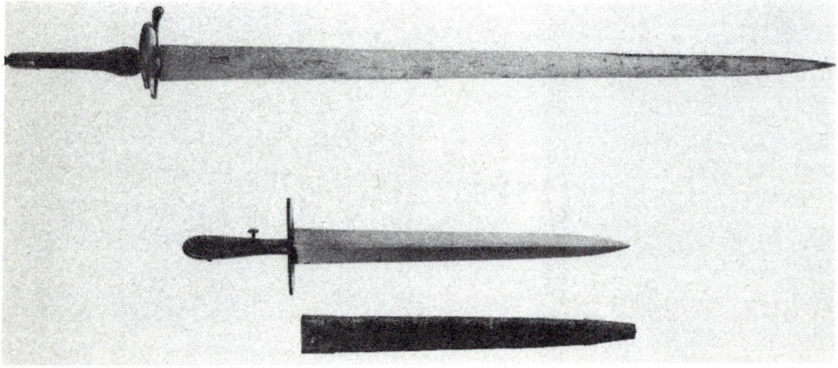

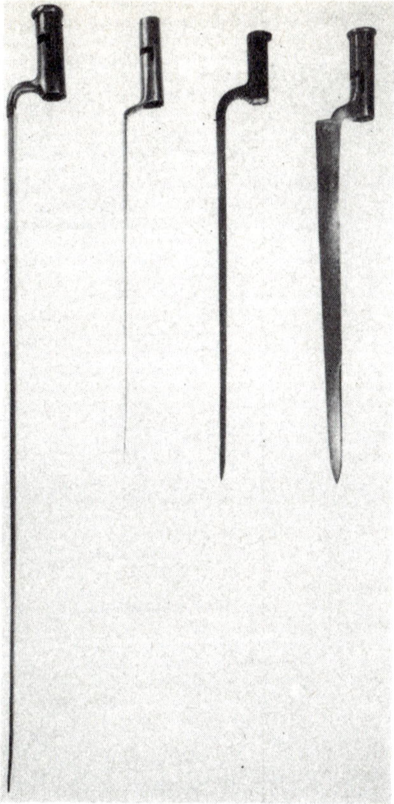

252

252 *British. Socket bayonets. Probins carbine 1750; Early socket* circa *1715; Brunswick rifle (Sergeants of Foot Guards) 1840;* circa *1720.*

253 *British bayonets. Baker rifle patts, Sword bayonet patt. 1801; Sword bayonet patt. 1800; hand bayonet patt. 1823; Socket bayonet 1819; Experimental hand bayonet.*

253

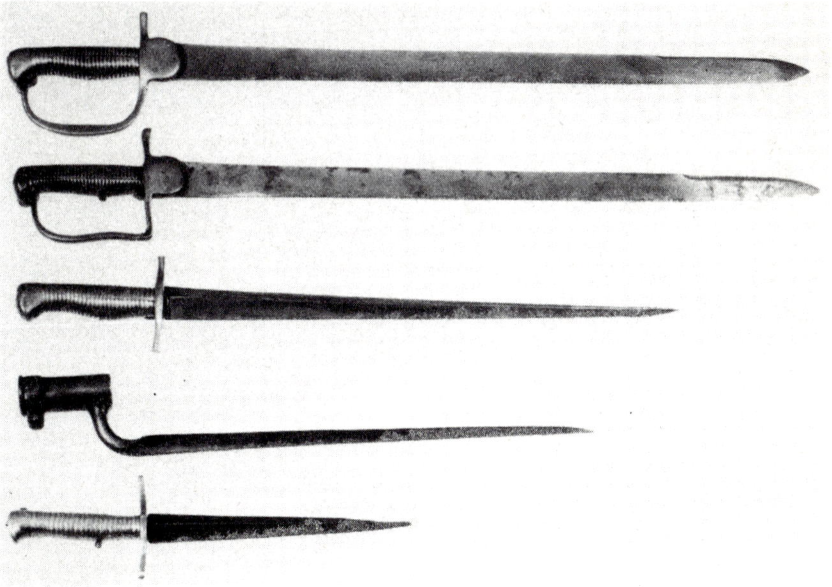

254

2

254 *British. Spear pointed socket bayonets for Eggs carbine 1784.*

255 *British. Volunteer sword/socket bayonet* circa *1796; Volunteer sword/ socket bayonet* circa *1790; Sappers and Miners sword/socket bayonet patt. 1841.*

256 *British. Sappers and Miners patt. 1843; Socket/sword bayonets* circa *1780;* circa *1740.*

257 *British. Sword bayonets for Brunswick rifle, patt. 1848; patt. 1836.*

258 *British. Socket bayonets with locking rings; Enfield patt. 1853; Martini-Enfield patt. 1895; Martini-Henry patt. 1876.*

259 *British. Sword bayonets, patt. 1856 with falchion blade; patt. 1856 with yatagan shaped blade.*

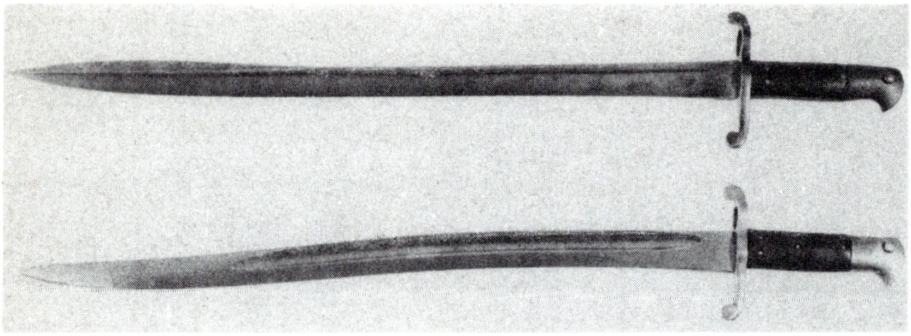

260 *British. Privately made sword bayonet for Jacob's double barrel rifle patt. 1856.*

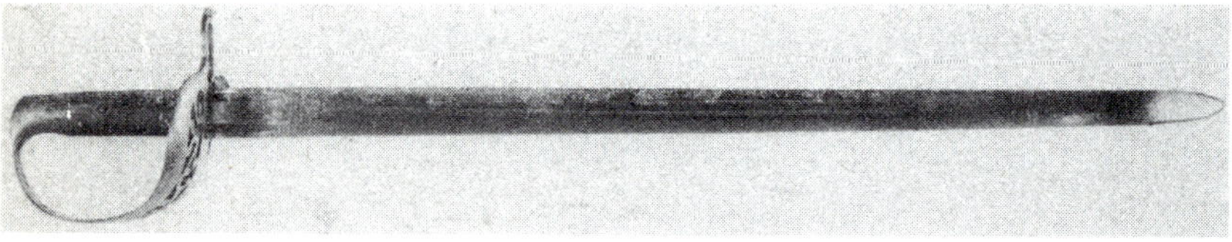

261 *British. Naval sword cutlass bayonet patt. 1859 (approved 18th April). This original pattern has six horizontal grooves in each grip which was replaced by chequering in the new pattern approved 1st May.*

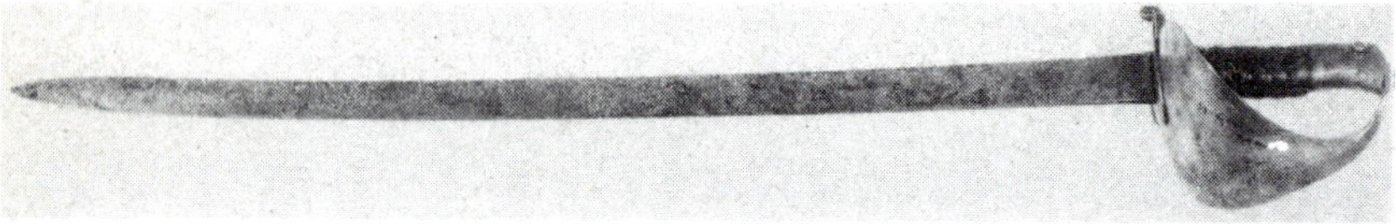

262 *British. Sword bayonets: Artillery patt. 1875; Elcho patt. 1871.*

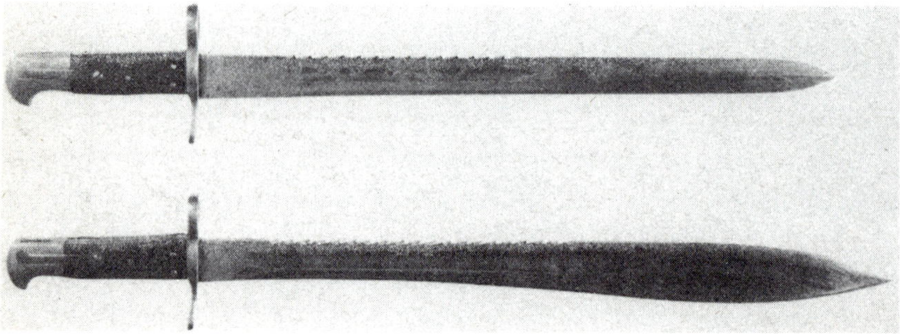

263

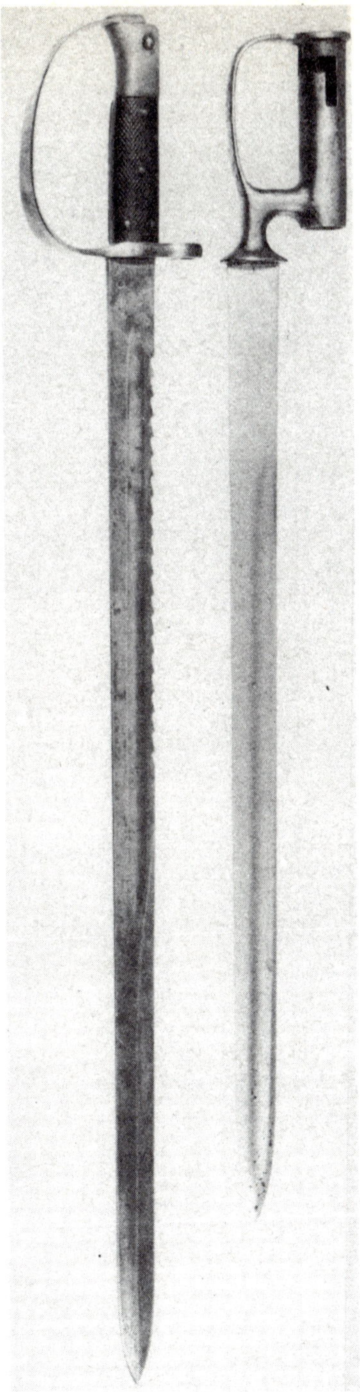

264

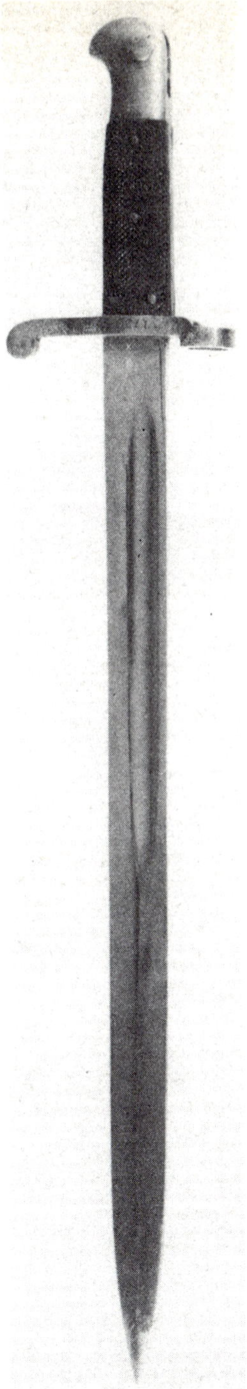

265

263 *British. Artillery sword bayonet patt. 1879; East India Company Sappers and Miners sword/socket bayonet patt. 1845.*

264 *British. Sword bayonet for Martini-Henry patt. 1886.*

265 *Canadian. Sword bayonet for Martini-Metford patt. 1893.*

266

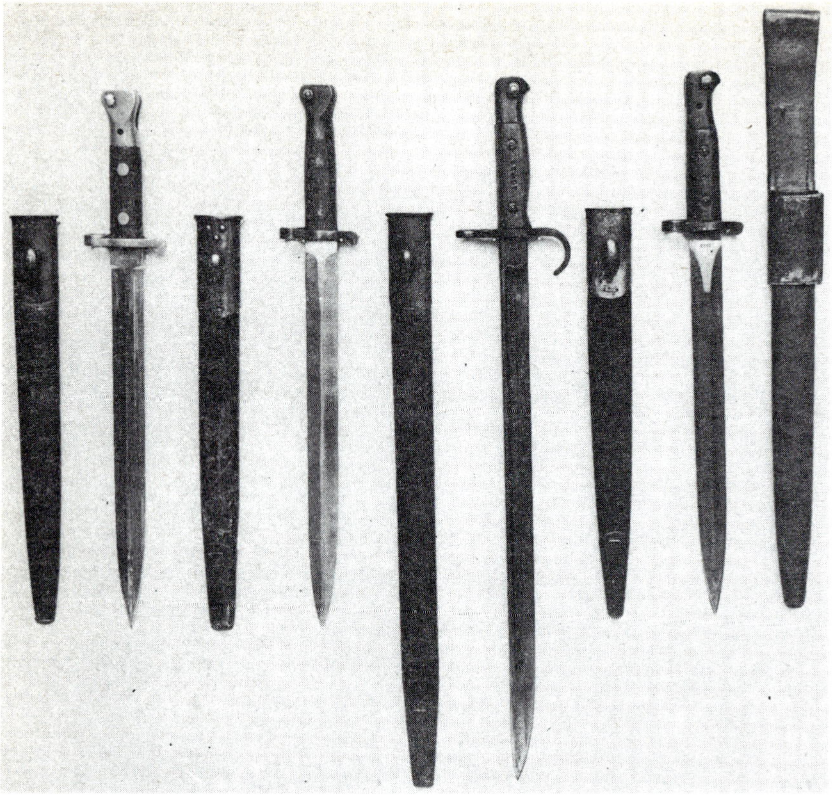

266 *British. Sword bayonets, patt. 1888 Mk II; Indian made patt. 1888; patt. 1913; patt. 1903.*

267 *British and Canadian. Sword bayonets; Canada Ross patt. 1910; British patt. 1907 (2nd model); patt. 1907 (original model); Canada Ross patt. 1910, pointed; Ross bayonet converted to hunting knife.*

267

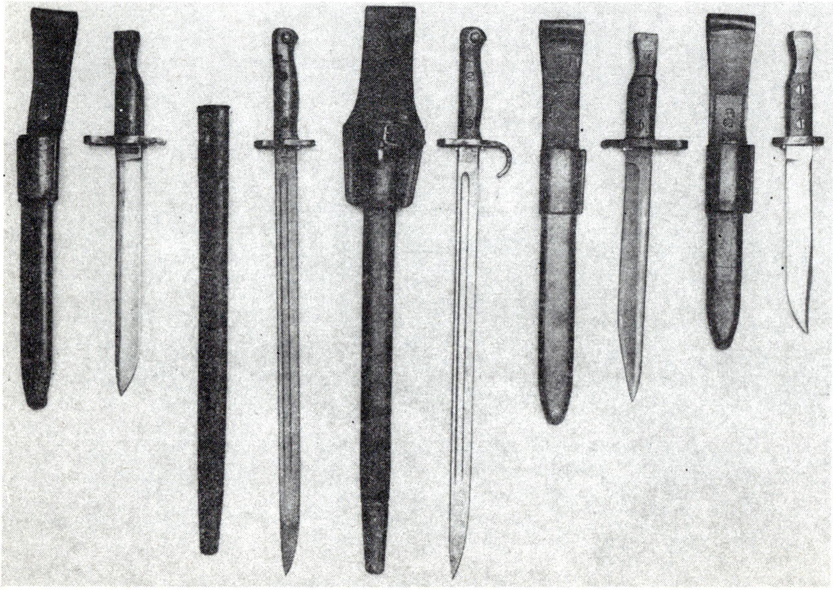

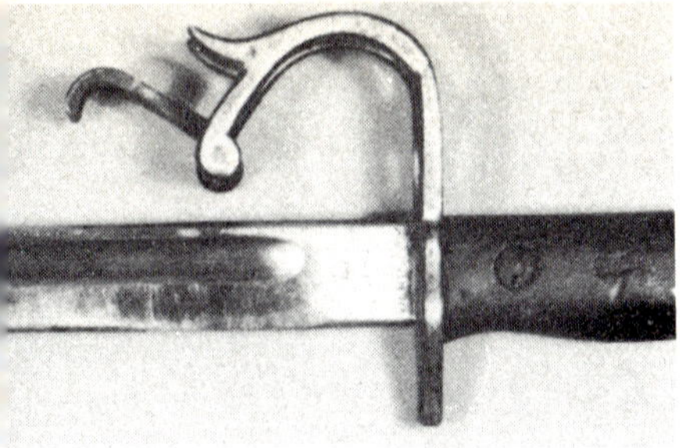

268 *British. Patt. 1907 adapted with wire cutting device.*

269 *British. Patt. 1907 with wire cutting attachment.*

270 *British. The various stages of manufacture of the patt. 1907 sword bayonet.*

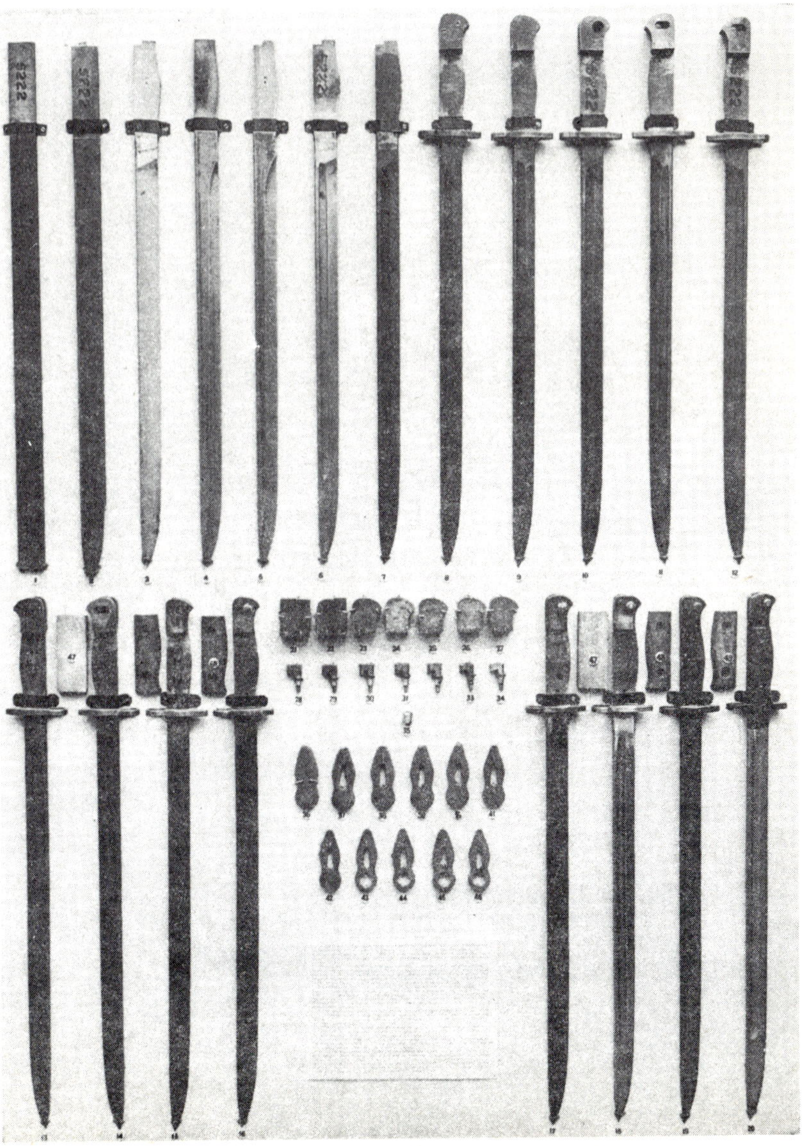

271

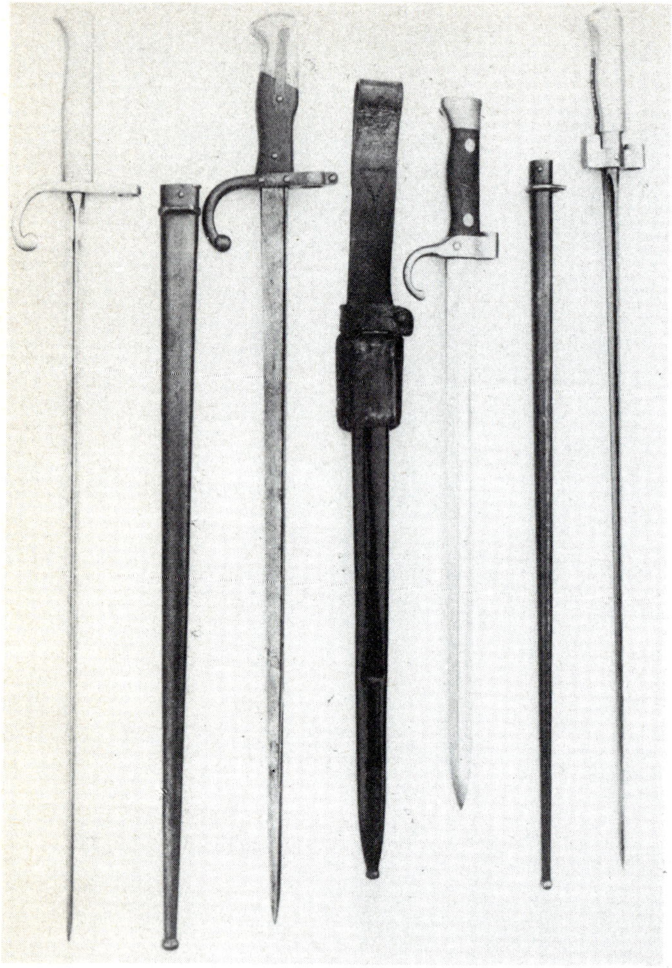

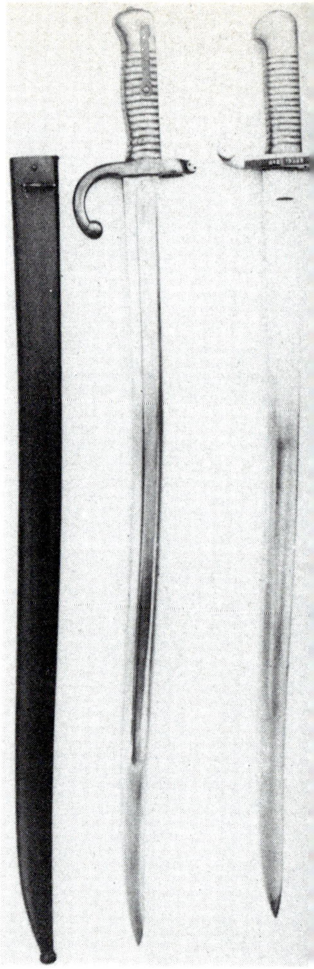

271 *French. Sword bayonets, patt. 1895 Daudetau; patt. 1875 for Gras rifle; patt. 1892 for Berthier carbine; patt. 1886 for Lebel rifle with quillon removed, 1916.*

272 *French. Sword bayonets, patt. 1868; patt. 1842.*

273 *French. Sword bayonet and carbine of the* Cent Gardes *1854–70.*

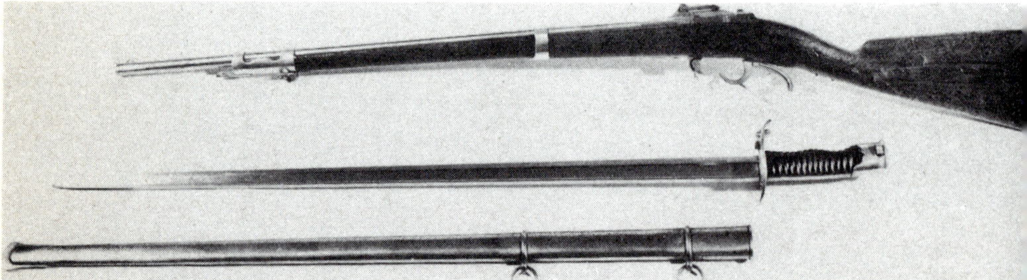

273

274 *French. Sword bayonet, patt. 1886 for Lebel rifle.*

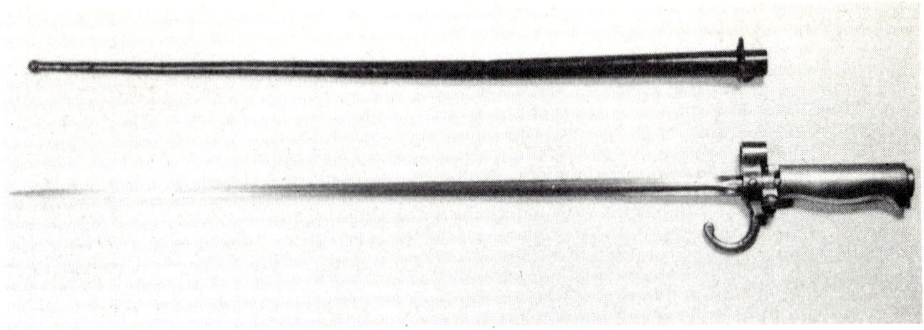

275 *Prussian. Sword bayonet or hirschfanger* circa *1812.*

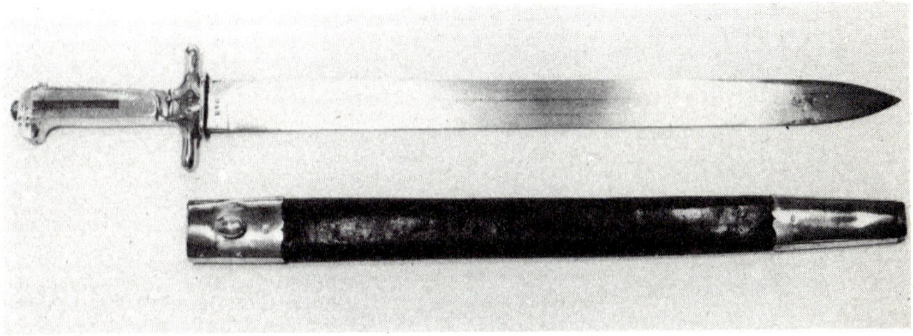

276 *German. Sword bayonets for Mauser rifle, patt. 1871; patt. 1871 dress bayonet with no pommel catch; patt. 1871 NCO's dress bayonet; patt. 1871–84.*

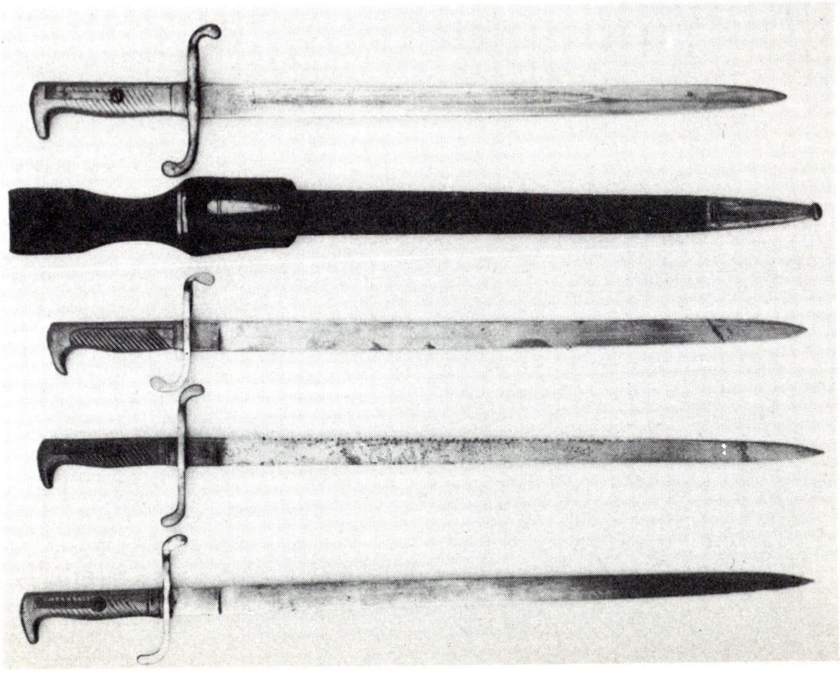

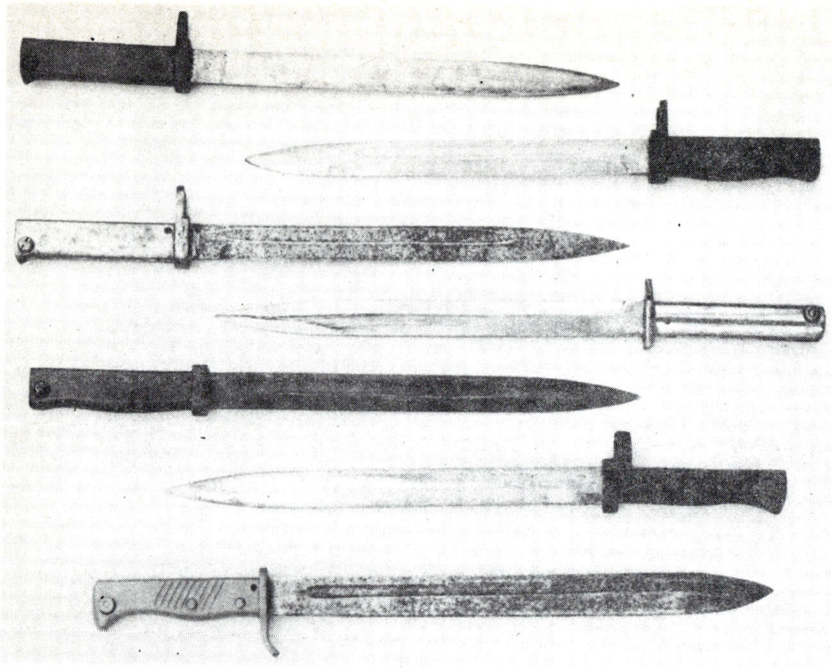

277

277 *German. Sword bayonets. A selection of World War I all steel emergency bayonets.*

278 *German. Sword bayonets, patt. 1898 with saw back for pioneers; patt. 1898–1905; patt. 1898–1905 emergency version with saw back; patt. 1898–1905 emergency version; patt. 1898 with saw back removed.*

278

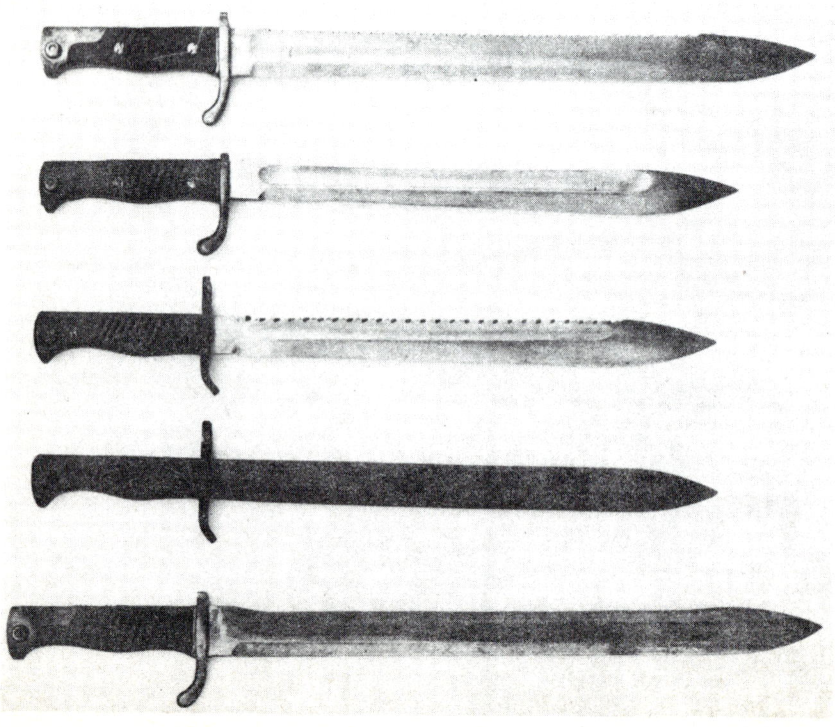

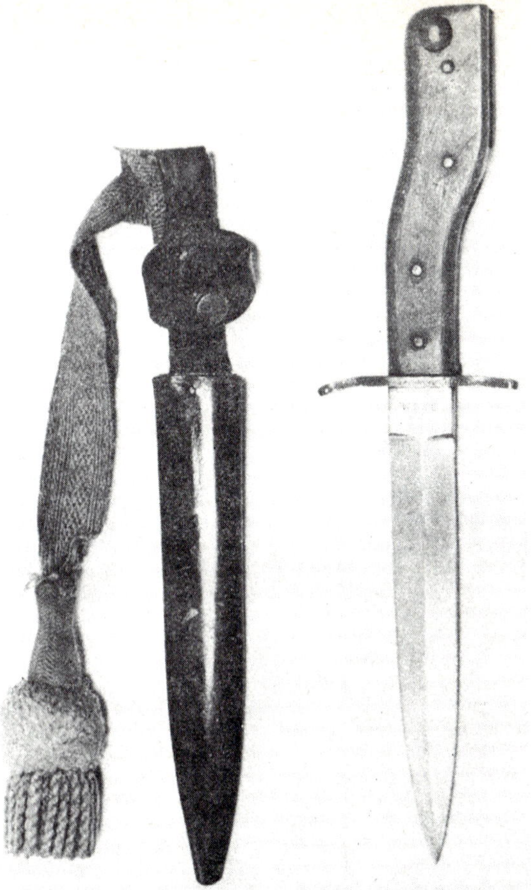

9

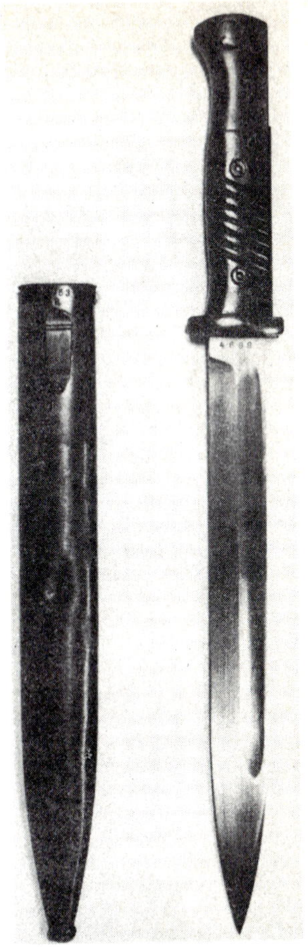

280

279 *German. Trench knife bayonet World War I with original dress knot and* **280** *German sword bayonet, patt. 1884–98 (this illustration is World War II vintage).*

281 *Danish. Socket and ramrod bayonets, shortened patt. 1794 with Khyl's leaf spring; patt. 1794 with Kyhl's leaf spring; patt. 1791 with Kyhl's locking ring; patt. 1789 ramrod bayonet; patt. 1785; patt. 1769; patt. 1769 long version.*

31

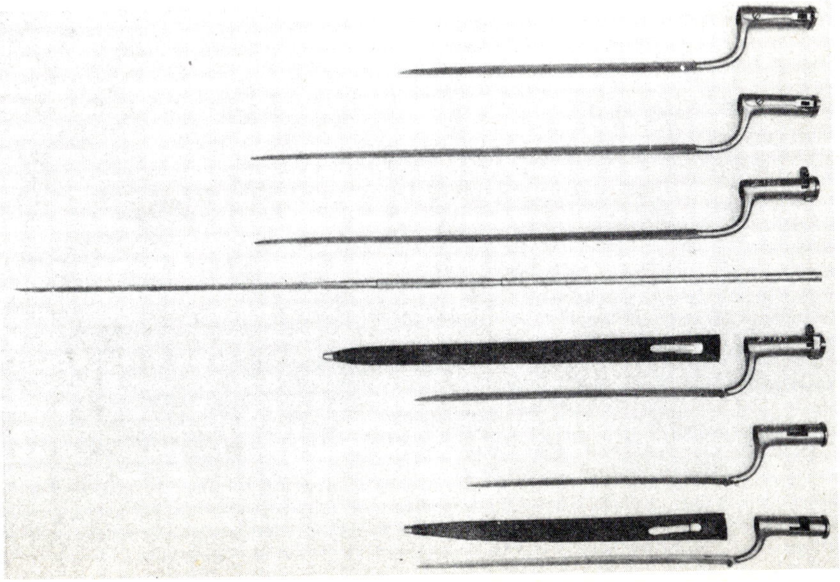

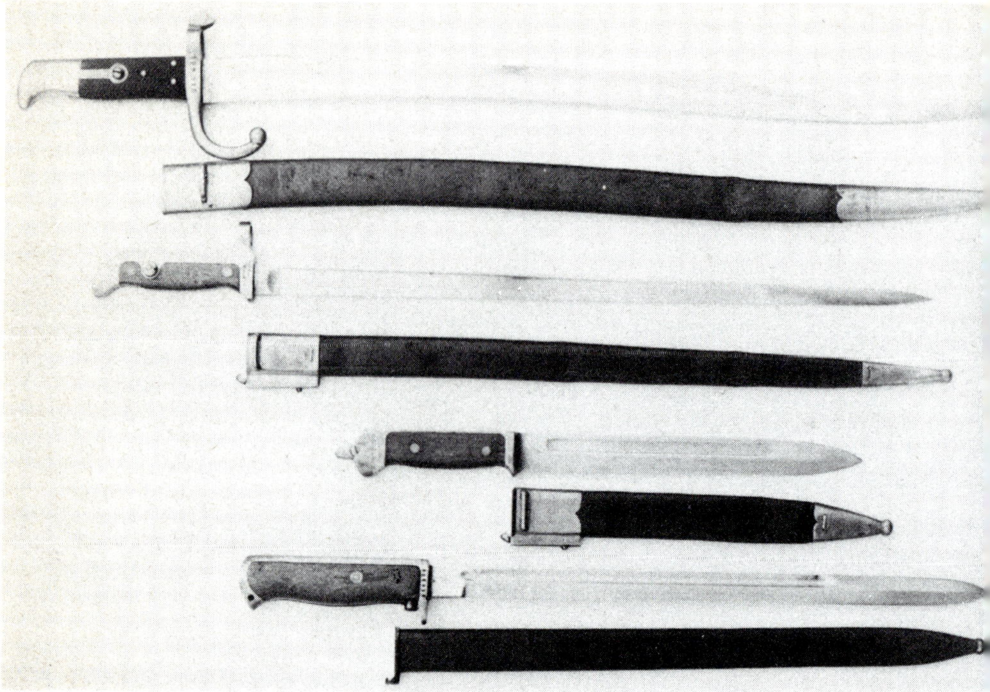

282 *Danish, patt. 1867; 1917; 1889; Norwegian, patt. 1912.*

283 *Norwegian, patt. 1894 with grips removed showing locking mechanism. This example shortened by Nazis during World War II*

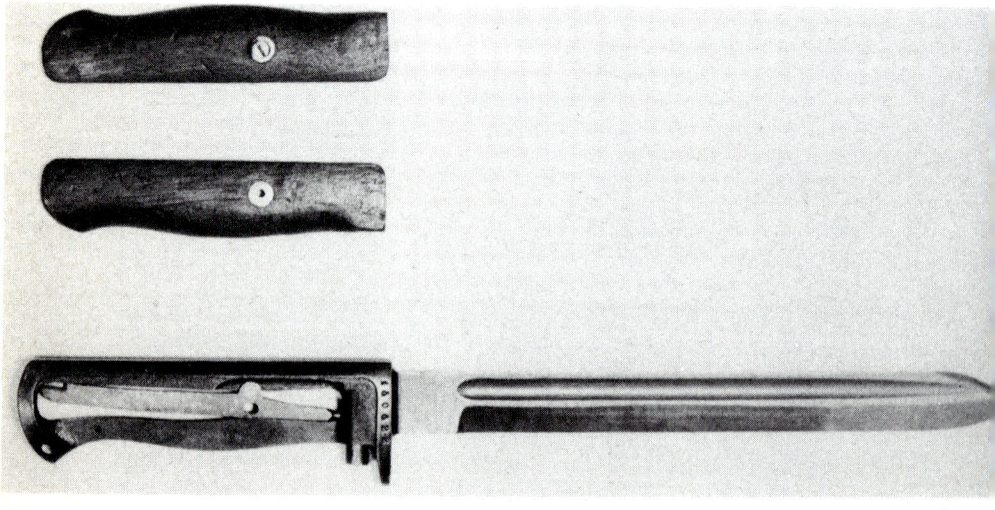

285

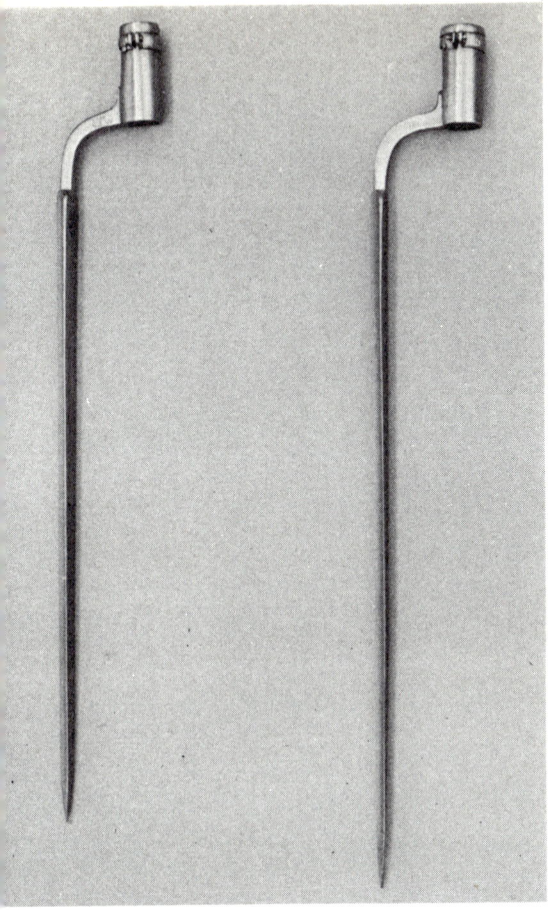

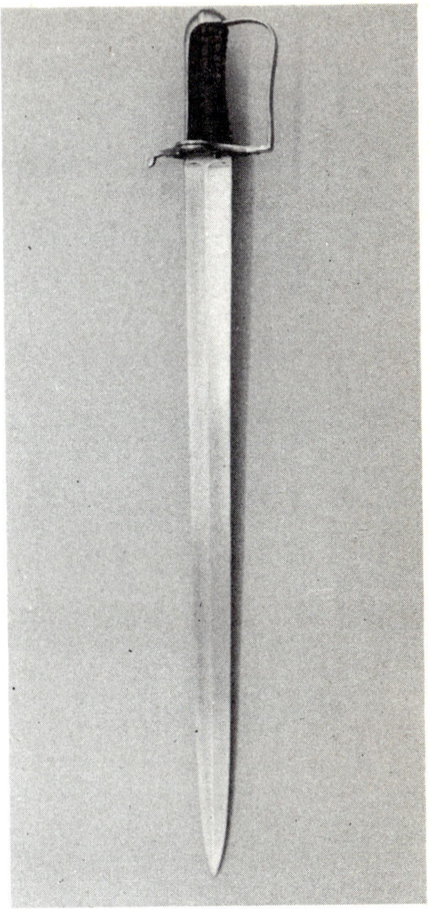

284 *Swedish. Socket bayonets, patt. 1815; patt. 1811,* and **285** *Swedish. Sword bayonet patt. 1815 for Jaeger rifle.*

286 *Swedish. Sword bayonet patt. 1896.*

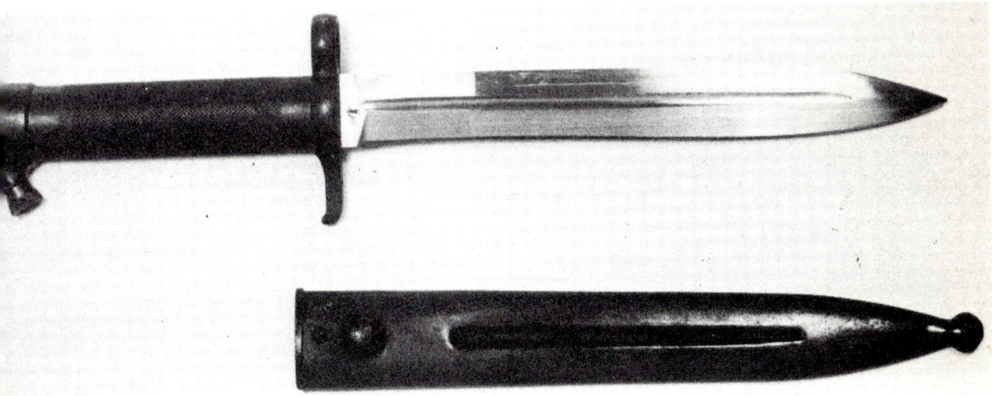

287

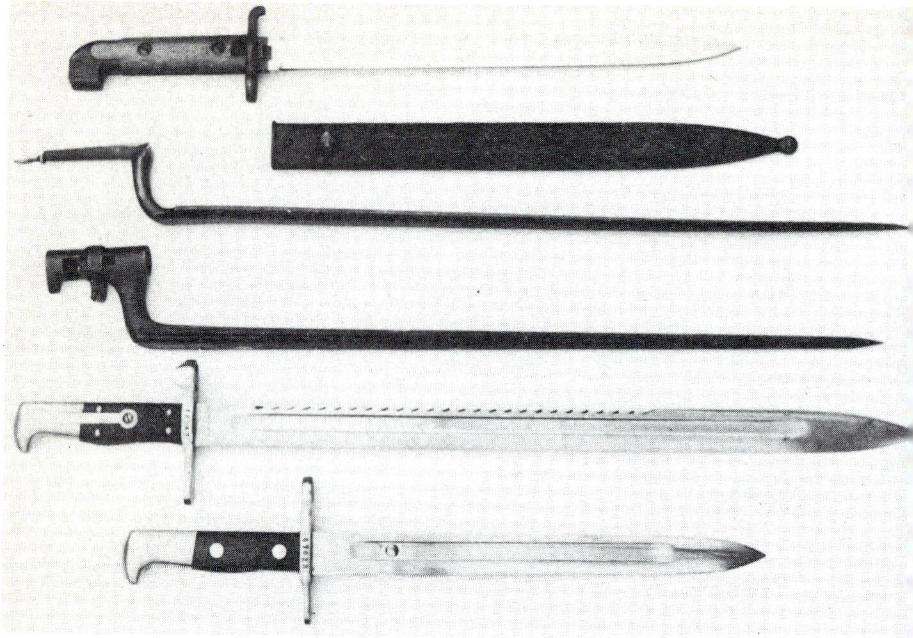

288

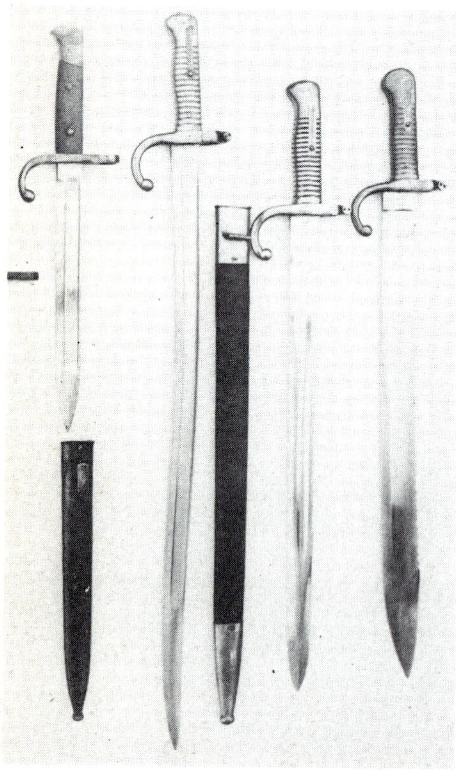

287 *Swedish sword bayonet, patt. 1898; Swiss. Sword and socket bayonets, patt. 1850 for Federal rifle; patt. 1868; patt. 1880–1888; patt. 1893.*

288 *Belgian. Sword bayonets, patt. 1889; 1868; 1880; 1880.*

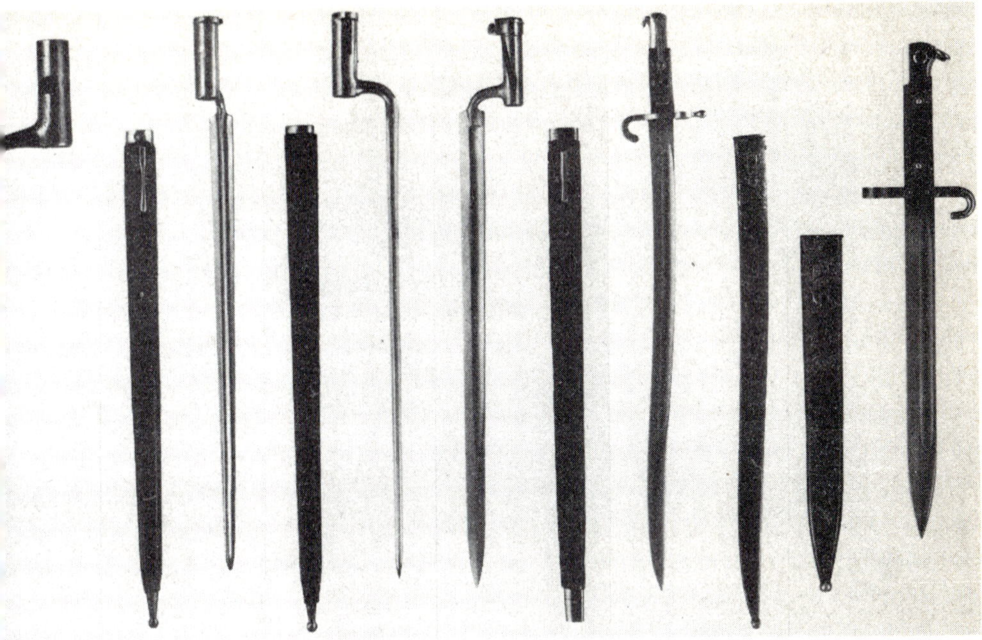

289 *Austrian. Sword and socket bayonets, patt. 1784; patt. 1799; patt. 1838; patt. 1854 Lorenze rifle; patt. 1867 Werndl rifle; patt. 1895 Mannlicher-Steyr rifle.*

290 *Spanish socket and sword bayonets, patt. 1916 Mauser, Artillery; patt. 1893–43 Mauser; patt. 1869 Remington; Swiss* circa *1860* (?).

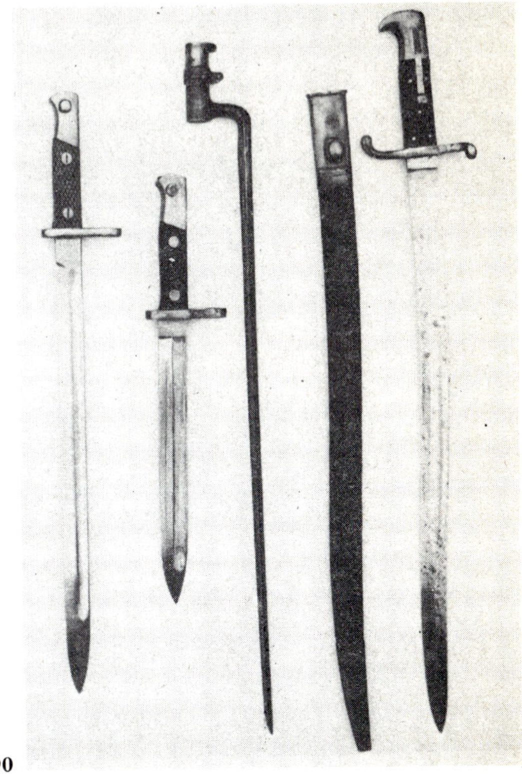

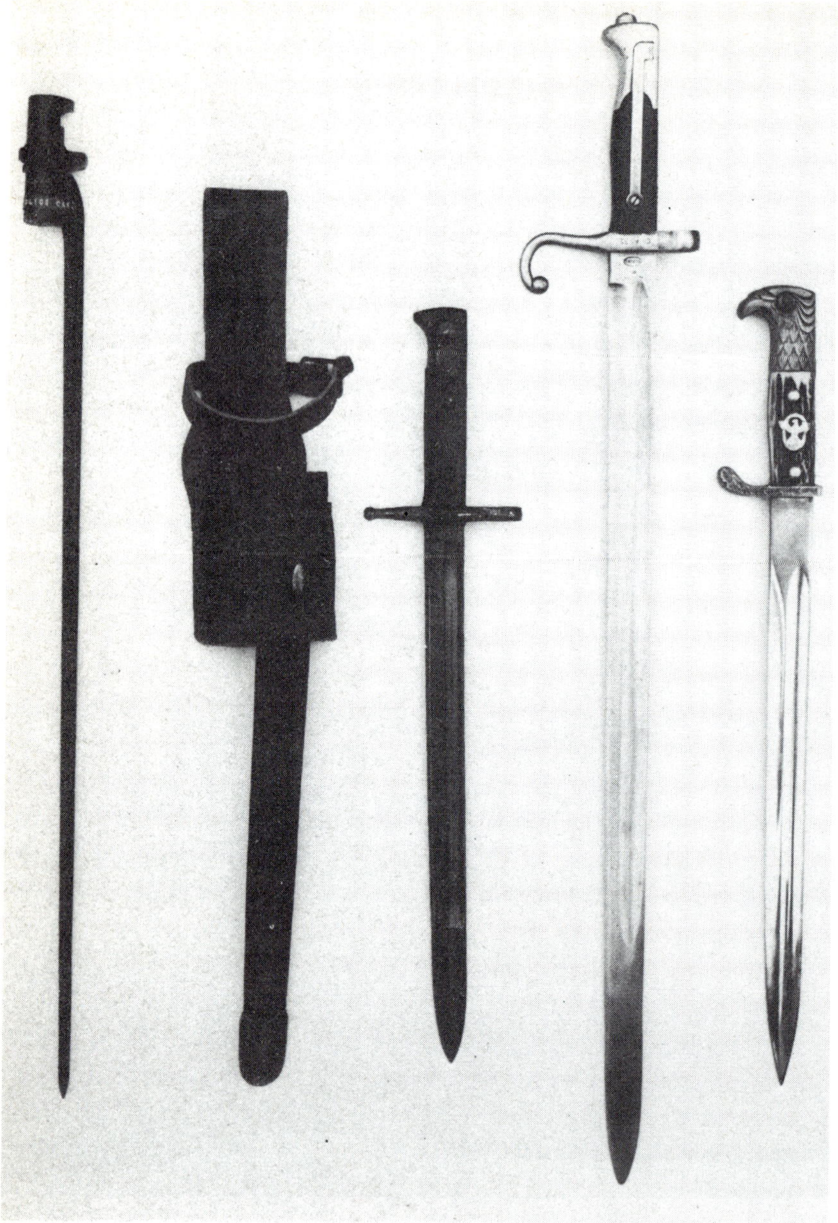

291 *Italian. Sword and socket bayonets, patt. 1897; patt. 1891 in Engineer pattern frog; patt. 1870 Vetterli. Nazi Police dress bayonet.*

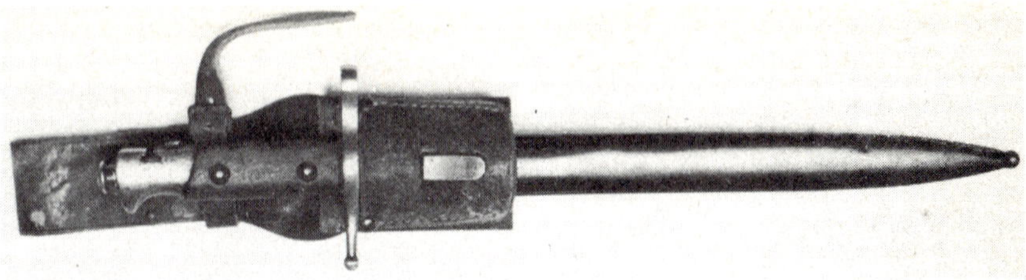

292 *Italian. Sword bayonet, patt. 1891–1897 with press stud on top of pommel.*

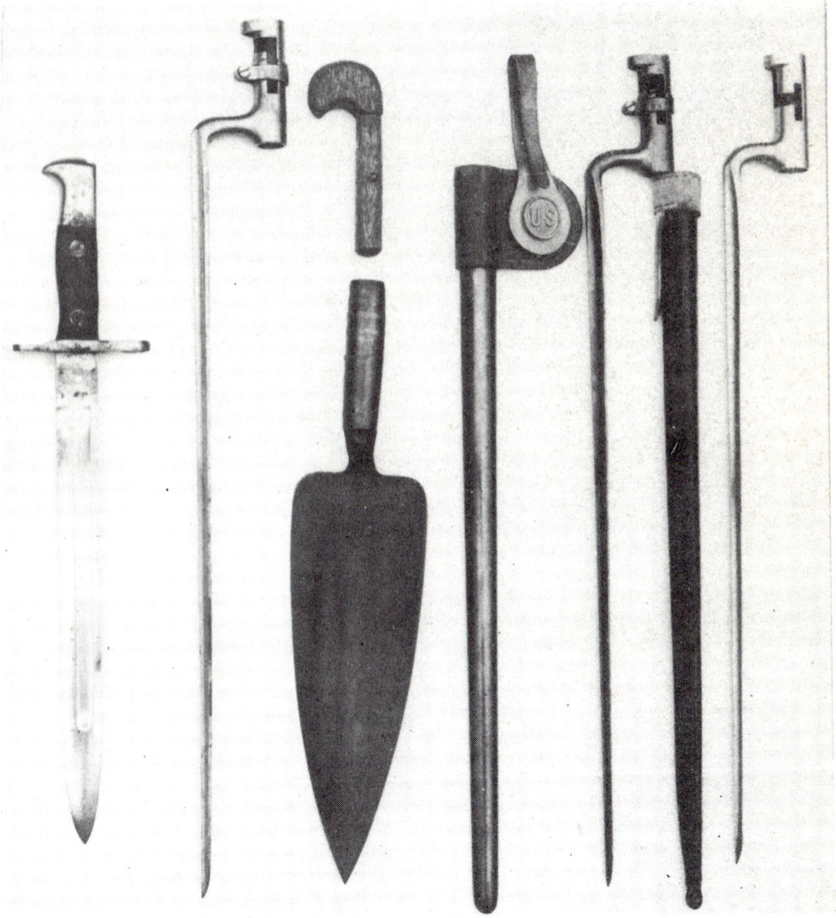

293 *USA. Sword and socket bayonets, patt. 1892 Krag; patt. 1866 Winchester; patt. 1873 Springfield trowel; patt. 1873 Springfield; patt. 1854 Maynard.*

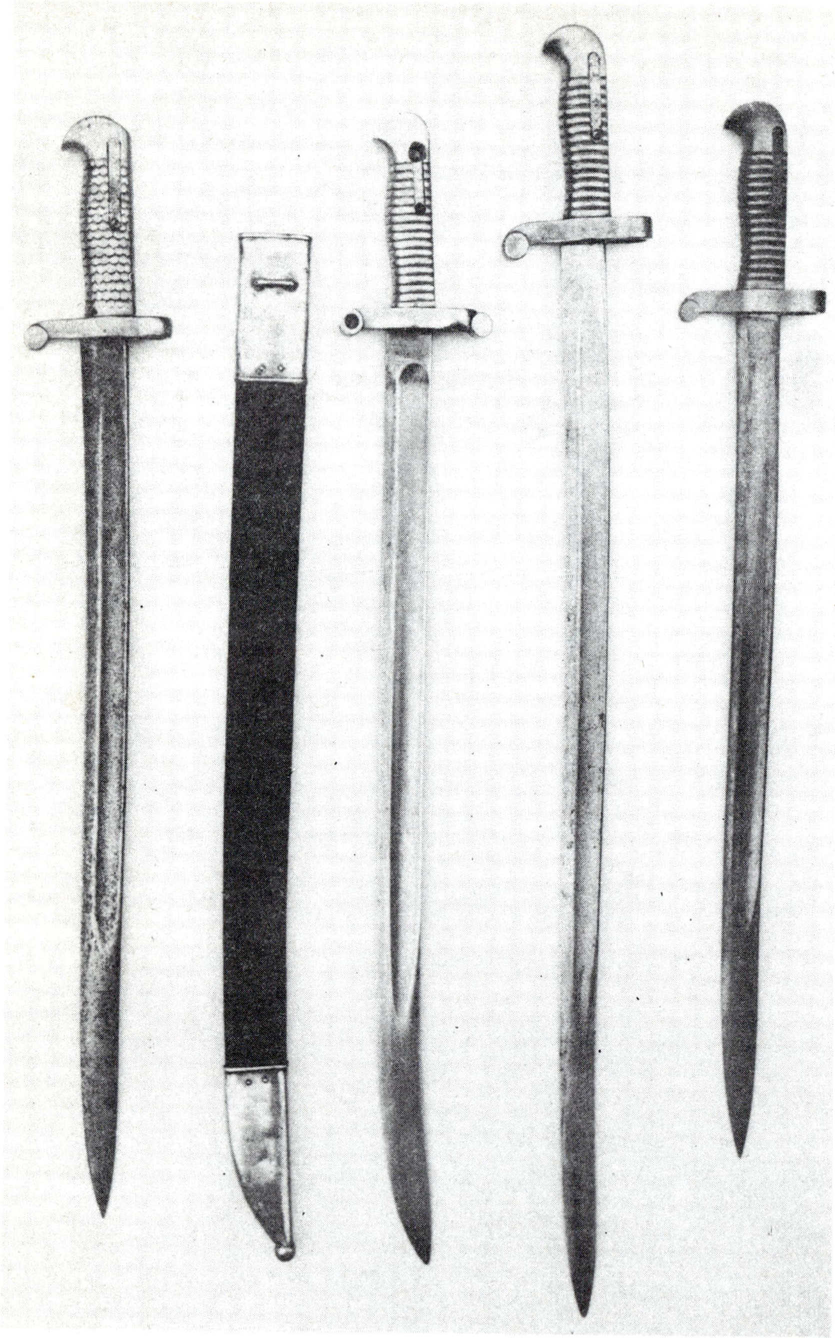

294 *USA. Sword bayonets, unknown Confederate patt.; patt. 1855 Mississippi rifle; patt. 1861 Merril rifle; patt. 1863 Remington rifle.*

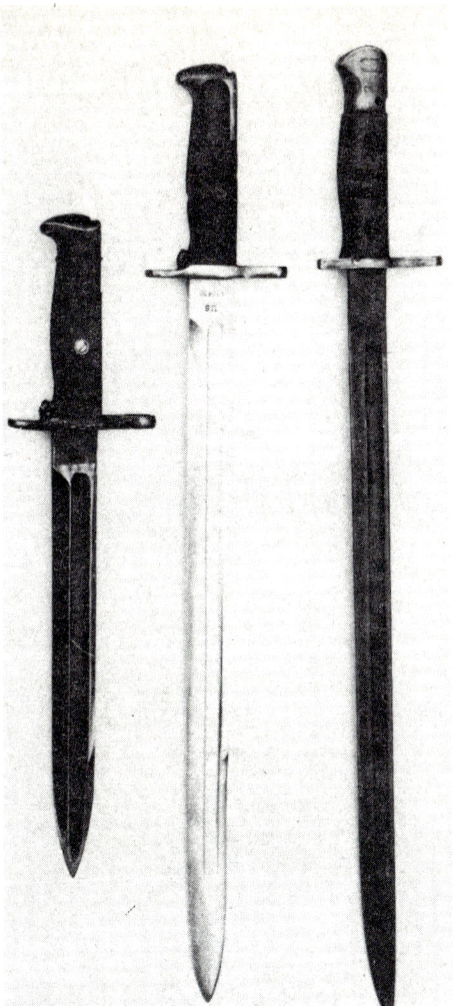

295 *USA. Sword bayonets, patt. 1905–43 Springfield; patt. 1905 Springfield; patt. 1917 Enfield.*

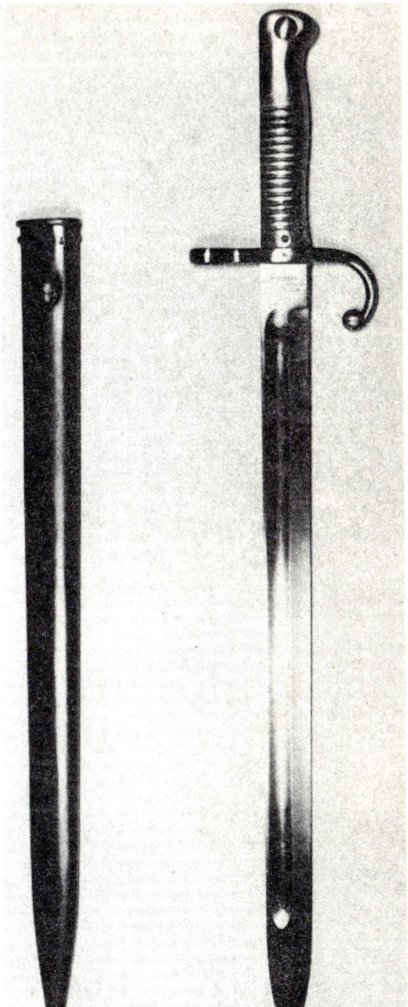

296 *Argentinian. Sword bayonet, patt. 1891 Mauser with all metal hilt; grips being brass. 1909 patt. was the same but with wood grips.*

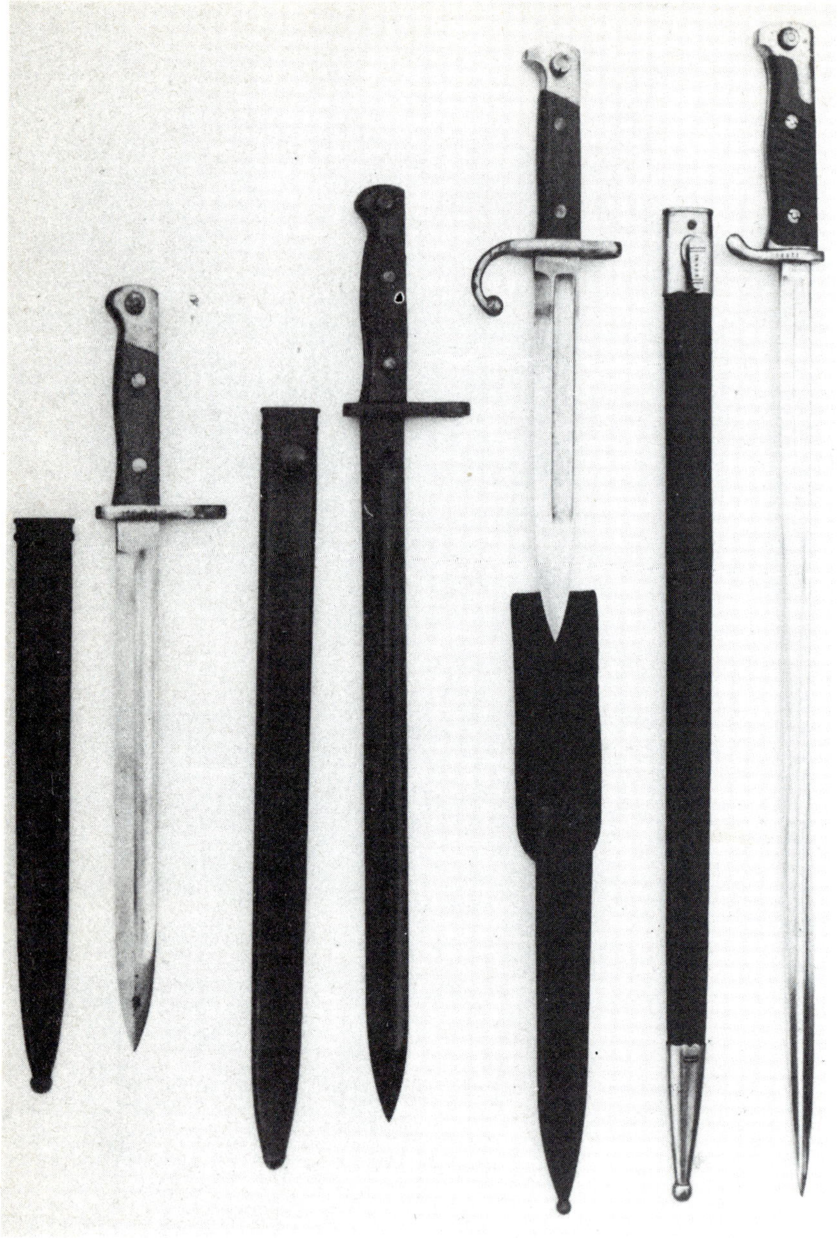

297 *Mexican. Sword bayonets, patt. 1898 Mauser; patt. 1954 Springfield/Mauser; patt. 1899 Remington; patt. 1898 Mauser (Standard German pattern).*

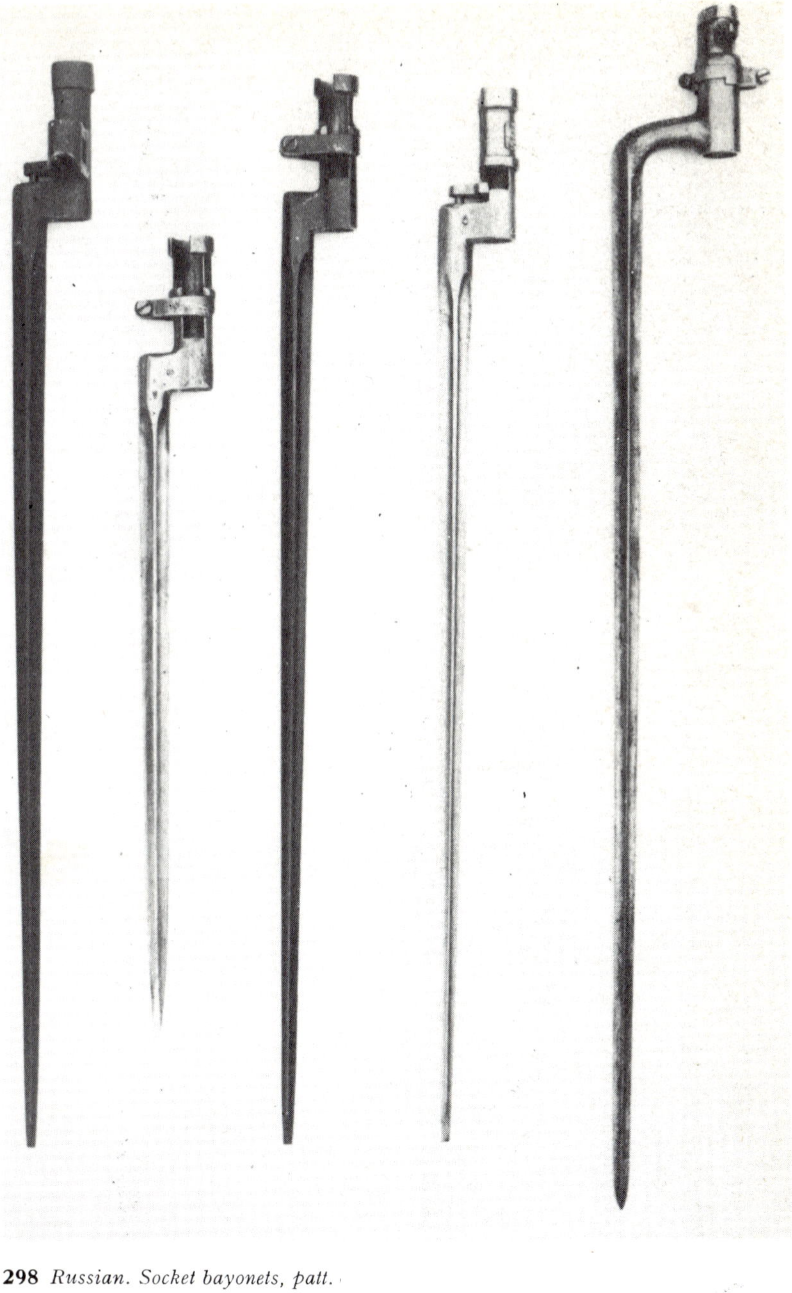

298 *Russian. Socket bayonets, patt. 1891–31 Mosin Nagent; patt. 1891 Mosin Nagent shortened; patt. 1891 Mosin Nagent; patt. 1931 Mosin Nagent; patt. 1871–91 Berdan Mk II. Finland also used the Mosin Nagent socket bayonet and adopted a sword bayonet for that rifle in 1927.*

299 *Japanese. Sword bayonet, patt. 1897 Arisaka.*

300 *Japanese. Folding bayonet, patt. 1911 Arisaka carbine.*

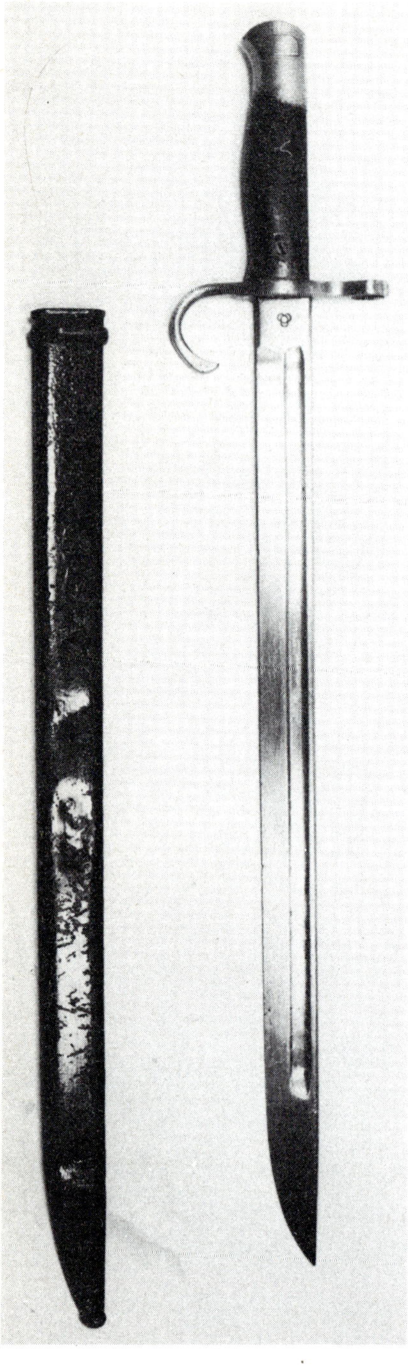

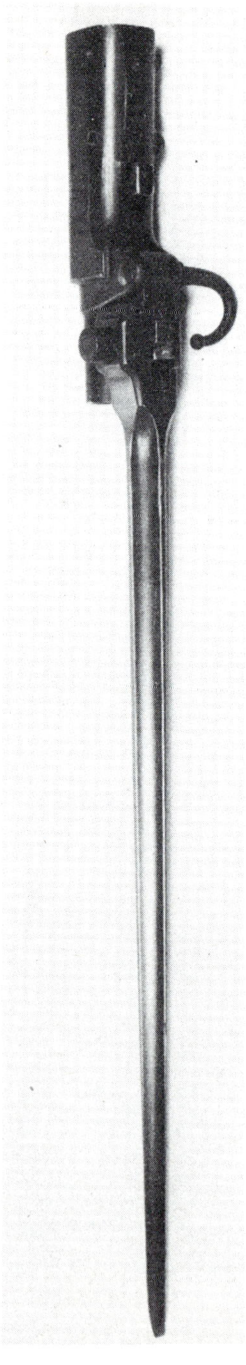